Sustainable Development Goals Series

The **Sustainable Development Goals Series** is Springer Nature's inaugural cross-imprint book series that addresses and supports the United Nations' seventeen Sustainable Development Goals. The series fosters comprehensive research focused on these global targets and endeavours to address some of society's greatest grand challenges. The SDGs are inherently multidisciplinary, and they bring people working across different fields together and working towards a common goal. In this spirit, the Sustainable Development Goals series is the first at Springer Nature to publish books under both the Springer and Palgrave Macmillan imprints, bringing the strengths of our imprints together.

The Sustainable Development Goals Series is organized into eighteen subseries: one subseries based around each of the seventeen respective Sustainable Development Goals, and an eighteenth subseries, "Connecting the Goals," which serves as a home for volumes addressing multiple goals or studying the SDGs as a whole. Each subseries is guided by an expert Subseries Advisor with years or decades of experience studying and addressing core components of their respective Goal.

The SDG Series has a remit as broad as the SDGs themselves, and contributions are welcome from scientists, academics, policymakers, and researchers working in fields related to any of the seventeen goals. If you are interested in contributing a monograph or curated volume to the series, please contact the Publishers: Zachary Romano [Springer; zachary.romano@springer.com] and Rachael Ballard [Palgrave Macmillan; rachael.ballard@palgrave.com].

More information about this series at
http://www.palgrave.com/gp/series/15486

Leena El-Ali

No Truth Without Beauty

God, the Qur'an, and Women's Rights

Foreword by Khaled Abou El Fadl

palgrave
macmillan

Leena El-Ali
Arlington, VA, USA

Foreword by
Khaled Abou El Fadl
UCLA School of Law
Los Angeles, CA, USA

ISSN 2523-3084 ISSN 2523-3092 (electronic)
Sustainable Development Goals Series
ISBN 978-3-030-83584-2 ISBN 978-3-030-83582-8 (eBook)
https://doi.org/10.1007/978-3-030-83582-8

This Palgrave Macmillan imprint is published by the registered company Springer Nature Switzerland AG.
The registered company address is: Gewerbestrasse 11, 6330 Cham, Switzerland

Read! In the name of your Lord who created,
created the human being from a clot.
Read! For your Lord is the Most Bountiful,
Who taught—by the pen—
taught the human being what it knew not.

Qur'an (96:1–5)
The very first verses revealed to Muhammad
by the Archangel Gabriel in 610 CE, according to Muslim belief,
while on a meditation retreat in a mountain cave near Mecca,
launching his mission as prophet. He died in 632 CE.

God is Beautiful and He loves beauty.

The Prophet, Muhammad

For women who love God and have always known deep down,
or have never doubted, that He loves them back.

For men who love God and have always known deep down,
or have never doubted, that He is Just.

FOREWORD

One of the chapters of the Qur'an is titled *al-Mujādila*, which can be translated as the arguing or disputing woman. The title of this chapter refers to an incident at the time of the prophet Muhammad in which a woman named Khawla bint Tha'laba argued with her husband, and apparently, the argument got out of hand. Khawla's husband lost his temper and yelled at her: "You are to me like the back of my mother!" This practice was known as *ẓihār* and according to pre-Islamic customs this oath counted as an irrevocable divorce. Reportedly, Khawla's husband regretted having uttered this oath, and Khawla herself was not convinced that this counted as a divorce because it was said in anger. Khawla sought out the Prophet and complained to him but was thoroughly disappointed when the Prophet informed her that the *ẓihār* was in fact effective, and that she was now forbidden to her husband. Unconvinced, Khawla continued to plead her case and argue with the Prophet but to no avail. The Prophet would only repeat that as far as he knew the *ẓihār* was effective and there was nothing that he could do. Having despaired of getting a different response, Khawla re-directed her appeals from the Prophet to God, saying, "Oh God, I complain and appeal to you." In response, the Prophet received a revelation stating the following: "God indeed has heard the words of the woman who argued with you about her husband, and who complained to God, for God hears your conversations, and truly, God is All-Hearing and All-Seeing. Those among you who commit *ẓihār* against their wives, those are not their mothers for none are their mothers save those who gave birth to them. Verily, what they say is indecent and calumny, and God is pardoning and most forgiving" (58:1–2). The Qur'anic revelation supported Khawla's position, proclaiming that *ẓihār* was not a divorce. The Qur'an stated that *ẓihār* was a serious sin and demanded expiation. Those who commit *ẓihār* must free a slave or fast two months or feed 60 poor people. Khawla, however, complained that her husband did not own slaves, was too old and frail to fast two months, and was too poor to feed 60 poor people. At this point, the Prophet raised the donations necessary for expiation and gave it to Khawla to feed the poor on her husband's behalf, and Khawla's marriage was saved.

This incident is not an outlier or unusual in the Prophetic tradition. At the time of the Prophet, women often actively exercised their agency in expressing their will, making demands, and negotiating solutions. What I consider striking about the *al-Mujādila* incident is that, as a woman, Khawla represented her demands and litigated her case and prevailed. As in so many other incidents at the time of the Prophet, women were not expected to stay in seclusion, guard their silence, and do as they were told. Women made demands upon the Prophet and God, and often obtained results that by the standards of the time can be described as socially equitable and progressive. This dynamic, where women acting as agents representing their own interests and litigating self-defined causes, can be seen time and again at the time of the Prophet. The problem, however, is what becomes of this dynamic after the Prophet dies, and the path to divine revelation is severed. In effect, early Muslim women made demands upon the divine will and achieved results that honored their agency and accommodated their perceived interests. But what becomes of women's agency after the age of revelation? How can women continue to make demands upon the divine will and still have their agency honored and protected? If the divine will is to be found in the cumulative folds of the Islamic interpretive tradition, how can this tradition continue to honor the integrity of women's agency in representing their own interests, making demands, and obtaining results?

Muslims believe that the Qur'an is God's revealed book, and that this revelation is relevant and valid for every place, time, and age. But if this is so then the revealed book must continue to address the ever-changing and evolving needs of men and women. In a sense, God's voice must continue to speak to the Khawlas of every age and place. These Khawlas must feel that as Muslim women, their agency is affirmed and validated by the

Islamic tradition, and that this agency is not persistently overwhelmed and defeated by the entrenched forces of patriarchy that dominated throughout Islamic history. Leena El-Ali insightfully notes that the Qur'an instituted an affirmative action methodology that revolved around the promotion, protection, and inclusion of women. But as Leena El-Ali recognizes, the male-dominated interpretive tradition of Islam has often frustrated and defeated the Qur'an's affirmative action and made the divine will largely unresponsive and unsympathetic to women's agency and autonomy.

What makes Leena El-Ali's *No Truth Without Beauty: God, the Qur'an, and Women's Rights* particularly valuable is that she is not afraid to exercise her agency as a Muslim woman, and she does it with remarkable strength, grace, and dignity. She is like a modern-day Khawla who brings an honest and brave voice interrogating the tradition and demanding that her agency as a Muslim woman be honored and respected. I dare say that like Khawla, Leena El-Ali appeals her case to the Divine, and with admirable integrity and transparency, she analyzes what God's book has to say in response. Not all Muslims will agree with Leena El-Ali's analysis, and some might even intensely dislike what she has to say. But this hardly matters. I submit that there are millions of Muslims around the world who will not only agree, but who will feel enlightened and inspired by her intellectual and ethical example. With enviable clarity and perspicuity, Leena El-Ali has written a very personable and highly readable introduction to what the Qur'an has to say about most issues that have a direct bearing upon women. She does not shy away from any topic and no issue seems to be too controversial. The reader will get a very lucid and honest introduction to all of the contentious and often very heated issues that relate to the Qur'an and women. Leena El-Ali discusses all the tough issues, such as the subordination of wives to husbands, the beating of wives, polygamy, the right to divorce, women and the right to leadership, inheritance rights, veiling, the segregation of women, and much more. As I said, nothing is too controversial. But what I especially valued in this book is the author's forthright personal narrative, and the sensibility and reasonability by which she takes on the task of interpreting the Qur'an. The Qur'an does not contain an amalgamation of disjointed and disembodied rules that happen to regulate women. All Qur'anic legal injunctions represent trajectories in the course of an entire moral and ethical project, and this project, as Leena

El-Ali argues, is best represented in the well-known Prophetic teaching that God is beautiful and loves beauty, and that God wants human beings to promote beauty in everything they say and do. It is this moral vision of Leena El-Ali's interpretive project that I find especially compelling.

Khaled Abou El Fadl,
Omar and Azmeralda Alfi
Distinguished Professor of Law
UCLA School of Law
Los Angeles, CA, USA
May 26, 2021

PREFACE

The decision to write this book was a difficult one for me to make.

The initial idea that entered my head in April of 2015 was that a new version of the Qur'an in English, one that also included footnotes for context, would be an incredibly helpful thing to have at this time of great confusion and misunderstanding. While it would be a formidable undertaking, I thought it would be more about time and labour than difficulty: thanks to the wonderful work of so many extraordinary scholars, we have all the information on context available already so it would be a question of consolidating and synthesising it for this particular purpose, in modern English, rather than leaving it so spread out that only a dedicated specialist or the most ardent researcher can benefit from it.

A few weeks earlier, I had been discussing the particular problem presented by English translations of the Qur'an with Amr Abdalla, whom I had crossed paths with years earlier in Washington, DC in the field of conflict resolution and peacebuilding, but only recently had the pleasure of getting to know. As native Arabic speakers—Amr of the Egyptian and myself of the Levantine dialect—and as native readers of classical Arabic who are at the same time very familiar with English translations of the Qur'an, we had experienced similar surprise at how certain words and phrases are commonly translated. So when I pitched him this initial idea and suggested we collaborate on it, he had no hesitation and replied that he was all for it.

A week later, I wrote Amr again, this time from Sri Lanka. I had just run a couple of workshops in English for a multi-national Asian group that included the topics of women in Islam and women's rights in the Qur'an, and I wanted to share with him two participants' questions in particular.

The first had asked if there was a Qur'an the participants could refer to that put all those women's verses we had just discussed in context.

The second had asked what Qur'an I had been reading the various verses from, because she found it surprisingly easy to understand.

The answer to the first question was essentially "no": I had never come across a version of the Qur'an in English—or Arabic, for that matter—that commented on all the verses relating to women while putting them in context *in a readily accessible way.*[1] Commentary on women's verses, yes, but nothing systematically analytical with regard to the topic of women's nature and rights, although there are of course many excellent books on the subject, without which I would not be able to even begin to write this book. These are highly scholarly and well-researched books, many written by contemporary academics who are exceptionally qualified to delve into the corpus of Islamic teachings going all the way back to the seventh century, and to whom we all owe a great debt of gratitude.

The answer to the second question was, in a sense, also "no", as I was not reading from any particular English translation, so there was no such Qur'an to recommend. This is because in preparing for the workshop, I was not myself convinced of the ease of comprehension to the average person of most of the verses as translated, and on occasion, I took issue with their accuracy. So after comparing six translations ranging from the rather old to the most recent, I decided to convert the classical 1930 Marmaduke Pickthall version (which sticks closely to the Arabic original) to modern English while borrowing as much as possible from the more recent translations. This is what I read out loud: a modernised Pickthall, as it were, and it seemed to do the trick. To my mind, it was the best I could do to ensure as much accuracy as accessibility while utilising *existing* translations. When distributing the women's verses to the group in print so they could have them handy for future reference, I included both the classical Pickthall and the Yusuf Ali translation that is so popular across Asia so they could get a sense of how translations can differ in implication

[1] Nasr, Seyyed Hossein (editor-in-chief) et al. 2015. The Study Quran: A New Translation and Commentary. New York: HarperCollins Publishers, published later that year in November 2015, and the monumentally insightful Asad, Muhammad. 2003. The Message of the Qur'an. Bristol, England: The Book Foundation, first published in 1980, are both exceptional resources for those able to commit the time and effort to investigating any Qur'anic topic.

and nuance, and recommended a couple of the more recent translations for further inquiry.

These two questions on context and language made me realise that given the large number of issues surrounding women in particular and their importance, perhaps a narrower attempt to tackle this topic alone is called for. In thinking through all of the specific issues to be addressed, I also came to realise that "context" should not simply mean the historical context of a particular verse or even how it relates to the verses immediately before and after it. It dawned on me that perhaps we are so focused on zooming in, as it were, on this or that verse that we often forget that it necessarily requires an act of *zooming out* to see the whole picture, which means going beyond immediate textual or historical context to consider the Qur'anic whole. We know the wisdom of this truth from the experience of our own lives, as captured in everyday expressions like "bird's-eye view" or "can't see the wood for the trees".

As an example, consider the following. If we were to line up all of the verses in the Qur'an that refer to women's issues, it would immediately strike the attentive reader that there is a persistent current of what in the United States is referred to as "affirmative action"—and in the United Kingdom as "positive discrimination"—with regard to women. In other words, one detects an agenda by the author—God—that revolves around the *recognition, protection, inclusion and promotion* of women. When detection of this undercurrent is further combined with the textual and historical contexts mentioned above, one comes away with an impression that is starkly at odds with what we have come to associate with Islam's religious institutions and customs, and their attitudes towards women.

To some extent, I regret having to resort to such a technical argument to make the case that the God of the Qur'an, as He tells us Himself at the beginning of 113 out of 114 chapters, is both "Mercy Itself" as well as its supreme manifestation, "The Ever-Merciful". In Arabic, he is the *raḥmān* and the *raḥīm*, usually translated into English as some combination of adjectives such as The Merciful, Compassionate, Beneficent, or Infinitely-Good, all of which are of course perfectly efficacious. I take a moment to point this out because I find it profoundly moving to hear God identify Himself so insistently as both (He who is) Mercy Itself *and* The Ever-Merciful—always the two together—as if to underscore to us what should be the evident fact that He will necessarily always manifest the quintessence of what He is. Elsewhere He also explicitly tells us that He has *decreed* Mercy for Himself towards us (6:12). And since this book is about women, let me just mention for the benefit of the reader who may have a penchant for linguistics or symbolism, that the Arabic word for womb—the medium of human creation—is *rahm*, which is the root word from which *rahma* (mercy) and *rahmān* (merciful) are derived. Food for thought for all of us, perhaps.

But I do not wish to overemphasise the preceding paragraph as a way of grasping the full picture in a visceral rather than technical or analytical manner, because it represents but one glimpse of the countless ways in which the Qur'an offers itself up to anyone who is truly listening. The Qur'an in its totality—not this or that verse—is what has captured the hearts of billions over the past 14 centuries, in whatever language they had to read it. Because whatever the shortcomings of any translation or whatever may be lacking in context of any kind has always been more than made up for by *the beauty and resonance of the whole.* Here it seems appropriate to mention the surprise that many Muslims and others often express when they learn that only about 5% of the Qur'an relates to regulations or legal rulings. The Qur'an is not a book of theology either: nearly two-thirds of it is devoted to recounting the lives of the Hebrew prophets, and of Jesus and Mary,[2] as expressions of the spiritual ideal. The remaining third sets out specific rules of conduct for the followers of the then-new religion, covering two major themes: good conduct in one's personal, social and familial life, and specific commentary on a past or present event. Thus looking at the picture in its entirety must once again form the foundation of our understanding of the Qur'an, before we delve into a specific verse or other. That is how we ensure that we see the wood and not just the trees.

Nonetheless, this book does in fact zoom in on specific verses' context (both historic and textual) and language in an effort to address the various themes relating to women, and numerous misconceptions. But I hope that this Preface, coupled with the compilation and classification of the women's verses provided throughout, will remind the reader that we must always keep the big picture in mind even as we grapple with specifics.

[2] For example the Qur'an mentions Moses 136 times, Abraham 69 times, Solomon 17 times, David 16 times, among others. Jesus is mentioned 24 times by name and various titles, Mary 34 times. See Moussa, Ali Helmy. 1982. Computer Application to Arabic Words in the Qur'an. Journal of 'Ālam al-Fikr (in Arabic), Volume 12, No. 2. Kuwait: Ministry of Information, 167–168.

My purpose in writing this book is to serve as a bridge between scholarly works that expound on the subject of women in the Qur'an and in Islam and the average reader of whatever background who may not have the time, inclination or ability to read these books directly, yet feels the need for answers. It is neither a work of scholarship nor of a scholar, but the fruit of a personal journey of belief and inquiry that, to my surprise, proved to be a most wonderful spiritual experience that also yielded a few new insights, often with regard to conventional interpretations. In the Qur'anic verses cited, I draw attention to these new insights, along with other important aspects, by underlining key words or by offering an [explanatory comment in *brackets*], with (added words that are necessary in translation shown in *parentheses*, per custom). The first four chapters (Part I) lay the groundwork for (re)establishing the Qur'an as the foremost source of scriptural authority in Islam, with the remaining 17 chapters (Parts II, III, IV and V) each delving into one particular topic that relates to women, or that has usually been interpreted in such a way so as to have a bearing on women. Some verses may appear in several chapters, a repetition I make so that each of these 17 chapters can serve as a standalone and useful reference on its topic, where all the relevant verses and associated myths, historical contexts, intra-textual contexts and other relevant information on that particular topic can be found.

Every last claim relating to Islam and women is addressed and countered, where applicable, with Qur'anic evidence to the contrary and with easy-to-pull-out tools (in the form of summaries) that everyone can use. How can a woman's testimony be worth half of a man's? How can men divorce their wives unilaterally by uttering three words? And what's with the obsession with virgins in Paradise? By looking up the chapter on any of these topics in this book, the reader will soon learn a) where the myth came from, and b) how to bust it.

The methodology pursued in doing this is simple. First, the Qur'an is given priority over all other literary or "scriptural" sources. Second, the meaning of its verses in the original Arabic is highlighted, often in contrast to English translations but sometimes also in contrast to widespread misunderstanding or misinterpretation. The book's objectives are that:

- The reader will learn that the Qur'anic God was a relentless advocate for women's rights who issued instructions that we would today call "affirmative action" targeting gender equality.

- The reader will grasp how culture, via patriarchy and interpretative custom, managed to turn the messages of many of these verses on their heads.
- Most importantly, the reader will become equipped with the tools necessary to restore Qur'anic verses on women's nature and rights to their original meaning, theme by theme, with no exception.
- Last but not least, the reader will hopefully find spiritual, moral and intellectual relief, and intellectual surprise.

In other words, I hope the reader will find this a compelling, clear and easy-to-use reference book, one that can help shift the conversation definitively around the nature and rights of up to 900 million women and girls around the globe, and to catalyse positive change. Any shortcomings are strictly my own.

For nearly a year and a half after the idea first came into my head that I should write something, I tried to ignore it. As I have mentioned, I felt that all the answers were already out there, beautifully presented in so many wonderful works, so what could I possibly add? After overcoming that hesitation by determining that I would only be bridging the gap by simplifying the presentation, the question then became: who am I to be attempting this at all? I had almost completely succeeded in pushing the idea out of my mind for several months when I woke up abruptly one morning in October 2016 at a strange hour, well before my phone alarm usually goes off, something that had almost never happened before. Unusually for me, I was lying flat on my back when my eyelids seemed to be flung open suddenly, and an absolute certainty that I must indeed proceed to write seemed to have been stamped *within* my chest, and was accompanied by an indescribable joy. When neither the certainty of what I had to do nor the accompanying joy let up even an iota in the next three days, I knew that for reasons I still only partially understand, writing this book is somehow part of my destiny. That night, my husband and I discussed the matter in greater depth, and though I felt extremely self-conscious and concerned about the loss of privacy that writing such a book entails, I knew I could not turn back the clock. My husband, bless him, had no reservations whatsoever and dismissed all notions of practical or imagined inconvenience with a priceless expression of his face that seemed to say "first things must come first regardless", and pledged to support me in the process in any and every way possible. Two days after our decision, when I was feeling quite reconciled with the idea of "coming out of the closet", to borrow an expression from another writer,[3] I received further confirmation of the task ahead and was shown how to integrate the effort into my ongoing spiritual journey.

In what follows, I have done my best to shine a light on God's love for all of us, meaning women as well as men. My one wish is for any reader of this book to emerge from the experience with a heart made more joyful by his or her ability to see more of God's beauty than perhaps they did before.

Arlington, VA, USA — Leena El-Ali

[3] Joseph, Theresa. 2014. Everyday Mystic: Finding the Extraordinary in the Ordinary. Theresa Joseph, 94–99.

Acknowledgements

I am boundlessly indebted to Shaykh 'Issa Nuruddin, aka Frithjof Schuon (1907–1998), for expanding my mind upward towards the heavens, and for his uncompromising and compelling insistence that beauty be the splendour of the True in every possible sense, in every sincere act.

My heart overflows with unearthly love and gratitude at the very thought of Shaykh Abu Bakr Sirajuddin, aka Martin Lings (1909–2005), a dazzling example of the ultimate possibility for the human spirit, a light that continues to shine as brightly today as it has ever done.

It would not be possible to overstate how much I owe the collective body of intellectually and morally courageous twentieth-century and contemporary scholars of Islam—both Muslim and otherwise—for their painstaking work and illuminating publications. Without their books, I could not have taken a single step in my own writing, for their erudition provided the bedrock of my inquiry.

I owe so much to Theresa Joseph, a gift that dropped into my life with immaculate timing. Her spiritual example, encouragement and generosity of spirit were ever-present companions from the inception of this project and throughout the process.

I am so grateful to Vasu Mohan for his spiritual instincts and for his trust, which is how my attention was inadvertently turned towards the subject of women in the Qur'an in the first place—and the rest, as they say, is history.

I am indebted to Amr Abdalla for not hesitating for an instant when I first broached the idea of writing this book, but cheering me on. While we did not end up collaborating on it as originally intended for various reasons, his advice and insights—and anecdotes—have certainly left their mark. It was also Amr who introduced me to the admirably detail-oriented Ammar Yasin, without whom I could not have possibly navigated the world of online *hadith* in Arabic effectively, nor identified many excellent sources in Arabic.

I am humbled by how much time Jorgen Nielsen was willing to give to this project, especially during the search-for-a-publisher phase. But it would be remiss of me not to mention how much it meant to me at the time to hear back from him after he read the draft manuscript—the first scholar to do so—and reportedly in a single sitting!

I cannot thank Linda Fallo-Mitchell enough for her incredibly on-point advice on the need for summaries, and her suggestions on how to restructure what had initially looked more like a manual into chapter format. This was no small feat, as organising the information when there were so many layers to every topic was a truly daunting task.

I thank the following friends, peers and scholars for taking the time to read the draft manuscript and provide valuable feedback, and for their contagious excitement: Amr Abdalla, Carlota Nelson, Daniel Calingaert, Farhana Mayer, Jorgen Nielsen, Joseph Fuentes, Linda Fallo-Mitchell, Theresa Joseph and Vasu Mohan.

I feel so lucky to have found Phil Getz, my conscientious publishing editor, who engaged with this project throughout with genuine consideration for both my purpose and its success. Thank you!

Last but not least, this journey would not have been possible without the unshakeable faith and unconditional support of Joseph Fuentes.

Praise for *No Truth Without Beauty*

"This is a book the world needs. Everyone in the diplomatic corps and international affairs at large will want to read it."

—Aud Lise Norheim, *Norwegian Ambassador to Iceland and former Ambassador to Iran (2014–2017), Lebanon (2007–2010), and Bangladesh (2003–2006)*

"Outside Muslim communities not many have heard the multitudes of Muslim voices, women and men, calling for equality. The author of this book is a lively representative of these muted voices. Based on years of work in organizations developing international and interreligious understanding, Leena El-Ali now turns her attention to what it means to be a Muslim woman in a modern society. She finds and builds on the extensive literature which takes the classical tradition to task. She shows that conservative interpretations favouring men do so because they were written by men in male-dominated cultures. The book is formulated in a language which is clear and unencumbered by excessive jargon or Arabic formulations. It will be a useful learning tool for young people facing these issues as they grow up. Book clubs and discussion groups in communities religious or not will find it a text worth studying and discussing."

—Jorgen Nielsen, *Professor Emeritus of Contemporary European Islam in Department of Theology and Religion, University of Birmingham, UK and Affiliated Professor of Islamic Studies, University of Copenhagen, Denmark*

"Much ink has already been spent on "Islam and women." But in this honest, witty, and erudite book, Leena El-Ali presents something really new and important: a brave overview of all the thorny issues, with sharp insights and even new interpretations. With sincere faith in the Qur'an, as well as reverent criticism toward the religious tradition, she shows how gender justice is foundational to a truly Islamic worldview. A must-read."

—Mustafa Akyol, *Senior Fellow in the Center for Global Security and Prosperity, Cato Institute and author of* Reopening Muslim Minds: A Return to Reason, Freedom, and Tolerance

"In this unique book, Leena El-Ali weaves her cumulative experience as a development professional with her diligent review of Islamic jurisprudence and history to produce a tapestry of grounded, well-informed perspectives on women's issues, guided by the universal principles of justice and equality, which are the essence of Islam. A must-read for those seeking Islamically-enlightened worldviews."

—Amr Abdalla, Professor Emeritus, *University for Peace, Costa Rica*

"Leena El-Ali's book is an absolute page turner. El-Ali leads us through complex linguistic, historical and geographical conundrums uncovering hidden gems, decoding centuries old symbolism, always presenting diverse perspectives with deep knowledge, sincerity and humility, and in the end leaving us with a collective "aha" moment: The equality of women and men is a central principle in the Holy Quran!"

—Vasu Mohan, *Senior Global Advisor for Conflict, Displacement & Minority Rights at the International Foundation for Electoral Systems*

"Based on the primary Islamic texts, Leena El-Ali offers a critique of misreadings and skewed interpretations regarding Muslim gender relations that have been perpetuated down the ages. Her book is an invaluable resource both for those working in this field and for laypeople too. The personal and highly readable style of Ms El-Ali's presentation will make it widely accessible.

No Truth Without Beauty is a much needed and very welcome contribution to dispelling commonplace misconceptions and factoids about the status of women in Islam."

—Farhana Mayer, *Senior Teaching Fellow and Lecturer at the School of Oriental and African Studies, UK (2010–2012) and Lecturer at the Institute of Ismaili Studies, UK (2010–2015)*

"Leena El-Ali has done a great service by correcting many misinterpretations of the Qur'an and showing how strongly the Qur'an supports equality between women and men. In stark contrast to the grim reality too many Muslim women suffer, the Qur'an conveys deep respect for women. This book is a joy to read."

—Daniel Calingaert, *Executive Vice President of Freedom House (2012–2017)*

"No Truth Without Beauty is a monumental work perfectly suited for our times. It should be read by everyone. El-Ali's work helps to redeem the reputation of the Muslim world, which is so disproportionately informed by radical ideology. You will learn, as I did, about the nature of the Qur'an. The author's loving treatment and respect for it shines a much-needed light on the misconceptions we have absorbed from patriarchal and radical interpretations. The world owes a debt of gratitude to El-Ali for the dedication, tenderness and love it took to birth *No Truth Without Beauty.*"

—Theresa Joseph, *founder of the Global Peace Movement and author of* Everyday Mystic: Finding the Extraordinary in the Ordinary

"A rare combination of a scholarly/activist take on gender justice in Islam. No Truth Without Beauty has a compelling narrative which takes the reader on a thrilling journey with loads of information and interesting facts to engage, educate and rethink women's place in Islam."

—Daisy Khan, *founder of Women's Islamic Initiative in Spirituality and Equality (WISE) and author of* Born with Wings: The Spiritual Journey of a Modern Muslim Woman

"The world needs this book and it needs it now. No Truth Without Beauty brings to light the truth about women and Islam through a painstaking verse-by-verse analysis and comparison between the words in the Qu'ran attributed to God and the interpretations of those words proffered by men. Whether as part of a school curriculum or on the "required reading" list for anyone interested in bringing about a new world, this book has the potential to educate and to transform perceptions about the Qur'an and Islam across cultures and faith traditions. It is a beautifully and lovingly written text by an author whose courage, scholarship and commitment to Truth is inspiring. Leena El-Ali has opened my heart and my mind. I was brought to a place of joy, a deeper appreciation and understanding of Islam, God's beauty and the power that we all have within our hearts to transform the world."

—Linda Fallo-Mitchell, Ph.D

"No Truth Without Beauty is powerful, compelling and highly relevant in today's world at a time of great confusion and misunderstanding. Combining profound knowledge on the subject with existing translations, scholarly works and personal stories, Leena El-Ali dismantles – point by point – the harmful myths about women in the Qur'an and in Islam to convey one of the most important messages of our time: the need for love, tolerance, peace and inclusiveness. The need for truth."

—Carlota Nelson, *Writer and Director of the film* Brain Matters: Putting the First Years First

Contents

About the Author

Leena El-Ali is a strategic thinker, social entrepreneur, and international affairs and development professional based in Washington, DC. For more than 16 years she has worked with a number of international and local non-profit organisations across South and South-East Asia, the Middle East and North Africa in several areas, including: conflict mitigation, governance and peacebuilding; Islam and democracy, human rights and women's rights; sustainable development and planning; and impact investing. From 2005 to 2012 she was also the editor-in-chief and publisher of the Common Ground News Service, commissioning constructive op-eds for Muslim-Western understanding that spanned the spectrum of cultural, historical, religious, political, contemporary and socio-economic topics, distributing them in six languages worldwide. She has published several of her own articles and essays, appeared on radio and TV talk-shows, and addressed diverse audiences globally on cross-cultural and interfaith dynamics in peacebuilding. A former investment manager with a successful career in the City of London for over a decade, Leena El-Ali is a Lebanese-British-American citizen who was educated primarily in Beirut as well as in England. She speaks Arabic, English, French and Spanish.

PART I

First the Qur’an, then Islam

CHAPTER 1

A Spiritual Journey

Embarking on a Personal Journey

It was a straightforward concept, really. So obvious that as soon as I heard it, I knew in my very core that it was of paramount importance—and that I had arrived.

I was between jobs and had only been back in London a day or so, after spending almost two and a half months in New York, when I asked a friend if he could get me an appointment with Dr Martin Lings. Over the previous seven years I had read all of Dr Lings' published books on religion per se and on Islam—often more than once—though none of his books of poetry or art and calligraphy yet. I had also read several of his teachers' and peers' writings, having come to hear of these writers from newly made friends in England after moving there from Lebanon in 1987 as a young economics graduate.

The reason for my visit was that I had been feeling a strong desire to be closer to God for many years, and I thought Dr Lings might be able to help. While in New York, I had finally come to the conclusion that no matter how much knowledge I acquired by reading the most exceptional books, I still needed help putting a plan in place to actually start the journey towards God in earnest.

For a long time, I thought I could do it on my own. After all, it was not like I was looking to convert to a new religion or anything, as I was born and raised Muslim and had always maintained a practice of sorts, and a

L. El-Ali, *No Truth Without Beauty*, Sustainable Development Goals Series, https://doi.org/10.1007/978-3-030-83582-8_1

connection. But I cherished my independence and was averse to the idea of engaging a "live" teacher, as opposed to one that only spoke to me through a book, as it would inevitably imply engagement with a community of some kind that must exist around every active spiritual teacher. I would no doubt bump up against an expectation to conform to many outward aspects of behaviour that were bound to clash with who I am, both culturally and personally.

But while in New York, the thought of "I must go see Dr Lings when I get back to London" entered my head at some point and remained lodged there, and somehow I was able to eventually stop sweating the small stuff, as it were, and take the step.

It was Thursday, the 28th March of 1996, and exactly one week after my return when I visited Sidi Abu Bakr,[1] as everyone in his immediate circle called him then, at his house in Westerham, in the county of Kent in south-east England. He was 87 years old. Once we had sat down I thanked him for seeing me, to which he promptly replied that I must tell him how he could help. I did just that, describing my need to move closer to God, how I had read his and similar books, and how I could do with some guidance. This time he responded by telling me his own story, how he ended up making the commitment I was now considering, and I noted as he spoke that he was 29 years old at the time—the same age I was then. At the end he asked me if I had any questions and after a brief exchange, the meeting was over and it was time for us to have tea with his wife, Sayyida Rabi'a (aka Lesley).

It was towards the end of tea, after a relaxed but far-from-frivolous conversation, that Sidi Abu-Bakr made the remark that struck me, and which I realise now has been a dominant feature of my journey and evolution.

He said: "Our way is not so much Islamic as Qur'anic."

As soon as I heard those words, I knew without a shadow of a doubt that somehow, I had found the right path. I had always been quite particular about how the adjectives Islamic and Muslim were used, often feeling

[1] *Sidi* is literally "my lord" in the North African Arabic dialect, and Abu Bakr was Martin Lings' adopted Arabic (composite) first name. As explained by the publisher in Lings, Martin. 2005. A Return to the Spirit: Questions and Answers. Kentucky: Fons Vitae, 85: "Traditional names are taken in many religious traditions to distinguish between a person's secular and sacred life. The term *sidi* (*sayyida* for women) is used as a term of spiritual respect. The Japanese, similarly, add the syllable '-sen' to the name of a person being addressed which indicates respect for that person's 'inner divinity'."

frustrated at how interchangeably many people seemed to use them. Surely "Islamic" should be reserved for the religion itself and its unquestionable perfection and beautiful manifestations, while "Muslim" is the adjective to be applied to us human beings and all our flawed productions! But on hearing that short sentence, I immediately understood that I had been fussing about the wrong thing. I had been nonetheless placing too much emphasis on Islamic *religious institutions*, whereas what I should have been concerned with is *God's word*, first and foremost. This is because religious institutions and associated fields of study, such as jurisprudence and law, are ultimately the work of us human beings in all our failings as well as our strengths, so what is "Islamic" is ultimately defined over time by Muslims themselves—no doubt doing our best—but not by God. God's only direct offering, all Muslims agree, is what we believe to be the perfectly preserved Qur'an itself as communicated by the archangel Gabriel to the prophet Muhammad in the seventh century over the course of 23 years.

Over the next five years, I committed to reading the Qur'an more thoughtfully during the fasting month of Ramadan, as opposed to rushing through just to finish it within the month, as had sometimes been the case. Up until then I had read it sporadically and only in the original Arabic, apart from sections I once read in English for one of the Civilization Sequence courses at the American University of Beirut that were required for all arts and sciences majors, a course which also covered Christianity and Judaism. But now I wanted to be sure I was not missing anything and the quickest way to do that, I thought, would be to read an English translation of the Qur'an side by side with the Arabic (as opposed to consulting an Arabic dictionary), given that English is effectively a second mother-tongue for me and my English vocabulary was far richer than my classical Arabic one. This meant being incredibly disciplined and focused if I was to keep the exercise going daily for a full month while fasting during the day, especially after I got back to work as a fund manager and later as an investment strategist, which meant 10 to 12 hours of being in the office five days a week.

Dr Lings was recognised as one of the world's greatest Arabists as well as a leading authority on Shakespeare and professor of English, having majored in English literature at Oxford University at both undergraduate and graduate levels, and having obtained a doctorate in Arabic studies from the University of London's School of Oriental and African Studies. But when some of his spiritual mentees would suggest he consider producing a new translation of the Qur'an into English, he would say that there was no need[2] because Marmaduke Pickthall's translation was very good.

I once heard him comment, though, that the much-repeated noun in the Qur'an that Pickthall translates as "those who ward off evil" could have been more simply translated as "the pious". I have also heard him say that one thing he regretted about Pickthall's translation, and that he would have done differently, is that he doesn't translate "Allah" to "God" but keeps the Arabic word throughout the English text. Clearly, Dr Lings was recognising the fact that to a complete newcomer who knew little or nothing about Islam, **this might give the false impression that "Allah" is the particular deity worshipped by Muslims, as opposed to simply the Arabic word for "God"**. My guess is that Pickthall kept "Allah" as is because he felt attached to how it sounded in the original (he had adopted Islam as his religion), but this does not serve the purpose of optimal communication through translation. Pickthall's decision not to translate "Allah" is ironic because at the same time, he does (correctly) translate the Arabic plural word *muslimūn* into "those who have surrendered (unto God)" as opposed to "Muslims", as such references in the Qur'an were unquestionably to *all* those who surrender to God regardless of their perceived religious affiliation. To underscore this definition and leave no doubt among future generations as to whom God considers to "have surrendered" to Him, **the Qur'an goes so far as to declare the pre-Islamic Abraham himself one "who had surrendered", or *muslim* in Arabic (3:67), and the same goes for the disciples of Christ (3:52, 5:111) who predated Islam by more than 600 years, among others**. This broader meaning of the Arabic *muslim* or *muslimūn* (pl.)—as an adjective rather than a noun—would have been evident to Muhammad's own generation also because the religion he established was not given the official name of "Islam", meaning "Surrender" or "Submission" (to God), till the very final passage of the Qur'an (5:3) revealed at the end of the 23-year process of revelation.

[2] In subsequent years, Dr Lings appears to have changed his mind about the need for a new translation of the Qur'an, and was in fact working on such a translation when he passed away in 2005. It was posthumously published in 2006 and presents his translations of Qur'anic verses as extracted from these previously unpublished writings and from all his other publications, with the Arabic original on the opposite pages. See Lings, Martin. 2007. The Holy Qur'an: Translations of Selected Verses. Cambridge, England: The Royal Aal Al-Bayt Institute for Islamic Thought and The Islamic Texts Society.

Pickthall's translation is in a formal, classical English style, so it is not a smooth experience for the modern reader, although it remains my go-to complete translation more than 20 years later, having compared it with all others I know of. It maintains an extraordinary degree of fidelity to the original text's structure, but in another language like English that ends up sounding clunky in many instances. And while it conveys the Arabic more accurately than most, the choice of wording at times is surprising, which makes me wonder if he would not have chosen differently had he lived among us today and been exposed to how easily an innocent word can have unintended consequences. Here I am thinking in particular of how he sometimes translates what essentially means allies or protectors as "friends" (5:51, 5:57), although at times he goes for the better option of "protecting friends" (6:14). But I very much like the introductions he has written to many of the chapters, which provide the context for a given chapter or explain some particular aspect of it, such as where its title came from. I just wished someone had thought to publish the Arabic original opposite each page of Pickthall's translation, as juggling two heavy books side by side with one index finger on a precise location in each book simultaneously and for hours at a time proved to be a tricky balancing act! As for the Arabic Qur'an, which comes in many hard-to-read though beautiful calligraphic styles, I would simply say that it can make all the difference to a reader to get hold of a copy in an easy-to-follow font that increases the chances of correct reading, and I was fortunate enough to have one: every reader of Arabic will know what I mean regarding the challenge of knowing where one word ends and the next one begins in calligraphic script, and which vowel should accompany a letter to ensure the correct meaning is extracted from the reading.

I never had any major issues with what I was reading in the Qur'an during those years, although a handful of verses in the English really were difficult to understand, which means that the Arabic was even harder. Taking the experience of reading the Qur'an as a whole while stopping to mull over both the verses and their translation, my faith only deepened.

The Journey Continues, in a More Distressing Environment

Like many people, I only started to hear of the more disturbing verses attributed to the Qur'an after September 11, and today it is pretty much everywhere I turn. They emanate from the East and the West, from Muslims and others, from politicians to religious leaders to lay people to extremists of all stripes, from the daily news to the latest TV series to anywhere you look on the internet. Who in the West today has not heard of the supposed 72 virgins awaiting a Muslim martyr (presumably male) in heaven? And what Muslim in any country on earth has not now heard of the verse allegedly telling husbands they can beat their wives?

It has been 18 years of this barrage in the 24/7 digital world we now live in. This has led some Muslims to distance themselves or turn away from their religious heritage altogether, while others have reacted with a combination of sadness, frustration, withdrawal and anger at what their beloved religion has been reduced to. Only extremists seem to relish the current atmosphere, and even thrive in it, whatever their background.

As my own personal journey has continued, I have also looked for answers to the seemingly inexplicable spread of such unsavoury ideas within and about Islam. I have searched for answers through investigative reading and experiential learning, the latter made possible by my work over the past 14 years in conflict resolution, peacebuilding and social entrepreneurship internationally. I have come to learn that the egregious ideas within Islam began to spread in earnest in the second half of the twentieth century in the Middle East, and that by the 1980s had been successfully exported to other regions. And that these ideas have continued to gain force since then, often displacing centuries upon centuries of more harmonious Islamic practice that had been perfectly at ease with a wide array of local cultures across the globe, replacing it with a spiritually dry version, one that is moreover increasingly homogenous in such visual manifestations as clothing, mannerisms and socio-religious customs.

The Challenge of *Hadith* vs Qur'an

I have also come to realise that most egregious claims within Islam can be attributed not to the Qur'an but to *hadith*, the collection of reports about the sayings and actions (the latter separately referred to as *sunna*) of the prophet Muhammad. This is no small technicality, for **all schools of**

Islamic jurisprudence draw heavily on *hadith* in formulating their moral guidelines (*sharia*) and establishing their Islamic laws (aka *sharia* law).

This set off an immediate alarm bell for me: the Muhammad of the Qur'an is a gentle being who is always concerned for others,[3] and his biography based on the earliest sources written by Dr Lings[4] himself had moved me to tears every time I neared its end, which of course recounts Muhammad's own peaceful end. In addition, all the *hadiths* I had ever heard or read about the Prophet were inspiring and beautiful, so where were all these ugly and sometimes bizarre ones coming from?

When I discovered that the most highly regarded collection of *hadith*, by Bukhari, had required the venerable man to sift through **no less than *600,000 reports*** as part of his monumental effort (which took him 16 years),[5] I began to see one possible source of the problem, not least because **Bukhari was born *178 years after* the Prophet's passing in the year 632**.

In Chaps. 2 and 3, entitled "*Hadith* Corpus" and "*Hadith* Content" respectively, I have tried to describe the key facts relating to *hadith* that I

[3] See Lang, Jeffrey. 1995. Struggling to Surrender: Some Impressions from an American Convert to Islam. Maryland: Amana Publications, 75–76, where the author sums it up beautifully: "When we read the Qur'an, however, much of that [worldly aspects] fades into obscurity, as does the character of the Prophet himself. What remains is a man who is very reluctant to insult his guests when they have stayed too long (33:53), who deals gently with his followers after the failure at Uhud (3:159), who perhaps too readily excuses others (9:43), and who prays for the forgiveness of his enemies (9:80). He is described as kind and compassionate (9:128), and as a "mercy" to believers (9:61) and to all beings (21:107). His anxiety and concern for the success of his mission and the fate of his fellow man (16:37; 16:127; 18:6) is such that he has to be reminded frequently that his duty is only to deliver the Message (6:107; 11:12), that only God guides people (2:272), and that it is not in his power to guide those he loves if God has decided differently (28:56). This is only a partial glimpse of Muhammad, but it is significant that this is the side of his character that is exposed in the Qur'an."

[4] Lings, Martin. 1988. Muhammad: His Life based on the Earliest Sources. London: Unwin Hyman Limited.

[5] Stowasser, Barbara Freyer. 1994. Women in the Qur'an, Traditions, and Interpretation. New York: Oxford University Press Inc.,105 and Brown, Jonathan. 2014. Hadith: Muhammad's Legacy in the Medieval and Modern World. London: Oneworld Publications, 32. And as the author relays in his Brown, Jonathan. 2015. Misquoting Muhammad: The Challenge and Choices of Interpreting the Prophet's Legacy. London: Oneworld Publications, 44, Ibn Hanbal's (d. 855) great collection contained 27,000 reports (of which a quarter are repetitions) that he sifted from 750,000 "*hadiths*" he came across on his travels!

have learned from some excellent books by Islamic scholars specialising in this field. This is critical information in a world inundated with all kinds of claims in the name of the Qur'anic God and His Messenger. Chapter 4 will then touch on the role of women in the development of the *hadith* corpus, a role that remained fairly active until the sixteenth century. A summary of *hadith* characteristics is then given at the end of Part I, including a bullet-point list of strengths and weaknesses. Some readers may prefer to skip straight to this summary of what *hadith* is and what it is not, not wanting to delve into the history and development of *hadith*, but if so I recommend at least glancing through the next two chapters to dissolve any doubt about where the summary comes from. The reason is simple: I feel it is better to clear the cobweb shrouding *hadith* before taking a fresh look at the Qur'an in the rest of this book in Parts II, III, IV and V, rather than walking through the cobweb toward the Qur'an while struggling with the web's sticky threads over our eyes, ears, and hearts.

CHAPTER 2

Hadith Corpus

The Fluid Boundaries of *Hadith*

It is important to recognise that the science of *hadith* collection that developed in the ninth century and ultimately gave us **the *completed* traditional collections of *hadith* more than 300 years[1] after the Prophet's death in the year 632** was an extraordinarily painstaking task undertaken by the most committed men of faith within mainstream, or Sunni, Islam. It is also important to highlight that the boundaries of this body of knowledge have never been fixed, with some referring to The Four Books of *hadith*, for example, others to The Six Books, and yet others to five or even eight[2] books. The most referenced six books[3] in Sunni Islam are by the following *hadith* scholars:

- Bukhari (d. 870)—The famous compilation known as the *Sahih of Bukhari* is said to contain 7379 *hadiths* with full chains of transmission, but given repetitions and different versions of the same report,

[1] Barlas, Asma. 2015. Believing Women in Islam: Unreading Patriarchal Interpretations of the Qur'an. Texas: University of Texas Press, 44.

[2] Oliveti, Vincenzo. 2002. Terror's Source: The Ideology of Wahhabi-Salafism and its Consequences. Birmingham, England: Amadeus Books, 28–29.

[3] Brown, Jonathan. 2014. Hadith: Muhammad's Legacy in the Medieval and Modern World. London: Oneworld Publications, 31–34 provides the ensuing summary descriptions of the six books of Sunni *hadith* collections.

L. El-Ali, *No Truth Without Beauty*, Sustainable Development Goals Series, https://doi.org/10.1007/978-3-030-83582-8_2

the actual number of Prophetic traditions is approximately 2602. The compilation also includes Bukhari's own comprehensive vision of Islamic law and dogma, backed up with relevant *hadiths*. The author also often includes his own commentary, and the commentary of Companions of the Prophet and later figures, on a given *hadith*. Bukhari did not claim that his compilation contained all reliable *hadiths*, but that he had focused on those relevant to his *legal* discussions.

- Muslim (d. 875)—The *Sahih of Muslim* collection contains nearly 12,000 *hadiths* but again given repetitions and multiple versions of the same report, the actual number of Prophetic traditions is estimated at around 4000. Muslim's compilation is more of a pure *hadith* collection than Bukhari's, containing no legal commentary by the author or commentary by any of the Prophet's Companions or later figures.

The compilations of Bukhari and Muslim have 2326 *hadiths* in common. Both men were students of the renowned scholar Ibn Hanbal. Both men broke with the then-prevailing willingness to use weak *hadiths* in law—in other words, **by the ninth century some laws had already been established and labelled "Islamic" despite their weak links to Islam**—choosing to focus only on *hadiths* with chains of transmission that they felt met the requirements of authenticity i.e. *sahih*, hence the two men's stature in Islamic history. However, **both men nonetheless were more concerned about authenticating a report's chain of transmission than about assessing or validating its content** as such, which will be discussed in Chap. 3, "*Hadith* Content".

The other four compilations also focus on *hadiths* with strong chains of transmission, but contrary to Bukhari's and Muslim's, **they include *hadiths* that the authors openly acknowledge as unreliable**. These unreliable *hadiths* might be labelled, among other categorisations, as "weak" or as "acceptable but unusual", the latter usually indicating that the chain of transmission seemed sound but the meaning less so due to lack of corroboration.

- al-Sijistani (d. 889)—The *Sunan of Abu Dawud*, as this scholar who was also a student of Ibn Hanbal is commonly known, is a compilation focused on *hadiths* used to derive law which cites around 4800 *hadiths*. As indicated above it does include weak *hadiths* but also alerts the reader as to which ones they are.

- al-Nasa'i (d. 915)—Two *Sunan* compilations were produced by this scholar: the larger one contains many *hadiths* the author acknowledged as unreliable, while the smaller one consists only of the 5750 that he considered reliable.

It is the *Sahih* collections of Bukhari and Muslim, and the *Sunan* collections of Abu Dawud and al-Nasa'i, that are often referred to as the four "core" books of *hadith* in mainstream or Sunni Islam.

- al-Tirmidhi (d. 892)—A student of Bukhari's, the *Jami*ʿ *of al-Tirmidhi* contains around 3950 *hadiths* and also focuses on *hadiths* used to derive law. He also does alert the reader to unreliable *hadiths* that he includes in his work.

- Ibn Majah (d. 887)—In the *Sunan of Ibn Majah* compilation, the author actually attempts to include only reliable *hadiths* as far as chains of transmission go, but later Muslim scholars noted that as much as a quarter of his 4485 *hadiths* were in fact unreliable.

The collections of al-Tirmidhi and Ibn Majah are the most often cited as forming part of The Six Books alongside the core four, but not always. And as indicated above, some will speak of five or eight books. Among the other scholars' works cited as references are those by Ibn Hanbal, Ibn Khuzaima, al-Daraqutni, al-Kurasani, al-Darimi and Malik bin Anas, the last three (Malik's in particular) being among the earliest compilations, to mention a few.

Between them, the Six Books of Bukhari, Muslim, Abu Dawud, al-Nasa'i, al-Tirmidhi and Ibn Majah are believed to contain no less than 19,600 different *hadiths* of the Prophet, yet their authors never claimed that they contain all *hadiths*. Nor did they claim that every *hadith* included in their books has a reliable chain of transmission, and indeed a huge number of other reports can be found in other works.[4]

Mention must also be made of **the Shia corpus of *hadith* reports which was compiled two centuries after the Sunni compilations in the eleventh century**, since approximately 10% of the world's Muslims belong to one of the Shia denominations within Islam. The primary Shia *hadith*

[4] Ibid., 58.

corpus (of the Imami or Twelver denomination) partially overlaps with the Sunni *hadith* corpus, including a notable overlap in transmitters,[5] but it also includes significant other material from the Prophet's family members and early descendants, also to be discussed in the next chapter on content. Here, one can speak of The Four Books of Shia *hadith* collections[6] by the following scholars:

- al-Kulayni (d. 939)—This compilation addresses all legal topics relating to the life of a Muslim, and the nature and origins of the Shia imamate. It is structured, like Bukhari's compilation, to deliver lessons to the reader, and claims to only include authentic *hadiths*.

- Ibn Babawayh (d. 991)—This collection is a comprehensive one by topic. The author does not provide full chains of transmission for the *hadiths* cited, but claims that only *hadiths* that are authentic are included.

- al-Tusi (d. 1067)—Two collections were produced by this scholar. The first is more of a commentary on a legal work by another scholar that focuses on that work's *hadith* citations. The second is devoted to sorting out and reconciling conflicting *hadiths*. Both books adopt a more rigorous approach to *hadith* authentication than al-Kulayni's or Ibn Babawayh's.

The above landscape tour of the *hadith* corpus is relayed here simply to highlight that from the beginning, **there was a vast amount of information to wade through and a very real element of temporal distance from the Prophet**, so that the body of *hadith* reports necessarily remains fluid and the study of *hadith* can never be an exact science, despite our collective best efforts.

In addition, the early *hadith* scholars were typically contemporaries who were also acquainted with one another, sometimes as each other's students or as peers who shared a central teacher. **This means that the widely recognised *hadith* compilations developed in the ninth and officially finalised in the tenth century came out of a specific time,**

[5] Ibid., 137–142.

[6] Ibid., 129–131, including for the ensuing summary descriptions of the four books of Shia *hadith* collections.

place and environment and not, as I had assumed growing up, from the Prophet's time, place and environment of the seventh century.

The Factual Case for the Qur'an Compared to *Hadith*

By contrast, the Qur'an does come to us from the Prophet's own time, place and environment. Its verses were memorised and **written down on parchments *as they were being revealed* over the course of the 23 years of revelation—and not 200 or 300 years later**—by early Muslim scribes, several of whom were among the Prophet's closest Companions. The scribes also received instruction from the Prophet near the end of his life regarding the order in which verses should be arranged, instruction he had in turn received from the archangel Gabriel, at which time he is known to have also recited the book in its entirety twice to them to ensure every word had been captured accurately.

Two years after the Prophet's death, in the year 634, the Companion and first caliph Abu Bakr ordered the gathering of the Qur'anic verses into a single volume to prevent their loss, as the first generation of Muslims who knew it all by heart, which included those who had served as its scribes, were dying off. Around the years 650–651, a new compilation was completed on the order of another Companion, the third caliph Othman, after he noticed slight differences in the pronunciation of the text as Islam spread beyond the Arabian Peninsula to non-Arab lands. This Othman compilation was based on Abu Bakr's volume and the two are accepted by Muslim scholars as being the same, only Othman's version provided the form that became the standard and that has been promulgated throughout the world to this day.

Thus around 19 years after the Prophet's death, the standardised Qur'anic form we know today was produced, based on the volume pulled together two years after the Prophet's death. Non-Muslim scholars agree with their Muslim counterparts that the Qur'an today presents the original verses as recited by Muhammad to his followers.[7]

As chance would have it, I visited a magnificent exhibition in February 2017 at the Smithsonian's Freer|Sackler Gallery in Washington, DC entitled "The Art of the Qur'an", where an impressive array of early versions

[7] Lang, Jeffrey. 1995. Struggling to Surrender: Some Impressions from an American Convert to Islam. Maryland: Amana Publications, 90.

of the Qur'an was on display. It was there that I first learned that early Arabic scripts such as the Hijazi script of the Othman era did not employ dots on letters that would help distinguish between two or more otherwise identical letters—I had certainly seen such unintelligible script before but just not thought much about it. A dot (or two or three) placed above or below a letter can make all the difference in Arabic as it can distinguish between several letters at a time. To demonstrate the point, consider that no dot above a certain letter yields *raḥīm* (merciful) whereas one dot below the same letter in the same word yields *rajīm* (accursed).

Nor did the early scripts show marks to indicate vowels, a less problematic omission for a native Arabic reader but still a significant challenge for easy or correct understanding when it comes to scripture, given its condensed articulation of unlimited divine wisdom into words that our relatively limited human minds can handle.[8]

This early absence of direction from dots and vowels made a reader's ability to correctly pronounce and therefore understand certain Qur'anic verses dependent on having access to the background or historical context of some verses, which is why the scribes often included notes to go with the verses they were writing down. Little wonder then that Qur'anic calligraphic script, such as the relatively early Kufi script, soon evolved, first by introducing the dots and then by adding the marks indicating vowels, from the end of the seventh century on.

[8] The great metaphysician of the twentieth century, Frithjof Schuon expressed this intuitively brilliant explanation of the complexity of the Qur'an and indeed all scripture in several of his writings. It is reminiscent of St Augustine's description of why scripture does not yield itself to the casual reader, requiring a genuine desire to understand for the layers to start peeling off.

CHAPTER 3

Hadith Content

Some of It Requires a Big Pinch of Salt

While acknowledging the limitations of the *hadith* corpus described above, it is a fact that without these *hadith* collections we would know very little about what the Prophet said or did during his lifetime besides relaying the Qur'anic verses, because the holy book itself references very few events from his life on a practical level.[1]

And where would we be without the moving and inspiring accounts demonstrating Muhammad's scrupulous fairness, admirable pragmatism, pronounced sense of empathy including towards animals, exemplary respect for other religions, generosity of spirit, touching gallantry, wondrous approachability, Job-like steadfastness in the face of immense personal sorrow every time he buried a young or adult child (six in total), humility with his wives and around housework, and love of nature and of his grandson, for that matter, whom he would happily allow to climb on his back while he prostrated in prayer, then gently set aside before arising

[1] Lang, Jeffrey. 1995. Struggling to Surrender: Some Impressions from an American Convert to Islam. Maryland: Amana Publications, 75–76. Or see Chap. 1, footnote 6 for full quote.

L. El-Ali, *No Truth Without Beauty*, Sustainable Development Goals Series, https://doi.org/10.1007/978-3-030-83582-8_3

and picking him back up to place on his shoulders as he went through the prayer motions?[2]

However if you are anything like me, at some point in your life (especially lately) you must have heard or read some *hadith* cited from one of the great *Sahih* compilations of Bukhari or Muslim or al-Nasa'i or al-Tirmidhi or some other reputable source that made you frown and drop your jaw at the same time, while leaving you tongue-tied in incredulity or exasperation. So having given the reader a sense of the fluid boundaries of *hadith*, let me now try to summarise some key points relating to the content of the *hadith* collections that I hope will be helpful.

As will have become evident from the previous chapter on the corpus of *hadith* reports, **if you have always assumed that any *hadith* cited from one of the two *Sahih* or other collections of the scholars listed above must:**

(a) **Be attributable to the Prophet,**
(b) **Have both a solid (unbroken) *and* sound (reliable) chain of transmitters, and**
(c) **Relay a verified saying or event,**

then like me, you would have been wrong. It must be noted here that at least part of the problem must surely come from the fact that the two most recognised compilations are called *Sahih*, which means "true" or "authentic" in Arabic.

In brief, here is what we must know about the *hadith* collections in terms of who transmitted the individual *hadiths*, the validity of the *hadiths* in these collections, and the process followed by early scholars in compiling their collections.

Attribution: Who Said That?

Alongside the reports attributed to the Prophet, the Sunni *hadith* collections often also include reports attributed to Muhammad's Companions and later figures, while the Shia ones always include reports attributed to

[2] al-Tirmidhi compilation (in Arabic). No. 3784. www.islamweb.net/ar/library/index.php?page=bookcontents&ID=3717&bk_no=2&flag=1.

the *imams*.[3] Additionally, the scholars' own commentaries are often included in the mix.

All these reports are commonly—and confusingly—referred to as *hadith*!

These *hadith* scholars did not seek to conflate the Prophet's sayings or actions with those of his Companions or successors or descendants or their own, and did label reports accordingly. It is *we* who stopped asking the question, freezing before anything someone might announce is a "*hadith*", assuming it must be both a verified quote or event *and* one attributed to the Prophet himself, and a binding directive at that (as opposed to even, say, a casual observation or act he might have made).

This is not to say that there is no value or truth in any of these other reports or commentaries by other figures—there often is—but to highlight a common yet critical misconception that can have negative implications.

For example, one of the great ironies of *hadith* history is that even as early Sunni Islam vociferously prioritised the rooting of law directly in the Qur'an and in the Prophet's example, **the result was that the first several centuries of Islam ended up placing more stock in the pronouncements of the jurists, "...often above or despite scripture...custom could *create* scripture and...the ulama [jurists] acknowledged this."**[4]

Basically, **the scholars/jurists did not shy away from openly using weak *hadith* to justify establishing a certain law if in their own minds they were doing so for the greater good**, in so far as they believed that

[3] Brown, Jonathan. 2014. Hadith: Muhammad's Legacy in the Medieval and Modern World. London: Oneworld Publications, 123–126. In Shia Islam, since the Prophet's authority was believed to live on in select members of his family known as *imams*, then the *imams*' own sayings constituted *hadiths* to be recorded in the corpus. The first *imam* was Ali, who was the cousin, son-in-law and Companion of the Prophet who became the fourth caliph after his death, and the eleventh *imam* was Hasan al-'Askari, who died in captivity in the year 874 with no apparent heir, although Twelver Shiism believes he did have a son (the twelfth *imam*) who went into hiding to escape the tyranny of the Abbasid caliph who had imprisoned his father. The Shia *hadith* corpus also places great stock in the *imams* themselves as transmitters of the Prophet's sayings and actions, whether alone or as part of a chain of transmitters, given their perceived authority as derived from the Prophet himself.

[4] Brown, Jonathan. 2015. Misquoting Muhammad: The Challenge and Choices of Interpreting the Prophet's Legacy. London: Oneworld Publications, 177.

prevailing custom carried an inherent legitimacy, or "lawfulness", in their societies.[5]

But the weight accorded to the opinion of the scholars at the expense of scripture—whether the Qur'an itself or the Prophet's genuinely recorded example—arguably had its most negative and lasting impact in matters relating to women:

> ...even in Bukhari and Muslim and other *Sahih* collections, contradictory traditions *(hadiths)* abound that give both sides of the argument, with the noteworthy exception of traditions on some women's issues—especially regarding matters of social status and rights—in which only one side of the argument, the restrictive, is documented.[6]

Needless to say, one wonders why women's issues were singled out for such a departure from the scholars' own methodological construct for compiling *hadith*. The only reasonable explanation I have found is the following: that **the scholars were determined to "regulate" as much of life as possible i.e. to act as jurists and not only as scholars, and in the process felt that customs relating to women that were widely held to be desirable had to have *solid* scriptural backing, meaning a single argument rather than several, to underpin their regulation, or institutionalisation**. After all as we have seen, it was typical of the ninth-century *hadith* scholars to openly declare that their primary interest in collecting *hadith* was to derive laws. And even the scholar Muslim, who resisted including any commentaries in his compilation, had declared (in self-defence) that he had left out authentic *hadiths* when he believed that not everyone would agree to their authenticity![7]

Even more alarming is the fact that it is in *hadith* that we find exceptionally offensive views on women, **many of which were inserted into the official corpus of *hadith* as late as the eleventh century—a full 100**

[5] It was somewhat reassuring to learn that while these efforts to derive and establish laws were loud and forceful, there is significant evidence to suggest that the majority of the thinking in those early centuries of Islam was that the Prophet as a role model is actually best honoured by applying the virtues and principles he exemplified to both secular and sacred challenges, outside of the realm of law.

[6] Stowasser, Barbara Freyer. 1994. Women in the Qur'an, Traditions, and Interpretation. New York: Oxford University Press Inc.,105.

[7] Brown, Jonathan. *Op. Cit.* (2014), 38.

years after the great compilations were officially concluded.[8] Among the most shocking are:

> ...images of women as 'morally and religiously defective,' 'evil temptresses, the greatest *fitna* [source of discord] for men,' 'unclean over and above menstruation,' 'the larger part of the inhabitants of Hell, because of their unfaithfulness and ingratitude to their husbands,' and as having 'weaker intellectual powers,' therefore being unfit to rule politically.[9]

Interestingly, **of the nearly 20,000 different *hadiths* or 70,000 total (i.e. including variations on the same *hadith*) in the official corpus, there are only about 6 offensive ones about women that are (somehow) designated as reliable,**[10] yet these have come to dominate the discourse at the expense of those *hadiths* that

> ...emphasize women's full humanity; counsel husbands to deal kindly and justly with their wives; confirm the right of women to acquire knowledge; elevate mothers over fathers; ...record women's attendance at prayers in the mosque during the Prophet's lifetime, including an incident where a girl played in front of him as he led the prayer; affirm that many women (including women from the Prophet's family) went unveiled in the later years of Islam; and record that the Prophet accepted the evidence of one woman over that of a man.[11]

We will see in later chapters of this book the extent to which the Prophet had been met with resistance to his extraordinarily emancipatory agenda with regard to women, even when a directive would have just come verbatim from God in the form of a Qur'anic verse on a particular issue.

Transmission: Weak *Hadiths* (and Bad Laws), Myths, Forgeries and Mixed Intentions

Most Muslims grow up believing, as I did, that all *hadith* attributed to the Prophet in any of the reputable compilations—whether the *Sahihs* or any of the works that came before them that they built upon, such as the

[8] Barlas, Asma. 2015. Believing Women in Islam: Unreading Patriarchal Interpretations of the Qur'an. Texas: University of Texas Press, 45.

[9] Ibid.

[10] Ibid., 46.

[11] Ibid.

musannafs, *musnads* or *sunans*—is 100% true as it was verified as such by the great scholars of the day.

But we have seen that *hadith* with weak and even doubtful chains of transmission were included even in the great *hadith* compilations, though most (not all, as in the case of Ibn Majah for example) were recognised as such at the time and so labelled. They were included not out of mischief, but because these scholars thought the weak and even suspect *hadith* might have a useful purpose nonetheless.

Yet we have also seen that the scholars with a juristic bent (not all were) had no qualms about going so far as to use weak *hadith* to derive laws when they thought the end justified the means. To their minds, a weak chain of transmission represented more of "an absence of evidence than evidence of absence."[12] To my mind this is unspeakably presumptuous, to put it mildly, because once a law is established anywhere it becomes close to impossible to revise or rescind it, especially if it has been assigned the label "Islamic" and come to be widely believed to be so.

At least as great as the harm caused by deriving laws from weak *hadiths* was the harm done by the everyday reach of weak *hadiths*, in so far as they undoubtedly influenced and arguably restricted what piety looked and sounded like. For example weak *hadiths* were regularly used by preachers, yet even the esteemed Ibn Hanbal, who had tutored all of Bukhari, Muslim and Abu Dawūd, is recorded to have said of such preachers:

> How useful they are to the masses, even though the mass of what they say is false.[13]

The scholars' laissez-faire attitude towards the use of weak *hadiths* by preachers reverberates to this day, as modern scholars mostly have no qualms about placing efficacy above accuracy:

> 'If a layperson comes to me off the street and asks me if there are mistakes in the Two Authentic Collections (*Sahihayn*) of Bukhari and Muslim,' admitted one modern Egyptian Hadith scholar privately, 'I'd tell them no. But among the ulama [jurists],' he added, 'we all acknowledge that the two books have errors—there is no perfect book but the Book of God.'[14]

[12] Brown, Jonathan. *Op. Cit.* (2015), 225.
[13] Ibid., 226.
[14] Ibid., 224–5.

So if the prevalence and use of weak *hadiths* was so widespread so early on, how many of them are there that we should be wary of?

When I first contemplated this question, I felt certain that these weak *hadiths* would represent a small portion, a tiny minority, of what was documented and is, of course, still out there. Alas, it turns out I was wrong.

The reality is that Muslim scholars themselves maintained that even if we look only at those *hadiths* that have been authenticated, i.e. determined to be of sound transmission, **only a few dozen Prophetic *hadiths* at most can be said to be reliable with absolute certainty, though many others can be said to be "most probably" reliable.**[15] **Still, contrast that, for a moment, with the 19,600 that the tenth century's Six Books of *hadith* ultimately come to, or with the 600,000 that Bukhari had started with or the 750,000 that Ibn Hanbal**[16] **had sifted through before him.**

This number—of a few dozen "absolutely reliable" *hadiths* and perhaps a few dozen more "most probably reliable" *hadiths*—rather than hundreds let alone thousands or tens of thousands, certainly rings true from my personal experience, as I have encountered wildly different types of *hadiths* on a given topic in communities across the Muslim world, many which clash disturbingly with my understanding of the message of the Qur'an and the beauty of God.

But if only the inclusion of weak *hadiths*, in terms of their transmission mechanisms, were the sole challenging issue with the *hadith* collections!

We have already seen that scholars of all backgrounds agree that the Qur'an has remained unchanged from when it was first written down. Conversely, all scholars also agree that there was massive *hadith* forgery, including the scholars and jurists of those first few centuries of Islam who produced the great *hadith* collections. In fact, those **early jurists readily admitted "that they had themselves uncovered thousands and thousands of forged *hadiths*."**[17]

Why would the early generations of Muslims, presumably more faithful than later generations due to their proximity to the Prophet and his immediate legacy, have wilfully forged *hadiths*, when the Prophet's every word (and deed) was deemed second only to God's?

[15] Ibid., 232.
[16] Ibid., 44.
[17] Ibid., 9.

A primary motive for forging *hadiths* has been found to be religious zeal. And even with the revered "authentic" *hadith* compilations we have been discussing, the compilers' motives were not only to record historical data but to also institutionalise the Prophet's exemplary behaviour as a model for the community.[18] In other words, it would seem that the approach of "the end justifies the means" was adopted even by the great compilers not only to establish desired laws, but also to prop up the Prophet as a role model—as though his true example needed any embellishment!

It should be clarified though that there was unanimous agreement among the scholars not to use *forgeries* to derive laws as such[19]—only for embellishing accounts relating to the Prophet. I suppose we should feel relieved by this, only it is hard to be grateful when they did not exhibit the same degree of responsibility when it came to using *weak hadiths* in legal matters, which can be just as harmful or possibly more so. In any case, this means that any forged *hadiths* found in the compilations are unlikely to touch upon legal issues. The scholars were willing to use forgeries if it served a good purpose outside of the legal sphere, and they did so even as they consistently condemned the intentional forging of *hadiths*, even if for a good cause, as did their successors without exception throughout the centuries.[20]

In everyday modern terms, consuming a product while at the same time condemning its very production seems not just contradictory but hypocritical, unless one takes the magnanimous view that the inherently immoral product was being turned against itself by being put to good use. The only problem with this is that a precedent would have been set, in this magnanimous interpretation, for future generations to embrace blatant untruths any time they deemed there to be a good reason to do so. I think many of us have known or heard of the negative consequences of such an approach in many of today's hyper-religious yet arguably irreverent environments.

A second motive for forging *hadiths* was, unsurprisingly, politics. The first 60 years after the Prophet's death were rife with conflict and outright civil war. To borrow a few words that convey the tragic point:

[18] Stowasser, Barbara Freyer. *Op. Cit.*, 104.
[19] Brown, Jonathan. *Op. Cit.* (2015), 225.
[20] Ibid., 224.

> Eager to insinuate their ideas and customs into the new religion, parties from every religious and political direction began placing their messages in the Prophet's mouth. Hadiths—reports of the Prophet's words and deeds—were forged by the thousands.[21]

Thus the Sunni-Shia split, as well as more secular political conflicts, spawned an industry of propaganda on both sides that indulged in forging *hadiths* to prop up each side's arguments. Ironically, the birth of the Sunni-Shia split is itself rooted not so much in the forgery of *hadith*—because both sides had heard the Prophet say the same thing honouring Ali, his cousin and son-in-law whom the Shia in particular revere—but in the fact that different people had interpreted such *hadith* differently.[22]

A third motive for forging *hadiths* was chauvinism in its various stripes,[23] including male chauvinism. While wilfully forging Prophetic *hadith* is outrageous whatever the motive, it is when aimed at demeaning women—literally one-half of humanity across the ages—that it hits the lowest rung of the human character. Ugly falsehoods about women and other topics were spread in earnest after the Prophet's death, along with perfectly good *hadith*, by at least one Companion of the Prophet (Abu Hurayra), who is recorded to have infuriated such towering Companions as Omar, Ali and Aisha (the Prophet's wife) to the point that they all angrily challenged and even threatened him, in one case, in response.[24] Yet these falsehoods are recorded, alongside the noble words of the Prophet, in the same *hadith* volumes. I cannot bring myself to relay any of these unsavoury claims here because I would be committing the act of consuming the product myself by propagating it, though I thank the Muslim scholars who have brought this evidence to light for us from the bottom of my heart. Besides, they are too ugly for a book trying to shine a light on the beauty of the Qur'anic message, one that's trying to scrape away the monstrous accumulation of man-made mould that has all but smothered it.

* * *

[21] Ibid., 22.

[22] Brown, Jonathan. *Op. Cit.* (2014), 70.

[23] Ibid., 71–73.

[24] Abou El Fadl, Khaled M. 2003. Chap. 7, Faith-Based Assumptions and Determinations Demeaning to Women in Speaking in God's Name: Islamic Law, Authority and Women. Oxford: Oneworld Publications.

For the record, it must be mentioned here that these *hadith* forgeries could take the form of either complete fabrications or of assigning someone else's sayings to the Prophet.

Also for the record, there were forgeries not only of Prophetic *hadiths* but also of chains of transmission, such as when someone wanted to establish a report as a Prophetic *hadith* or boost the credibility of a particular existing *hadith*.[25] This is no secondary issue: Chap. 2, "*Hadith* Corpus", alluded to how the compiling scholars Bukhari et al. were more concerned with assessing the chain of transmission than with assessing the content of *hadiths*, which will be discussed further below.

Lastly, for the sake of completion, we should know that Shia Islam had to grapple with similar forgeries stemming from similar motives, which is primarily what led al-Kulayni and Ibn Babawayh in the eleventh century to produce their *hadith* compilations after the twelfth *imam* had vanished (whether through death or occultation is irrelevant for our purpose here). In the absence of a living *imam* (direct heir-descendant of the Prophet) whom the Shia community could cross-check everything with, a need to safeguard true *hadith* became evident. Having said this, the Sunni and Shia *hadith* traditions have never been totally separate bodies of knowledge, as they share common origins and overlap significantly, especially with regard to devotion to the Prophet's family.[26]

Process: Far from a Perfect Methodology

The amount of energy and depth of commitment involved in the process of collecting and sorting *hadith* is hard for me to even begin to wrap my head around. It truly was a monumental achievement by all these scholars, one that is a rightful source of pride for all Muslims, even if I am drawing attention here to its imperfections.

One of the disconcerting issues with the process of *hadith* collection is the fact that the compiling scholars prioritised verification of a *hadith*'s chain of transmitters over and above verification of its content. **To put it simplistically, they felt that tracing the path of the courier-pigeon and scoring that path for *likelihood* was more important than assessing the nature and implication of the delivered package**. I have to believe that they did this in a bid to remain as neutral as possible about any

[25] Brown, Jonathan. *Op. Cit.* (2014), 75.
[26] Ibid., 133–137.

"*hadith*" they may have come across, but in light of their ultimate willingness to use weak *hadiths* to derive laws and in light of the massive number of forgeries they themselves were uncovering along the way and watching preachers propagate, it seems to me that more emphasis on assessing a *hadith's* message was called for in determining authenticity. Ultimately, authenticity must stem from compatibility with the Qur'anic message, and not from tracing a centuries-long chain of who said what to whom about the Prophet having said or done something.

A second troubling feature of *hadith* collection, which at this point should come as no surprise to the reader, is that **the compiling scholars dwelt more on verifying the chain of transmission for a *hadith* with *legal* implications than they did for a *hadith* relating to morality or manners.**[27] We have already seen that the ninth-century *hadith* compilers were driven by an interest in legal matters and in acting as jurists. This was something they openly acknowledged:

> Ibn Hanbal drew on the words of one of his teachers when he stated, 'If Hadiths are related to us from the Prophet concerning rulings of the Shariah and what is licit and prohibited, we are rigorous with the chains of transmission.' 'But if we are told Hadiths dealing with the virtues of actions, their rewards and punishments [in the Afterlife], permissible things or pious invocations,' Ibn Hanbal qualified, 'we are lax with the chains of transmission.'[28]

It is this unequal rigor in the treatment of legal and moral matters when collecting *hadith* from the beginning—**which caused a far greater proportion of the compiled *hadith* dealing with morality to be classified as weak *hadith***—that made possible the psychological inclination of these very scholars to be lax with preachers spreading dodgy *hadiths* to make whatever point they had in mind.[29] I suppose they must have felt that on balance, more good would result than bad from these dodgy *hadiths* on morality and manners, never mind that any dodgy *hadith* on morality was likely to stick and stand out, and many have surely come back to haunt us today.

Thirdly, it was inevitable and is perfectly understandable that the compiling scholars of the ninth century would agree to the use of paraphrasing in recording *hadith*. Were they to insist on a word-for-word account of

27 Brown, Jonathan. *Op. Cit.* (2015), 259.
28 Ibid., 231.
29 Ibid., 259, 231.

what the Prophet had said exactly, very little material would have been collected on his sayings. After all, many of the *hadiths* conveyed were things that the Prophet had only uttered once, or were heard by only one person. Thus **rather than verbatim, they had to focus on conveying the general meaning of what the Prophet had said, and there was implicit acceptance that this assumed that *all* the transmitters in a chain had understood the meaning of the Prophet's utterance, or act for that matter, in the first place.**[30]

A fourth issue with the process of compiling *hadith* is a most fundamental one and has been discussed at some length already in the latter part of Chap. 2, "*Hadith* Corpus". Briefly, the *hadiths* were not compiled as they were happening nor immediately after the Prophet's death, but two centuries later after many conflicts and several civil wars had taken place. I do not think this fact warrants further comment, though I was interested to learn that there are several *hadiths* relaying that **the Prophet himself had told his followers not to write his words down, lest they be conflated with the Qur'anic verses that were still being written down as they were being revealed by several scribes and in many personal documents**.[31]

Finally, it must be mentioned that there are a few supposed "*hadiths*" included in the final tenth-century compilations that scholars past and present consider utterly absurd, and any sane person would agree. **While Arabic is a language that lends itself to hyperbole and the Prophet certainly spoke in parables and metaphor, there is no amount of bending over backwards for either fact that can lend meaning or purpose to these ridiculous and sometimes vulgar reports**.[32] Many medieval scholars had tremendous difficulty with the fact that the compilers of the ninth century had allowed such material, *which in any case made no sense whatsoever*, anywhere near a compilation about the Prophet. But ultimately these scholars managed to shrug off their concerns, though some later scholars from the nineteenth and early twentieth centuries are known to have lost their faith in the entire *hadith* corpus as a result.[33]

[30] Brown, Jonathan. *Op. Cit.* (2014), 23.

[31] Ibid., 21.

[32] For illustrative examples, see Brown, Jonathan. *Op. Cit.* (2015), 69–71.

[33] Ibid., 70–71.

CHAPTER 4

Women and the Development of *hadith* Literature

Unsung Heroines

The role of women as sources, and later as scholars, of *hadith*, managed to be significant as thankfully the more extreme currents of misogyny were widely rejected by the majority.

Around 12 women served as sources of 20 or more *hadiths* each, most notably Aisha, who is the fourth most-prolific source overall with over 2000 *attributed* to her (a total of over a thousand sources are recorded though only about 500 of these relayed more than a single *hadith*).[1] As to women scholars of *hadith* and other Islamic "sciences", as they are referred to:

> History records few scholarly enterprises, at least before modern times, in which women have played an important and active role side by side with men. The science of *hadith* forms an outstanding exception in this respect… .**At every period in Muslim history, there lived numerous eminent women-traditionists [*hadith* scholars], treated by their brethren with reverence and respect**. Biographical notices on very large numbers of them are to be found in the biographical dictionaries [of *hadith* transmitters and scholars]…

[1] Siddiqi, Muhammad Zubayr. 1993. Hadith Literature: Its Origin, Development and Special Features. Cambridge, England: The Islamic Texts Society, 15–18.

L. El-Ali, *No Truth Without Beauty*, Sustainable Development Goals Series, https://doi.org/10.1007/978-3-030-83582-8_4

..many.....excelled in delivering public lectures on *hadith*. These devout women came from the most diverse backgrounds, indicating that neither class nor gender were obstacles to rising through the ranks of Islamic scholarship. For example, Abida, who started life as a slave..... learnt a large number of *hadiths* with the teachers in Medina....It is said that she related ten thousand traditions [in Andalusia] on the authority of her Medinan teachers ..... Zaynab bint Sulayman (d. 759), by contrast, was a princess by birth...[she] acquired mastery of *hadith*, gained a reputation as one of the most distinguished women-traditionists of the time, and counted many important men among her pupils.[2]

Some women travelled widely in pursuit of *hadith* and are known to have delivered lectures at their destinations to students also travelling far and wide to hear them, including in gender-mixed classes. Nor did women restrict themselves to *hadith* but some also excelled in theology, law, history and grammar. But references to women scholars in the biographical dictionaries of eminent people began to dwindle noticeably from the sixteenth century on, with the last woman scholar of top rank from pre-modern times said to be Shaykha Fatima al-Fudayliya (d. 1831), whose students would receive certificates from her and who founded a rich public library in Mecca.[3]

Reflections

I have heard my friend Amr Abdalla, as part of a course on Islam[4] that he gives annually at the Wesley Theological Seminary in Washington, DC, opine that the rise of the Ottoman Islamic Empire marked by its expulsion in 1453 of the Byzantines from Constantinople combined with the subsequent expulsion of the last Muslims from Andalusia in 1492 gave rise to an increasingly militaristic approach by Muslim rulers. Indeed, at the height of its power in the sixteenth century, the Ottoman Empire reached south-eastern Europe and Western Asia/Caucasus and the Arab heartland, and remained a force to be reckoned with until its defeat four centuries later in World War I and its subsequent disbandment. Against this

[2] Ibid., 117–118.

[3] *Ibid.*, 122–123.

[4] Amr Abdalla is Professor Emeritus of Peace and Conflict Studies at the University for Peace, Costa Rica. He has published articles and other works on Islamic perspectives to conflict resolution.

backdrop, I can see how resources and the environment may have shifted towards outward preoccupations, whether of desire for power or survival, at the expense of scholarship and erudite pursuits in general.

Today, however, Islamic scholarship is back and I would say at its historic peak, at least qualitatively speaking. In an increasingly interconnected world where no one can live in isolation from other ideas or from questions about one's own inherited ones, Islamic scholars of all backgrounds, most of whom are Muslim either by birth or by choice as adults, have risen to the challenge, and we owe them all an enormous debt of gratitude. Many of these scholars, though not all, live in the West. And it is increasingly among these that we see a resurgence of women scholars of Islam, whether they are native Muslims (such as among the African American community), Muslim immigrants, descendants of Muslim immigrants, non-Muslim scholars of Islam, or recent arrivals to Islam: I never like to use the word "convert" because it implies that a person rejects whatever religion they came from to adopt Islam, whereas for many who take this step it is an act of adding (not subtracting) a dimension, one that comes in the form of adopting a message from yet another one of God's messengers.

The point is that we have all we need qualitatively today in terms of answers and guidance in these trying times. What remains is for us to make this top-quality information as accessible as possible, to as many people as possible.

AT A GLANCE: First the Qur'an, then Islam

Why the Qur'an Must Come First

As a matter of faith, **we must assess any *hadith* through the lens of the Qur'an. It is astonishing that we have allowed the reverse to become the norm, whereby *hadith* has taken precedence over the Qur'an and even overturned some of its messages**, as has been explained in Part I and will be shown in the rest of this book, topic by topic.

The direct word of God, as we Muslims believe the Qur'an to be, must surely take precedence over all else for a believer. This is both logical from a faith perspective and what *hadith* itself, as a matter of fact, tells us that the Prophet instructed us to do. He told his followers that many words would be put into his mouth after his passing:[1] if they are consistent with the Qur'an, he said, we should accept them, but if they conflict with the Qur'an, we should discard them.[2]

As a matter of plain logic or agnostic assessment also, the Qur'an surely surpasses *hadith* for accuracy. Recall that the Qur'anic verses were being written down as they were being revealed to the Prophet over the 23 years of his mission, and that before he died he gave instruction regarding the order in which the verses should be arranged. Two years after Muhammad's

[1] Al-Qari, Ali, and Al-Tabrizi, Muhammad. 2001. Mirqāt al-Mafateeh: Sharh Mishkāt al-Massabeeh (in Arabic). Dar al-Kutub al-Ilmiyya, Vol. 1, 239. www.islamweb.net/ar/library/index.php?page=bookcontents&flag=1&bk_no=79&ID=318.

[2] Al-Mubarakfuri. 1421H. Tuhfat al-Ahwadhi bi-Sharh Sunan al-Tirmidhi (in Arabic). Egypt: Dar al-Hadith, 175, reference no. 2906. www.islamweb.net/ar/library/index.php?page=bookcontents&ID=5596&bk_no=56&flag=1.

death, the caliph Abu Bakr gave instruction for the verses to be gathered into a single volume, and this forms the base of the standardised form we know today that was produced, by the caliph Othman, 19 years after the Prophet's death. By contrast, the *hadith* compilation effort took place roughly 200 years after the Prophet's death and the final form we have today was produced around 300 years after his death.

Hadith in Its Totality: Strengths and Weaknesses

From the exploration in Part I of the *hadith* literature produced by a variety of predominantly Muslim scholars dedicated to this specific field, the following points seem appropriate to reiterate in summary:

1. Of the tens of thousands of Prophetic *hadiths* to be found in the officially recognised compilations of both Sunni Islam and Shia Islam—which share a lot of common material—only dozens are considered "absolutely true" *hadiths* of the Prophet's words and deeds by scholars past and present, with possibly a few dozen more considered to be "most probably true."
2. This is primarily because the traditional compilations of Sunni Islam were not begun till the ninth century and not put into final form till the tenth, three centuries after the Prophet's death.
3. Other reasons why only a small proportion of the Prophetic *hadiths* in the great compilations is reliable are:

- the inclusion of weak *hadiths* (i.e. with weak traces back to the Prophet)
- the inclusion of recognised forgeries (scholars decided to err on the side of caution and include everything they came across, even a few absurd accounts and even a particularly notorious one popularly labelled "the satanic verses"[3])

[3] To quote Lang, Jeffrey. 1995. Struggling to Surrender: Some Impressions from an American Convert to Islam. Maryland: Amana Publications, 114: "The incident of the 'satanic verses,' in which Muhammad supposedly compromised his message to suit the pagans of Makkah, has been judged by Muslim orthodoxy as entirely fictitious, even though it appears in *Sahih al Bukhari*."

4. The great compilations included sayings by others, which may be of value but which must not be conflated with the Prophet's words (such as by his Companions or less-close contemporaries, descendants, scholars).
5. On women's issues, only restrictive *hadiths* were included, contrary to the scrupulously balanced policy on all other topics where the included *hadiths* reflect a variety of positions on a given subject.
6. Weak *hadiths* were used freely by early scholars who would be jurists to derive laws.
7. Recognised forgeries were *not* used to derive laws by early scholars, *but* were tolerated in preaching from early on.
8. *Hadiths* were not assessed or rated according to the degree of their compatibility with the Qur'anic message: tracing the path of transmission and scoring it for likelihood was more important to the compiling scholars than assessing the nature, Qur'anic compatibility and implication of the delivered *hadith*.
9. The compiling scholars were diligent with verifying chains of transmissions for *hadiths* with legal implications, but not so much for *hadiths* relating to morality and manners (nor for those on the life or *sīra* of the Prophet), reflecting their own freely admitted interest in deriving rules and regulations.
10. Recording *hadiths* necessitated the use of paraphrasing since verbatim was impossible, which means that the message that a *hadith* ultimately conveyed was dependent on the conveyers' own understanding of what was heard or seen.

Having said all the above, we must be careful not to discard the good with the bad, for lack of a better expression. We have a duty to open our eyes with regard to deficiencies in the compilations overall, but they still contain a treasure, and we are fortunate to have them.

Nor did those early Muslim scholars seek to deceive us. As described in some detail already, they carried out an immense task, and they never claimed to have arrived at a perfect record of the Prophet's words and deeds. Rather, they maintained that they had collected a body of information whose authority was *second* only to the Qur'an's for deriving laws, which was their prime motivation as outlined above.[4] Personally, I would have been more interested in pursuing the information on morality and

[4] Ibid., 104.

manners than the information that could form the basis of one law or another. But I am a product of my time and the problems we see today with trying to dictate to people through man-made religious laws, just as these scholars were a product of their time, when doing precisely that would have seemed a very logical thing to do.

Additional Challenge: Twentieth-Century "Corrections" to Ninth-Century *Hadith*

Whatever the challenges presented by the *hadith* collections in terms of the need to sift the "good" from the "bad", it remains a fact that they are the closest thing we have to a record of the Prophet's life and works. So I was stunned to learn that there had been a massive and systematic *re-writing* of the *hadith* corpus in the twentieth century, specifically by followers of Salafi Islam.

> The Salafis...have a process whereby their 'scholars' systematically but inscrutably 'correct' these ninth-century collections...The most famous of these Salafi *Hadith* 'experts'...died only in the year 2000 ... thanks to him and his successors and students...—and of course to millions of Salafi dollars which print and give away his books free all over the world—the Salafis now have an entire 'revised' corpus of *Hadith* that says exactly what they want it to. Needless to say, moreover, this revised corpus is one that paves the way for a radical and politicized reinterpretation of Islam.[5]

Painfully aware of the dangers of "re-writing" old texts as demonstrated by the Salafi revisions, many orthodox Muslim scholars of Islam today reject the suggestion that Islam needs to be "reformed" or "modernised", insisting rather that what is needed is to reclaim its true heritage by "re-establishing" the spirit of its original message. This would be done by **educating the general populace about the mixed characteristics of the *hadith* compilations along the lines described above, alongside a re-prioritisation of the Qur'an above all other sources** so that *hadith* is assessed through the lens of the Qur'an rather than the other way round, as has astonishingly been the case. After all, God left Muslims this one, inviolable book till the end of time, so presumably He expects us to look

[5] Oliveti, Vincenzo. 2002. Terror's Source: The Ideology of Wahhabi-Salafism and its Consequences. Birmingham, England: Amadeus Books, 28–29.

to it for guidance above all other sources, which need not diminish the unquestionable added-value provided by much *hadith* and the teachings of our betters by word, deed and example. And did not the Prophet himself say, in a well-recognised *hadith*, that after his passing many words would be put into his mouth, and that what we needed to do was measure them against what the Qur'an says to know whether to accept or discard them?[6]

It must be said that it is highly unlikely that most people who identify with Salafism—whether officially or implicitly—are aware that the body of *hadith* that circulates amongst them has been subjected to such editing. Rather, it is most likely that they receive such *hadiths* in good faith, and that many would be aghast to learn quite how much "correction" had taken place.

[6] See footnotes 1 and 2.

PART II

The Nature of Women

CHAPTER 5

Women Were Not Created of Inferior Celestial Material

Why Treating Women as Second-Rate Beings Is Illogical

To be fair, I have not myself come across anyone making the argument that God created women from an inferior essence or substance as such relative to men.

But since women are often treated as second-rate beings in many Muslim communities, it unfortunately seems necessary to begin by addressing this issue. The view that women are intrinsically inferior to men may not be openly articulated, but perhaps it is what shapes the mind-set that enables some societies that claim to follow a religion of "justice" to nonetheless subdue and even subjugate half of their population.

So how might this have happened? *How can any follower of a religion so explicitly focused on the question of justice feel at ease with treating women so differently to men*, including on such fundamental issues as dignity and spirituality?

One logical conclusion would be to assume that the prophet of Islam, Muhammad, must have treated women as inferior and so set the tone for all but the most enlightened and independent of his followers through the centuries. The problem with this theory, however, is that the historical record unambiguously shows the diametric opposite of such a conclusion, depicting a leader and family man with the comportment of both a thoughtful and conscientious individual with respect to issues of women's dignity and inalienable capacity. Many Islamic scholars—both Muslim and

L. El-Ali, *No Truth Without Beauty*, Sustainable Development Goals Series, https://doi.org/10.1007/978-3-030-83582-8_5

otherwise—have touched on the topic of Muhammad's interactions and dealings with women, usually as part of a book, chapter or article covering a broader theme. These references leave us in no doubt that Muhammad's attitude and agenda regarding women were highly evolved for the seventh century and represented nothing short of advocacy in a far-from-compliant environment. Yet despite the pushback he encountered, women appear to have had more rights under his leadership than they do in some Muslim communities today, fourteen centuries on—surely a veritable betrayal of his example and, therefore, of his understanding of the Qur'an.

Another logical conclusion would be to assume that the holy book of Islam, the Qur'an, simply neglects to discuss women, much less address them in any way, leaving a vacuum that could easily be filled by whatever trends in a given society. Yet the Qur'an mentions, discusses, and addresses women as a group often, with one of the longest chapters in fact entitled "Women".

A third logical conclusion would be to assume that the Qur'an actually establishes women's intrinsic inferiority in no uncertain terms, making the matter definitive for ardent Muslims. Yet once again, this is not the case and in fact, nothing could be further from the truth, as will be shown in the following section by examining specific verses from the Qur'an as they relate to the nature of women.

Qur'anic Verses on the Creation and Origin of Women

Here are some verses from the Qur'an that specifically touch upon the question of women's nature as created by God, in the order they appear in the Qur'an. Both the name and number of the chapter (*sura*) are listed, followed by the number of the verse cited within that chapter. So the very first verse shown below comes from the chapter entitled "Women", which is Chap. 4, and is verse 1.

✓ <u>Women, 4:1</u>

Oh humankind: Reverence your Lord, who created you (pl.) from a single soul and from it created its mate, and from the two of them disseminated multitudes of men and women; and reverence God, Whose name you invoke to one another, <u>and the wombs [i.e. the human creation]</u>; for God is always watching you.

This is the foundational verse on the creation and nature of women ; so warrants somewhat detailed attention, partly because its more usual translation-cum-interpretation renders the last part of it essentially as follows:

> × ... and reverence God, in Whom you make claims of one another, and the wombs [i.e. family ties]; for God is always watching over[1] you.

But I also say this because I feel that often, this verse is inadvertently glossed over so that some of its foundational content is missed, as unpacked below.

It is widely accepted that the first part of the verse is a reference to Adam and Eve, given the declaration that *from the two of them* countless men and women were then spread forth. Notice that in this and other articulations on the creation and nature of men and women (also shown in this section), the Qur'an never says anything about who came first, Adam or Eve, so that the emphasis remains solidly on the declaration that all men and women—Adam and Eve's descendants—come from the same soul i.e. are spiritually the same. Now we do hear of Adam referred to as though he is the representative or godfather of humankind, but that comes elsewhere in such verses that recount Satan's fall from grace for refusing the divine order to bow to Adam, verses addressing humankind as the Children of Adam, and so on, which is unsurprising given the predominant cultural custom of linking descendants to their *male* ancestors.

If we read this verse carefully, part by part, this is what it tells us regarding the origins of the human race:

- Adam and Eve were created from the same soul
- Adam and Eve were created as "mates" i.e. together forming "a pair"
- All men and all women emanate from Adam and Eve, the original human pair
- Thus all men and all women emanate from the same soul as Adam and Eve

[1] Most translations of the last sentence of verse 4:1 render it essentially as "...truly God is watching *over* you" instead of simply "...watching you", as I have. The former is a literal translation from Arabic to English which unfortunately overlooks the fact that to "watch over" in English (at least today) has a very different meaning from "to watch". Moreover, it makes a lot more sense that God would demand reverence *three times* and then warn us that He is always watching us, rather than insistently demanding reverence and suddenly switching tones to say that He is always protecting (watching over) us anyway.

Therefore **this verse clearly establishes the spiritual sameness of men and women, and indeed of all human beings** regardless of gender, race, or other physical or indeed mental differences.

It also establishes the concept of a mate (*zawj*), which literally means "one member of a pair" or simply "pair", depending on how it is used, and is also the word for "spouse".

But the verse does not end there, which would have made for a natural stop. No: having established the spiritual sameness of all human beings, the Author then continues, within the same verse, with the following:

- That we must reverence God as we contemplate Him
- That we must reverence every member of His human creation (the wombs)
- That He is ever-watchful

It is hard for me to think of a more comprehensive or clearer articulation of the spiritual or "human" equality of all men and women in God's eyes.

But the standard interpretation of "wombs" in this verse has not usually been "womb *contents*", so to speak, but rather "womb *relations*" or family ties. I can understand why this has been the norm: in other verses where "wombs" appears in a metaphoric way (8:75, 47:22, 60:3), indeed the reference cannot be to anything but "blood relations" or family ties. But I find it hard to relate to such an intention for the word "wombs" in this case for three reasons:

- In this verse, God is demanding no less than reverence—*that we be in awe*—which is an attitude we as human beings are to have towards Him and no other. This is an exclusivity every Muslim instinctively understands, but is one that I feel has been lost in conventional attempts to communicate this particular verse.

  To put it differently, **it sounds uncharacteristic for God to be demanding reverence (*taqwa*) for Himself as our Creator *and for our relatives.***

  Whereas demanding reverence for Himself as our Creator and for all His human creation (the wombs) is surely both profoundly fitting in the context, and of immense significance.

- In this three-part verse on the origin of the human race and its creation process, it seems natural to keep the focus on God *the Creator*, His creation *process* and His creation *results*, while demanding a corresponding attitude of reverence or awe from us. **To mention other people here, like our relatives, seems rather incongruent as part of the creation narrative**.

- Lastly, **that this is the very first verse one encounters in the Qur'an on the subject of the creation and nature of women, and that it is the opening verse of the chapter entitled "Women" which deals with a large number of women's issues, is surely no coincidence.** Where would be a more fitting location in the Qur'an for establishing the fundamental nature of women?

In its totality, surely this verse contains everything we need to know about human spirituality and the intrinsic worth it bestows equally on each one of us, whatever our gender or indeed colour, ethnicity, culture or social class.

A note is in order on the divergence of custom from scripture regarding verse 4:1.

In popular custom, people will usually quote only the first half of the first part of this three-part verse, specifically "**...(He) created you from a single soul and from it created its mate....**".

The problem with this abridging habit—which I have long been guilty of myself, thanks to the sheer weight of collective repetition—is threefold:

- While this is lovely in and of itself, **it does not necessarily convey the spiritual equality of *all* of the descendants of Adam and Eve—nor allow the tracing of women's nature back *to the divine breath*** (since we are told elsewhere that God fashioned the human being from clay and water and then breathed into it of His Spirit—15:28–29, 32:7–9, 38:72).
- On its own, **the abridged form of this verse can even sound as though one gender (the male) was the main act of creation and that the other (the female) was only created to be his mate, and as though men were an extension of Adam himself** rather than of *both* Adam *and* Eve.
- And obviously, **the abridged version cannot possibly convey the correlation God establishes between the intrinsic nature of our souls and our attitude towards all that comes from His**

> **creation process—and how both things are so important to God that He warns that He is always watching us.**

This is a good example of the importance of reading a verse in its entirety. But it is also an example of how important it is to take note of the Qur'anic context, as mentioned in the Preface, which can include taking note of the actual location of a verse.

> ✓ The Cattle, 6:98
> And it is He who made you (pl.) from a single soul, thus a dwelling-place and a repository [i.e. for you in one another]. We have spelled out the verses/signs clearly for those who understand.

I have always understood verse 6:98 to be about the human couple, as shown in the brackets above, primarily because the first part of the sentence "He made you from a single soul…" is essentially the exact wording usually deployed in the Qur'an just before describing human beings as having been created as "mates to one another" or as "pairs"[2] (see previous verse and other verses in this section). In fact, one particular verse—30:21—is virtually identical also in structure, in that the second sentence claims that the first sentence is a sign for people who reflect or understand. Here is 30:21 for comparison:

> And among His signs is that He created mates for you (pl.) from your own souls so that you may find tranquillity in them, and established between you love and compassion. In this there are signs for people who reflect. (30:21)

However in looking up the English translations of this verse, I did not come across any that took it as a reference to the relationship between men and women, but rather to the human condition in general: rather than "thus", these translations use "and" to link the two parts of the first sentence, thereby severing the correlation between them that I hear. The most common translation of verse 6:98 is essentially the following:

[2] There is only one verse, 31:28, that speaks of the creation of human beings from a single soul in a completely different context, namely the creation and resurrection of humankind in its entirety as a single soul. And as I will explain in this section, the usual interpretations also regard verse 6:98 as not referring to the relationship between human couples, although I disagree.

× And it is He who produced you (pl.) from a single soul, and (has given you) a dwelling-place [i.e. womb or life on earth] and a repository [i.e. male loins or final resting place after death].[3] We have detailed/expounded the signs for people who understand.

This more common interpretation totally erases verse 6:98's tender description of the intended relationship between the human couple, replacing it with a combination of philosophical and eschatological meanings that do not resonate at all, for two reasons:

- Other verses in the Qur'an that begin in a similar way usually proceed to tell us that God's creation of human pairs from the same essence is so that they may dwell together in tranquillity, love and mercy (besides the virtually identical 30:21 above, see also 7:189 below), so it makes sense for God to be telling us here that we were made for being together in stability (dwelling-place) and trust (repository): **as the Qur'an tells us throughout the book, it speaks to us in analogy (including parables)[4] and not just directly or literally**, and it is prone to repeating fundamental themes over and over again for emphasis.

- As we shall see, the three verses before 6:98 and the one immediately after it are a list of the "proofs of God", so to speak, through His transcendent omnipotence and beneficence—for those who know, understand, believe. Several verses in the Qur'an—shown in this section—tell us that one such proof is God's creation of the human couple from the same essence, so the first interpretation fits the context perfectly. Here are the points made in verses 6:95–6:99 in brief to help the reader get **a sense of the flow**:

[3] There is one other verse in the Qur'an that mentions "a dwelling-place and a repository", 11:6, where the context is explicitly about God knowing everything about every creature on earth, including its "dwelling-place and repository". In that case, I agree with the rendering of these terms as "life on earth" and "place after death" given the context, but cannot help but find them somewhat unintuitive for 6:98.

[4] References in the Qur'an to God "striking an analogy" to make things clearer to us, and the deployment of certain parables, are too many to list, but examples include 30:58, 39:27, 47:3 and 59:21.

- It is God who splits the grain and the pit, and who brings forth the living from the dead, and the dead from the living: how then are we still drawn to perverted beliefs?
- It is He who causes the dawn to break and who made the night for resting and the sun and moon for measuring/reckoning
- It is He who made the stars for us so we can be guided in darkness on land and sea: these are clear signs for people who know
- *And it is He who created us from a single soul, thus a dwelling-place and repository: these are clear signs for people who understand (6:98)*
- And it is He who causes rain to fall from the sky, causing all plants including vegetation, grains, fruit etc. to grow: these are clear signs for people who believe

Given the reasons above, **I find the most intuitive meaning of 6:98's "dwelling-place" and "repository" to be a description of the reciprocity between members of the human couple due to their very nature: since they come from a single soul.**

I find it impossible to relate to the most common interpretation, which holds that they refer to the female womb and loins of the male,[5] not least because it would then basically mean the verse is literally saying that we were created from Adam (the single soul) and a female and a male—surely a most peculiar sentence construction. I find it easier to relate to the other popular interpretation of "dwelling-place" and "repository" as our temporary life on earth and final resting place after death, but *not* as they appear in this verse partly because of how similar it is to 30:21, and partly since issues of human life, death and resurrection as "proofs of God" have just been covered in the first verse in this very series, 6:95: "...He brings forth the living from the dead, and the dead from the living...".

I might also add that not connecting with the interpretation that relates to human "pairs" or "mates" would be a missed opportunity, because I find it a wonderful reiteration of the intimate partnership intended by God when fashioning the human couple.

I believe this to be **a good example of the importance of reading a verse within the context of the verses before and after it, but also of listening for the nuances of the Qur'an overall on a given theme—in**

[5] See commentary on different interpretations of verse 6:98 in Nasr, Seyyed Hossein (editor-in-chief) et al. 2015. The Study Quran: A New Translation and Commentary. New York: HarperCollins Publishers, 376–77.

this case, the intended relationship between the human couple. To do this, a reader must be willing to allow both the mind and heart to relax sufficiently so as to be able to enter what I think of as the "psychological mood" of this book of scripture. Not to compare the sublime with the profane, but the attitude in question is not dissimilar to what is required to appreciate an "atmospheric" novel or film, one where the beauty lies in entering the mind-set of the time and place as opposed to following a gripping and sequential plot. Only then can we realise the truth contained in the saying, "the whole is greater than the sum of the parts."

> The Heights, 7:189
> It is He who created you (pl.) from a single soul and from it created its mate so he may find tranquillity with her. Then when he covered her, she bore a light burden that she carried easily. Then when she grew heavy, they called upon God "If You give us a healthy child, we will be among the grateful."
>
> ..continued in 7:190
> Then when He gave them a healthy child, they ascribed Him partners in what He had given them. God is exalted above the partners they ascribe.

Verse 7:189 is the only verse on the creation of human beings that seems to specifically address the male human being, since it is a precursor to describing the act of procreation as shown by the flow of the verse: the point being, as the rest of 7:189 and the subsequent verse 7:190 show, to denounce those men and women who renege on their promise to God after He has answered their most ardent prayer—in this example, that they be granted a healthy child. These two verses are an inevitable prompt for a couple of further remarks:

- **There is no suggestion, in other words, in any of the verses on human creation** (shown in this section), **that men were God's primary object of creation, their "mates" a secondary act**.

- **Nor can men claim exclusive descent from Adam and attribute women's natures exclusively to Eve:** as we have already seen in earlier verses, **all men and all women come from *both* Adam *and***

Eve, and the nature of all men and all women (including Adam and Eve) traces back to the divine breath.[6]

I raise these two fallacies as they are not uncommon in the popular parlance here and there, despite the Qur'anic evidence against them.

> The Bees, 16:72
> And God made for you (pl.) mates from your own souls, and made for you from your mates children and grandchildren, and provided you with good things.....

> The Byzantines, 30:21
> And among His signs is that He created mates for you (pl.) from your own souls so that you may find tranquillity in them, and established between you love and compassion. In this there are signs for people who reflect.

The above verse was already cited in the discussion of 6:98 and the natural meaning there of men and women being a "dwelling-place" and a "repository" for one another.

> Creator, 35:11
> And God created you (pl.) from dust, then from a drop, then He made you into pairs...

Verse 35:11 is striking because it skips over all mention of one soul coming from another or all souls coming from a single (original) soul to describing God's creation of humankind as a project of creating human couples, period. Here, **the male and female are explicitly equal parts of the whole**.

> The Throngs, 39:6
> He created you (pl.) from a single soul and then made from it its mate...

> Consultation, 42:11
> Creator of the heavens and the earth, He has made for you (pl.) mates from your own souls...

[6] On God breathing of His Spirit into Adam, see Qur'an 15:28–29, 32:7–9 and 38:72.

The Private Rooms, 49:13
Oh humankind: We have created you (pl.) from a male and a female, and made you into nations and tribes so you may get to know one another. Surely the most honourable among you in God's eyes is whoever is the most reverent among you. And God is All-Knowing, Ever-Aware.

Verse 49:13 re-frames what we have already heard in several of the earlier verses: that all men and women come from Adam and Eve equally. It proceeds to spell out that human equality cuts across cultures and ethnicities, with the only difference among us in God's eyes stemming from the quality of each person's faith. Perhaps most interestingly—though not the subject of this book—God is explicit here that our cultural diversity and racial diversity exist by divine decree and were intended to enrich and inform the human experience.

The Star, 53:45
And that He created the two mates—the male and the female.

Resurrection, 75:39
And (He) made it (the human being) into two mates—the male and the female.

The Tiding, 78:8
And we created you (pl.) in pairs.

As with 35:11 above, the reference in 78:8 is directly to the creation of the human couple as the consequential act of creation, with the male and female as equal parts of the whole.

Moreover this verse is the third of eleven consecutive verses listing "proofs of God", as it were, reminiscent of the flow of 6:95–99 discussed above, once again underlining the human pair of male and female as a pillar of creation. The points made in **the flow of verses** 78:6–16 are as follows:

- God made the earth a place of rest
- and the mountains firm.
- *And He created us in pairs.*
- And made sleep for repose
- and made night a covering
- and made day for livelihood.

- And built seven strong heavens above us
- and made a radiant lamp
- and sent water pouring down from rain-clouds
- to produce grain and plants
- and lush gardens

The Night, 92:3
By Him who created the male and the female.

This is another of those verses that is part of a list of "proofs of God", for lack of a better phrase, where the two genders or the human couple is again cited as an example of God's unique transcendence and beneficence. But this is a more succinct list than the previous examples as this opening argument of chapter 92 then proceeds to make very direct "good vs bad" statements. The points made in **the flow of verses** 92:1–11 are as follows:

- By the night as it enshrouds,
- By the day as it brightens,
- *By Him who created the male and the female:*

Followed immediately by

- Truly people's endeavours are diverse.
- As for those who give and are reverent
- and who believe in goodness,
- their path will be eased unto a state of ease.
- But as for those who are miserly and think themselves self-sufficient
- and who have no faith in goodness,
- their path will be eased unto a state of hardship,
- and their wealth will not help them when they die.

The Pushback of Alleged *Hadith* on Women's Origin: Crooked as a Rib!

Now **given all these references in the Qur'an to Adam and Eve having been created from the same soul containing the divine breath, and to all men and women emanating equally from Adam and Eve, and to**

the equality of both members of the human pair, what should be our reaction if someone cites an alleged *hadith* from Bukhari's compilation where the Prophet supposedly said that woman was created from a crooked rib[7] and so if one tries to "straighten" her, she will break just as surely as a rib would, therefore man would do best to accept her flaws so he can enjoy her for what she is? Insult aside, no matter who supposedly transmitted this and no matter how strong or weak the transmission chain was declared to be in Bukhari's and other *hadith* compilations,[8] it makes no sense to accept this supposed "*hadith*" when a) it flies in the face of everything the Qur'an tells us about the fundamental nature of women and b) history, our current world and my own life experience are replete with many admirably principled and moral women in my life and across the globe.

"From Your Own Souls"

A note on the translation of one particular phrase that recurs in several verses above is in order here. The Arabic phrase "from your own souls" so often used in the Qur'an in reference to the creation of human "mates" or "pairs" has often been translated as "from yourselves". This may convey a good enough meaning, but it does not convey the level of intimacy clearly intended by the Author in verses that convey ideas like "He created you (pl.) from a single soul and *from it* created its mate", which readily conjures up the familiar notion of a soul-mate.

But I am more disheartened by translations that render "from your own souls" into "from *among* yourselves", as this seems to thoroughly rupture the intimacy I hear in the Arabic original, moving the meaning of the phrase from the spiritual to the sociological realm. I have to believe that many English translations rely and build on one another—as I have in fact done myself to a good extent—and in the process of such a mammoth

[7] The biblical story of Eve's creation from the rib of Adam cannot be found in the Qur'an. That said, I do not necessarily find this a contradiction as "rib" also depicts intimacy and sameness in my view, and human creation is both a tangible and an intangible process as seen in Qur'anic references to the creation of the human being from clay and water but also from divine breath. The problem with the "crooked rib" *hadith* though is that Jewish lore (the *Isra'iliyyat*) then in circulation and accessible to *hadith* compilers arguably had its own biases, and "*hadith*" seemed to borrow from it selectively, as has been widely noted even by early Islamic scholars such as Tabari, among others.

[8] Stowasser, Barbara Freyer. 1994. Women in the Qur'an, Traditions, and Interpretation. New York: Oxford University Press Inc., 32.

task as translating the entire Qur'an, perhaps some nuance existing in the Arabic has sometimes been lost as linguistic/translating custom has asserted itself.

Lastly, it must be mentioned that the word for "soul" (*nafs*) is a feminine noun in Arabic (there are no gender-neutral nouns). So it is particularly telling when some English translations refer to the soul using the masculine "he", obviously not even content to adopt the grammatically correct gender-neutral form "it" that I have used. Anything to move as far away as possible from "she", it would seem!

All Life on Earth Was Created in *Pairs*

In combing through the Qur'an for references to women, I could not help but notice the large number of times the word "pair" or "mate" occurs[9] (this is the Arabic *zawj*, which as a reminder can denote both "pair" and "one of a pair" i.e. mate or spouse, depending on context). However, not all such references relate to men and women or even to animals, as the reference is often to plants and fruit. Where this is the case, English translations usually render "pair/mate" as "kind", as in "kinds of plants or fruit", as it would sound too weird to say "*pairs* of plants or fruit".

I came across an enlightening footnote about this issue in one of the more interesting English translations and commentaries of the Qur'an,[10] which brutally exposed to me the fact that I had never paid much attention in biology class. As most readers will likely know though, plants usually have both male and female sex organs co-existing within themselves, though some will have them in separate flowers of the same plant. In rare cases, the reproductive organs are found in separate, unisexual plants of the same species. Anyway, I was relieved to find an explanation for what had seemed to me a strange deployment of the concept of the male and female pair in the Qur'an!

It is significant that the Qur'an makes reference to all of God's earthly creation in terms of two sexes, explicitly making "the sexual pair" the fundamental building block in its creationist narrative. And if the human pair

[9] The word for "pair" or "mate" (*zawj*) appears in numerous references to the natural world beyond humans and animals, such as in 13:3, 20:53, 22:5, 26:7, 31:10, 50:7 and 55:52.

[10] Asad, Muhammad. 2003. The Message of the Qur'an. Bristol, England: The Book Foundation, 399.

is at the apex of this creation, then both members of that pair—men and women—are in an exceptionally privileged position. Here are just a few of the many examples of this to be found in the Qur'an:

> Ya Sin (uncertain meaning), 36:36
> Glory be to He who created all the pairs—those that grow from the earth and those from their souls—and those they do not know about.
>
> Ornaments of Gold, 43:12
> And He who created all the pairs.
>
> The Scattering Winds, 51:49
> And of every thing We have created two mates, so that you (pl.) might reflect.

What Explains Societal Deviation from the Qur'anic Pillars of Creation?

In light of the evidence above from the Qur'an itself regarding the essential nature of women being identical to that of men, what could possibly explain the treatment of women as second-rate beings in some Muslim communities? I can think of a number of possible explanations.

- **Many Muslims do not actually read the Qur'an, and local or imported trends fill the vacuum**.
  Scripture always requires a significant effort on the part of a reader due to the density of its content and complex structure, making it anything but an easy read whatever the religion in question. And while the tradition of reading the Qur'an from beginning till end every Ramadan is widespread among Muslims, I know from personal and others' experience how one can read it yet miss out on key messages when the focus is on finishing the book within a month.
  Additionally, it is a most unfortunate fact that much of the Muslim world is illiterate, a sad irony for the followers of a religion so directly based on a book. While literacy rates vary widely from one Muslim-majority country to another and many across the Middle East and Asia are in fact highly literate by global measures, some of the more populous or strategic countries (for varying reasons) nevertheless have very high rates of illiteracy including Afghanistan (61.8%), Mali

(61.9%), Pakistan (41.3%), Bangladesh (38.5%), Yemen (29.9%), Morocco (27.6%), Egypt (24.8%), Sudan (24.1%), Iraq (20.3%), Algeria (19.8%), and Tunisia (18.2%).[11] Elsewhere, populous countries with significant Muslim populations where the illiteracy rate is also high include Nigeria (40.4%) and India (27.9%). Contrast that for a moment with overall illiteracy rates in regions such as Latin America and the Caribbean (6.8%) or Europe and Central Asia (1.9%).[12] Some reports have suggested that close to 40% of the Muslim world is illiterate.[13]

A further complication is that even among the literate in many countries, such as in South Asia, many people prefer to spend their time listening to and memorising the Qur'an as the word of God in the original Arabic for its intrinsic divine blessing (*baraka*), which they feel becomes an act of internalising God far superior to reading the Qur'an in another language. This makes many people particularly dependent on *hadith*, however relayed or selected.

The point is this: it is most probable that relatively few of the world's Muslims read the Qur'an anyway, never mind their degree of commitment or concentration when they do.

- **Many Muslims read the Qur'an technically but not reflectively, because they are familiar with the Arabic alphabet but not with Arabic as such.**

For example, readers of Urdu or Farsi or Uzbek may recognise the Arabic script sufficiently well to read it, but unless they have studied the language, they would have to rely on others to tell them what it actually says—such as others who may have their own agenda or be themselves influenced by others' agendas or who are simply misinformed. This is like someone who knows only English trying to read French, German or Portuguese, all of which use the Latin alphabet. Why would Muslims who do not know Arabic even try to read the Qur'an in the original Arabic, one might ask? Again, because Muslims believe that there is an intrinsic divine blessing (*baraka*) in repeating the direct word of God as He chose to communicate it to us. I should

[11] United Nations Development Programme. 2017. Human Development Report 2016, 230–233. The illiteracy rates cited are for the population aged 15 years and above.

[12] Ibid., 233. Central Asia consists of five Muslim-majority countries with highly literate populations.

[13] The Union of News Agencies (UNA, formerly The International Islamic News Agency). 2015. www.iinanews.com. January 14.

add the clarification that this *baraka* nonetheless requires that the heart be sincere in the effort and one is not simply going through the motions, otherwise surely the blessing will not be forthcoming whether one understands the Arabic language or not.
But I also believe just as firmly that this reading effort—or indeed the rote memorisation of the Qur'an so common in many religious schools—does not absolve anyone of the duty of trying to genuinely understand what the Qur'an says, that we must try to meet God half-way, so to speak, by doing our bit and making the effort not just to read, recite, or repeat—but also to understand!

- **Many Muslims (and others) read translations of the Qur'an that are either heavily influenced by an agenda, or predominantly influenced by accepted cultural norms**.
In today's world, this is in fact the issue of greatest concern with respect to Muslims' relationship with the Qur'an. Although the vast majority of egregious ideas within Islam today appear to have come out of the Arabic-speaking world in the latter part of the twentieth century, with Arabs tending to read the Qur'an through the lens of modern Arab experience with statehood and governance, it is a fact that less than 18% of Muslims in the world are Arab. This means that any spreading of such ideas globally must be primarily taking place in other languages. Passive ignorance or limited knowledge because of not being able to read or fully understand the Qur'an is one thing, but discrimination, intolerance and perhaps even violence due to misinformation is quite another. As explained in the Preface, my experience with some English translations, for example, is a significant factor shaping this book.

Once the essential nature of something is established, there really should be no confusion over its worth as such. Thus in an ideal world, this book on women in the Qur'anic worldview would end right here.

However our world is far from ideal, and women in particular have borne the brunt of unfavourable treatment, time and again, across history and cultures. It is bad enough for society to discriminate against some of its members, but positively egregious to do so while claiming that it is what God wants, adding insult to injury. And it is this that makes it necessary for me to continue writing, which I regret to some extent. I say this because while it is important to address the myths and other perversions we have all heard of, I genuinely resent having to raise unpleasant topics in a book that is ultimately about God, who is all things beautiful to me and who could not be further removed from the unsavoury blame assigned to Him for our own shortcomings.

CHAPTER 6

Eve Is Not Blamed for the Fall from Eden, Nor Are Women Guilty by Association

Qur'anic Verses on the Fall from the Garden

The Qur'an describes God's creation of the human being and its infusion with His Spirit multiple times, as we have already seen. In 25 other verses the first male, Adam, is referred to by name. Reference is also made to Adam's mate and spouse though her name, Eve (*Hawwa'* in Arabic, as in Hebrew), is not mentioned. Once again, this is no doubt a reflection of prevailing customs—neither Sarah nor Hagar are mentioned by name in relation to Abraham, for example, and so on.

Importantly, the Qur'an does not single out Eve for blame in the matter of the original couple disobeying God and thus being exiled from the Garden for a time. **If anything, the Qur'an actually singles out *Adam*—unsurprising given that he is the representative of humanity with whom God had made His covenant—though the overall message is firm in that both Adam and Eve did wrong of their own free will** and were therefore accountable. Thus there is no premise for women to be considered "guilty by association".

There are three groups of verses that show, in an almost identical way, the free will and accountability of *both* Adam and Eve. I am including them all here to highlight the number of times the Qur'an could have singled out Eve for special blame for the Fall from the Garden, but did not. I also want to show how the Arabic original explicitly addresses both Adam and Eve by using the dual-plural, which does not always come

L. El-Ali, *No Truth Without Beauty*, Sustainable Development Goals Series, https://doi.org/10.1007/978-3-030-83582-8_6

across in English translations since "you" in English applies to the singular, the dual-plural, and the communal-plural. Also I have underlined some phrases for a reason, which will soon be made clear.

Group 1: The Cow, 2:35–38

And We said: Oh Adam, dwell with your spouse in the Garden and eat from it freely from whatever you both like but do not approach this tree, either of you, for then you would become wrong-doers.

Then Satan caused them both to slip and removed them from the (ideal) state they were in. And We said: Descend, all of you. You [pl. that denotes three or more] will be enemies to one another. And you shall have a dwelling-place on earth, and enjoyment for a while.

Then Adam received words from his Lord, for He relented towards him. Truly He is the Ever-Relenting, Ever-Merciful.

We said: Descend from it, all of you. But you will surely receive guidance from Me, and those who follow My guidance shall have nothing to fear, nor shall they grieve.

Group 2: The Heights, 7:19–24

Oh Adam, dwell with your spouse in the Garden and eat from whatever you both like but do not approach this tree, either of you, for then you would become wrong-doers.

Then Satan whispered to them both so as to make them aware of their private parts, of which they had not been conscious. And he said: Your Lord has only forbidden you both this tree so you cannot become angels, nor join the immortals.

And he swore to them both: I am your sincere adviser!

Thus he lured them both with delusion. And when they tasted of the tree they became conscious of their private parts, and they went about covering themselves with leaves from the Garden. And their Lord called out to them: Did I not forbid you both this tree, and tell you both that Satan is a clear enemy?

They both said: Our Lord! We have wronged ourselves. And if You don't forgive us and have mercy on us, we shall surely be lost.

He said: Descend, all of you. You [pl. that denotes three or more] will be enemies to one another. And you shall have a dwelling-place on earth, and enjoyment for a while.

And finally, this is where Adam is singled out for blame, to some extent:

Group 3: Ta Ha (uncertain meaning), 20:115

And We had made a pact with Adam in the past, but he forgot, and We did not find him to be of firm resolve.

...continued in 20:120–123

Then Satan whispered to him saying: Oh Adam, shall I show you the tree of immortality and infinite power?

So they both ate from it and thus their private parts became apparent to them, and they began to cover themselves with leaves from the Garden. Adam disobeyed his Lord, and so he lost his way.

Then his Lord chose him, and relented towards him, and guided him.

He said: Descend from it, both of you—all of you. You [pl. that denotes three or more] will be enemies to one another. But you will surely receive guidance from Me, and then whoever follows My guidance will not lose their way, nor suffer.

Now, an important word on the underlined parts beginning with "Descend" in the verses above.

As briefly mentioned, in Arabic there are two plural forms for "you": the first denotes "two", while the second denotes everything above two, i.e. three or more. So it is always clear whether two people are being addressed, or three or more.

But English translations of these verses usually use "you" without additional clarification as to how many people are being addressed.

The problem with this is that although it is linguistically correct English, it can leave the reader or hearer of verses 2:36 and 7:24 thinking that the

Qur'an is saying that Adam and Eve, and by extension men and women generally, will be pitted against *each other*.

Such translations essentially convey those parts of 2:36 and 7:24, which are part of the story of Adam and Eve's Fall from the Garden, as follows:

> × Descend, each of you an enemy to the other / enemies unto one another

rather than

> ✓ Descend, <u>all</u> of you. You will be enemies to one another

or some such equivalent, which would have made it easier for the reader to realise that those being addressed are in fact not just Adam and Eve, but Adam and Eve and Satan—as is in fact widely agreed by Qur'anic commentators—as well as Adam and Eve's progeny, by extension.[1]

But I am more concerned about how the other "Descend" verse, 20:123 shown above, is usually translated:

> × Descend from it, <u>both of you together</u>, each of you an enemy to the other / enemies unto one another

rather than

> ✓ Descend from it, <u>both of you—all of you</u>. You will be enemies to one another

In other words, most translations of 20:123 translate the "both" part but not the "all" part of the first sentence, perhaps because it is odd to be addressing "both" and "all" at the same time. On its own this omission is not a big issue given that the last part of this verse does point to all of Adam and Eve's *descendants*. But once "all of you" is omitted in the first sentence, it becomes necessary to also translate the second sentence on "enemies" as addressing "both" Adam and Eve—or at least ambiguously—rather than absolutely everyone, even though the Arabic is clearly in the communal-plural to correspond to the preceding "all of you".

[1] See commentary on 7:24–25 in Nasr, Seyyed Hossein (editor-in-chief) et al. 2015. The Study Quran: A New Translation and Commentary. New York: HarperCollins Publishers, 414.

Again, the problem with these translations' decisions is that they can leave the reader or hearer of 20:123 who is not also aware of the totality of the other verses cited in this section with the possibility of hearing the second sentence as God saying that Adam and Eve—and so their descendants also—will be naturally pitted against one another *by gender*, rather than generally.

The Pushback of Alleged *Hadith* on Eve: Guilty and Solely Responsible!

"*Hadith*" references to Eve, however, turn the Qur'anic story of Adam and Eve's Fall from the Garden on its head. While the Qur'an faults both parties even as it places a little more emphasis on Adam's guilt—presumably as the representative of humanity as I have noted—multiple and varying *hadith* references all put the blame squarely on Eve's shoulders, and turn quite speculative after that. **By the time the famous *hadith*-based Qur'anic commentary by Tabari is written in the ninth and tenth centuries, these contradicting and creative *hadiths* are in such wide circulation that Tabari himself quotes a large number of them in his work even as he frequently expresses reservations about their reliability.**[2] Here is a summary of the environment at the time and the kind of "*hadiths*" he referenced:

> …it was the majority opinion of theological experts by Tabari's time that it was only through the woman's weakness and guile that Satan could bring about Adam's downfall…Iblis (Satan)…approached Hawwa' (Eve) with the words: 'Look at this Tree! How good it smells, how good it tastes, how nice its color is!' Hawwa' succumbed, then went to Adam and addressed him with Satan's very words; and Adam ate. Other traditions report that Hawwa' commanded her husband to eat, or that she urged him on by saying: 'I have just eaten of it, and it has not harmed me'. Else, sexual desire or intoxication are made to explain the absence of Adam's rational powers at this critical moment: Satan made Hawwa' appear attractive to Adam, and when he wanted her for his desire, she refused to obey unless he first ate of the Tree, or: she gave him wine, and when he was drunk and his rational faculties had left him, she led him to the Tree and he ate.
>
> …God then put His curse on the woman…, but He did not curse the man, only the earth from which he had been created…[and God] banished

[2] Stowasser, Barbara Freyer. 1994. Women in the Qur'an, Traditions, and Interpretation. New York: Oxford University Press Inc., 28.

> Adam to a life of want and work...God's curse on the woman, however, was *ad personam* and severe; it involved the constitution and mental abilities...Because Hawwa' had tempted God's servant and had made the Tree bleed when she picked its fruit, she was condemned to bleed once a month, to carry and deliver her children against her will, and to be often close to death on delivery. God also made the woman foolish and stupid, while He had created her wise and intelligent. 'Were it not for the calamity that afflicted Hawwa', the women of this world would not menstruate, would be wise, and would bear their children with ease.' ...On the question of the humans' repentance after their disobedience, some traditions quoted by Tabari indicate that both the man and the woman acknowledged their sin and asked God's forgiveness and mercy, but a larger number of reports specify that the prayer for forgiveness and God's promise of eternal life involved Adam alone.[3]

I believe the above quick tour of the anti-Eve "*hadith*" reports speaks for itself, as does the fact that such a respected scholar as Tabari had doubted their reliability. But more important is the fact that ***hadith*** **leaves us with a diametrically opposite impression of Eve as our primordial Grandmother—Jeddah in Arabic, for whom the city is named—and of women's capacity to that given by the Qur'an. To accept these** ***hadith*** **reports, one would have to disregard the Qur'anic narrative on Eve and on women, something surely no believing Muslim would do knowingly**.

CHAPTER 7

Women Are Not a Constant Source of Social Discord: Nor Naturally Conniving!

Qur'anic Verses on Social Discord, or *Fitna*

One of the strangest cultural twists I encountered on my travels was the discovery that in some Muslim communities, women are believed to personify *fitna*.

Now *fitna* in Arabic denotes such big-picture concepts as **social discord or divisiveness, often due to oppression or persecution**. Examples from the Qur'an are:

> <u>The Cow, 2:217</u>
> ...And oppression (*fitna*) is worse than killing...
>
> <u>Repentance, 9:48</u>
> They (who do not believe) had sought to sow discord (*fitna*) and had upset things for you...
>
> <u>The Spider, 29:10</u>
> There are people who say: We believe in God. But when they are hurt because of (their belief in) God, they mistake their persecution (*fitna*) by others for punishment from God...

On a personal or more micro-level, *fitna* in the Qur'an refers to a **trial (personal ordeal) or affliction, often due to our own character flaws or as a consequence of our choices**. Examples:

L. El-Ali, *No Truth Without Beauty*, Sustainable Development Goals Series, https://doi.org/10.1007/978-3-030-83582-8_7

> Spoils of War, 8:25
> And beware of an affliction (*fitna*) that does not only befall wrong-doers, and know that God is severe in punishment.
> ...continued in 8:28
> And know that your wealth and your children are but a trial (*fitna*), and that with God is an immense reward.
>
> The Pilgrimage, 22:53
> That He may make that which Satan proposes a trial (*fitna*) for those whose hearts are diseased and hard...

The above is but a sampling of how the Qur'an uses *fitna*, a ubiquitous word appearing both in noun and verb form dozens of times—**while never having anything to do with women** as such.

But oh, for the power of cultural insinuation!

When I re-met Amr Abdalla in March 2015 after having crossed paths with him a couple of times years earlier, it was at a lunch-time talk he was giving at Georgetown University on some topic related to Islam. His experience as a sharia-trained prosecutor in Egypt was a fascinating one to hear about, containing valuable insights for today's challenges. But what I remember the most that will probably always make me think of him is one word: ***kayda-kunna***. Let me explain.

Amr asked our small group if we were familiar with the story of Joseph in the Qur'an. Some of us nodded: Chap. 12 actually carries the prophet Joseph's name and tells his entire life story, and is moreover famous for being the longest continuous narrative in the book.

Were we familiar with the story of how his master's wife had tried to seduce Joseph? Nods all round...

And when Joseph tried to resist her, how she grabbed his shirt and it tore in the process? Yes...

And when Joseph and his master's wife ran into the husband at the entrance and she accused Joseph of having made advances at her, what happened then? We mumbled that someone suggested that if Joseph's shirt were torn from the front, then the master's wife was telling the truth—but if it were torn from the back, then she was lying and Joseph was telling the truth. And of course it was torn from the back...

And what does the Qur'an then say, Amr asked?

And this is where eager-beaver me blurts out: *kayda-hunna 'adheem!* ... just as I realise that I was the only one who spoke, because I was the only Arabic-speaker in the group who knew the famous line.

Are you sure, Amr asks me?

Why, yes!

Are you sure it is *kayda-hunna* (all women, who are all schemers), not *kayda-kunna* (you women who scheme), that are said to be terrible?

Here I gradually begin to realise what is going on...but surely not! Everyone, all my life, has always said *kayda-hunna* when deploying that supposed idiom!

But Amr was not done: he asks me who I think uttered those words, and now I can no longer be quick to reply. Eager Beaver is suddenly pausing for thought.

He is gracious, dear Amr, and offers it up: Do you think this phrase was uttered by God, or by the master of the house?

And of course the answer has to be by the master of the house (12:28), not God, except that people usually cite the phrase as if it were uttered by God Himself. The story then continues with a group of women being invited by the master's wife to check out Joseph's beauty for themselves, and the accusation is repeated by Joseph (12:33) and once more by his master (12:50), both times clearly in reference to *this* group of scheming women.

I will never forget this cautionary tale, which was a brilliant way to make a point about the cultural impositions on religion. **An uttering by one man to a scheming woman a long time ago is verbally perverted through the change of one letter and presented as a negative utterance by God Himself about all women**. Amr told our group that every time he used this example in a class, he got the same reaction from the native Arabic speakers present as he had from me. Just think about that for a moment.

Perhaps it is the mis-reciting of this phrase, which relates to the attempted seduction of Joseph, that has led the word *fitna* to become mis-associated with the idea of "women as constant sexual enticement" and as "naturally conniving" in so many corners of the world. This is an oddly specific and narrow association given the broad, existential concept that *fitna* is in the Qur'an. I cannot say for sure, but this mis-recital cannot have helped matters.

Interestingly, this matter of how a single letter can change the meaning of a word in Arabic is one I have been aware of for many years in relation to another verse, but one that has no bearing on our topic here. I mention this nevertheless because it makes me wonder how many more suspect verbal departures from Qur'anic verses we have absorbed into our everyday Arabic speech as proverbs without realising it.

The Pushback of Alleged *Hadith* on Women's Character: Hell Is Full of Women!

Supposedly, the Prophet has said that the majority of the inhabitants of hell are women, because they are ungrateful (to their men) and in other more flowery versions, also because they are deficient in intellect and religion, and they often slander and curse.[1]

The first time I read about this "*hadith*" from Bukhari's compilation, I was initially dismissive. But the ensuing discussion made me realise that it has quite a bit of currency even in some influential quarters,[2] and soon my amusement turned to shock. Shock then turned to incredulity when I found some efforts to explain it by "putting it in context", the thrust of the argument being that the Prophet had used exaggeration and even humour to offer women very good religious counsel![3]

How could this be? Who could possibly have wished to go this far in their desire to discriminate against, and oppress, women? Who would risk their soul to put such counter-Qur'anic words into our beloved Prophet's mouth, or perhaps into the mouths of his contemporaries—who knows?

As I think of this, there can only be two answers as to how this could have happened. Either those responsible did not fully believe in Muhammad's message, or they did but thought they were acting in the interest of the greater good as defined by their own prejudices.

In any case, **several overburdened Muslim experts[4] have since taken on this alleged *hadith* and done us the service of exposing its shortcomings, whether technically or substantively**. I feel grateful to them, but also regret that their formidable skills had to be applied to something

[1] Abou El Fadl, Khaled M. 2003. Speaking in God's Name: Islamic Law, Authority and Women. Oxford: Oneworld Publications, 225.

[2] Ibid., 225.

[3] Ibid., 229.

[4] Prominent Muslim scholars challenging the alleged "women are the majority of hell's inhabitants" *hadith* include Fazlur Rahman and Khaled Abou El Fadl. See also Al-Matroudi, Ibrahim bin Salman. 2013. Al-Riyadh newspaper No. 16326. www.alriyadh.com/815375 (in Arabic). March 6.

so sordid. I regret that so many of us are no longer content to refer back to the Qur'an or our conscience and would rather waste our precious scholars' time on tedious rebuttals of the absurd, rather than free them up so they can reach more of us with their spiritual example and inspiration.

Finally with regard to a supposed *hadith* claiming that the Prophet had said that men face no greater threat of social discord—*fitna*—than women, we should know that this is a "*hadith*" that has been roundly shown to be unreliable.[5]

[5] Reda, Nevin. 2005. Women Leading Congregational Prayers. Canadian Council of Muslim Women paper, 12.

CHAPTER 8

Women Were Created with the Exact Same Spiritual and Intellectual Capacity as Men, So of Course They Can Lead

Qur'anic Verses on Women's Spirit and Intellect

It is hard not to cringe at having to state the obvious, especially when the opposite suggestion is so downright offensive and plain wrong, both factually and morally. But what can one do?

If the Qur'an tells us as we've seen in the verses discussed in Chap. 5 that all men and women were essentially created from Adam's soul, and that Adam's soul contained no less than the divine breath because God breathed into Adam of His Spirit when giving him life, then surely any differences between human beings spiritually and intellectually can only come from personal differences—never from one's gender, or race for that matter. These personal differences may stem from our individual characteristics or from our environments, but they cannot—by definition—stem from our God-given existence! So how can anyone say that women cannot or must not serve as religious leaders or *imams* or judges or heads of state? If women *can* lead, why can't they?

There is no justification whatsoever on a Qur'anic basis for preventing women from fulfilling their potential or any of these roles, with a large number of verses addressing men and women making it clear that **both bear equal responsibility for making their societies flourish**. This is so evident in the Qur'an that for me to show it in this particular chapter of the book would require re-presenting a large number of the verses I already include in other sections—in particular, see the verses cited in Chap. 11 in the section entitled "Participation".

L. El-Ali, *No Truth Without Beauty*, Sustainable Development Goals Series, https://doi.org/10.1007/978-3-030-83582-8_8

But I will say this, to demonstrate the point: one of the most remarkable discoveries for me personally was to learn quite how responsive God was being at the time, via the Qur'anic verses, to sometimes very personal concerns. I had imagined the Qur'an as being driven solely by big-picture concerns, placing vision for the new religion and community above individual interests at all times. But I was wrong, and as I read on, I came to realise that on occasion, **verses were revealed in response to a specific individual's concerns or predicament—in several instances a particular woman's predicament, as we shall see later, on such varied issues as unjust divorce, the right to earn, not being heard, and sexual slander—clearly issues God was signalling He took very seriously.** Qur'anic studies indeed place great emphasis on the "reasons for a revelation" (*asbab al-nuzul*), whatever they may have been. But my favourite story and the one which is relevant here has to be the following.

It appears that some women had raised a concern to the Prophet that the Qur'anic verses being revealed always addressed people in the generic plural form,[1] which is linguistically masculine in Arabic just as it is in French and Spanish and possibly hundreds of other languages. A noun in Arabic, and in fact a verb also, when referring to a group of women is readily distinguishable from when it refers to a group of men, but when the group is mixed-gender it is the masculine plural that is used. I get goosebumps as I recall the impact this report[2] first had and still has on me, because God's response was the metaphorical equivalent of Him getting off His throne and taking ten steps towards these women who cared enough to ask, a response which came in the following verse:

> <u>The Confederates, 33:35</u>
> For submitting men (to God) <u>and submitting women</u>, believing men <u>and believing women</u>, devout men <u>and devout women</u>, truthful men <u>and truthful women</u>, patient men <u>and patient women</u>, humble men <u>and humble women</u>, charitable men <u>and</u> <u>charitable</u> <u>women</u>, fasting men <u>and fasting women</u>, chaste men <u>and</u> <u>chaste</u> <u>women</u>, men who remember God often <u>and women who remember God often</u>—for them God has prepared forgiveness, and a great reward.

Nor was the above the only Qur'anic verse to go to such lengths, as I hope the reader will notice from other verses cited in this book and, of course, when and if they next read the Qur'an.

[1] Abou El Fadl, Khaled M. 2003. Speaking in God's Name: Islamic Law, Authority and Women. Oxford: Oneworld Publications, 230.

[2] Ibid., 255.

Objectors to women's leadership usually push back against women's advancement primarily by citing supposed *hadith* denouncing women as such, most strikingly such alleged *hadith* that re-define women first and foremost as a constant source of sexual enticement and so a moral danger to a presumably otherwise innocent society of men, thereby requiring them to be kept out of sight. And then to prop up their position, objectors point to allegedly Qur'anic obstacles to women's leadership via a combined extrapolation of (a) what the Qur'an meant by *hijab* (it meant curtain or screen) and (b) how the Qur'an regarded the Prophet's wives (unlike all other women) to arrive at broad gender segregation. The baselessness of these claims laid at the door of the Qur'an, and which are used to limit women's full participation, will be covered in Part IV.

The Pushback of Alleged *Hadith* on Women as Heads of State: But Women Are "Losers"!

In light of women's natural spiritual and intellectual capacity according to the Qur'an and our own experience of the world, if someone cites a *hadith* where the Prophet supposedly said that no nation or community would succeed if it had a woman as its leader, what should our reaction be? To me, even if the transmission chain of this *hadith* was deemed reliable (though scholars have highlighted that this *hadith*'s chief source was a recognised slanderer and rabid woman-hater from the caliph Omar's time)[3] and no matter which compilation it appeared in (it was even in Bukhari's), it makes no sense as (a) it contradicts the Qur'anic message of the essential sameness of the two sexes and (b) it represents a generalisation that flies in the face of historical and contemporary evidence in many countries and cultures. But I am most likely to respond with the more potent reminder that if this were truly the case, then God would surely not have devoted a block of two dozen or so verses to telling the story of **the powerful Queen of Sheba's wise leadership as she interacted with her court as well as with King Solomon, whom she voluntarily joins in submission to God because, as the Qur'an puts it, she *chose* the right path (27:22–44)**. And if I were in a cheeky mood, I might point to the dozens of countries in the world—starting with Muslim-majority

[3] Ibid., 111–113 and Stowasser, Barbara Freyer. 1994. Women in the Qur'an, Traditions, and Interpretation. New York: Oxford University Press Inc., 65–66.

ones—that are led by men but are doing miserably on virtually every indicator of both worldly and spiritual success possible.

The impact of this strange myth cannot be underestimated. While working with a group of civil society activists recently in North Africa, the question of women as heads of state came up. All the men in the group were against the idea as were most of the women in fact, though some of the women as well as men stated that their reason was that a woman president would not succeed at her job given the culture of their countries. But one man offered a different argument that a few others agreed with: Even in America, he said, people say that the American Ambassador to Libya, the late Chris Stevens, would not have died if Hillary Clinton had not been the Secretary of State at the time. No mention was made of this egregious *hadith* allegedly saying that no nation shall succeed with a woman at its helm, but the illogic of this reasoning leaves me in no doubt that this is the only place the man in question could have been coming from.

If this supposed *hadith* on the certain disaster that would befall a people who choose a woman as their leader is not a complete fabrication, how might we explain its existence in light of its Qur'anic opposite, as conveyed by the story of the Queen of Sheba, and by Qur'anic gender principles in the holy book?

Perhaps the historic context of this *hadith* can shed some light:

> ...this Hadith was narrated from the Prophet by a Companion who recalled that, 'When it reached the Prophet that the Persians had placed the daughter of [their former king] Chosroes on the throne, he said, 'A country that entrusts its affairs to a woman will not flourish.'[4]

To my mind, the fact that this *hadith* was a response to a particular development and was not an out-of-the-blue declaration makes all the difference, and causes me to sigh in relief. As believers, we err not only when we take a general principle and then try to clip its wings so as to restrict it to what is convenient for us, but we also err when we do the opposite: when we take the specific and try to extend it into a general principle. In fact, **the version of this *hadith* narrated by Bukhari indicates that the Prophet was simply predicting the fall of Persia, and moreover not all the compilers classified this *hadith* under their "governance" section,**

[4]Brown, Jonathan. 2015. Misquoting Muhammad: The Challenge and Choices of Interpreting the Prophet's Legacy. London: Oneworld Publications, 138.

which clearly shows that they did not think it had anything to do with who could or could not become a ruler.[5]

But I will let the words of a great Islamic jurist and scholar speak for themselves in conclusive commentary on this bizarre *hadith*:

> ...it is possible that Abu Bakrah [the narrator of this *hadith*] was, in fact, someone who saw little value in women[6]. If that is the case, is it possible that the Prophet had commented on the developing situation in Persia by saying, 'A people who are led by *this* woman will not succeed?' Is it possible that Abu Bakrah misheard the statement because he was receiving it through his own subjectivities? But if the Prophet did make a statement such as the one reported by Abu Bakrah, why was he the only one who seems to have heard it? If, as in some versions, the Prophet made this statement in the presence of Aishah [the Prophet's wife and prolific *hadith* narrator], why did she not report it?[7]

The Pushback of Ir-rationalisation on Women as *Imams*: Grasping at Straws

The question of women as congregational prayer leaders, or *imams*, warrants some attention as it has been firmly held almost everywhere in modern times that this is a role that is off-limits to women no matter what. This is despite the opinion of the likes of Tabari, the widely respected tenth-century *hadith*-based Qur'anic commentator, as well as historical evidence that suggests it is perfectly acceptable, as we shall see below. Justifications for this objection are sometimes anchored in the alleged "women leaders bring failure" *hadith* and/or by pedantic, puritan and even physiological arguments for good measure.

- The **pedantic objection** to women leading the prayers goes like this: since women used to line up in rows behind the men's rows during congregational prayers, and not alongside the men, then it must

[5] Abou El Fadl, Khaled. *Op. Cit.* (2003), 136.

[6] The narrator of this bizarre *hadith* on women as leaders, Abu Bakrah, is reported to have said: 'The death of a father breaks the back, the death of a son splits the heart, the death of a brother severs the wings and the death of a woman deserves no more than one hour of grief." See Abou El Fadl, Khaled. *Op. Cit.* (2003), 113.

[7] Abou El Fadl, Khaled. *Op. Cit.* (2003), 113–114.

mean that a woman is not supposed to ever be *in front of* a man.[8] This argument conveniently omits mention of the fact that during the Prophet's time, when some men arrived late to the congregational prayers they would simply line up in rows behind the women's rows and proceed to join in the rites.[9] Notice that there was no mention of separate, curtained-off or walled-up areas called the "women's sections" in those days, as has become depressingly widespread throughout the Muslim world today.

- The **puritan objection** to women leading the prayers maintains that men could not possibly focus and social strife would arise if they had a woman standing in front of them—or worse, if they could hear her voice reciting the prayers or giving the Friday sermon—since women are allegedly a constant source of sexual enticement, apparently even when they are immersed in the worship of God. Notice that the framing of the issue exonerates men from responsibility for their possible actions, placing it squarely on women's shoulders and, some would argue, their implied ever-present ill-intent.
- The **physiological objection** to women leading the prayers argues that since women cannot perform the prayer or fasting rites during menstruation—according to custom, not the Qur'an—then they cannot act as prayer leaders at *any* time. The illogic of this argument is glaringly obvious. Some conveniently extend this custom to maintain that women must not utter God's verses either during this time, a significant chunk of a woman's life, nor touch the holy book. Yet the Qur'an mentions menstruation only to say that sexual intercourse should be avoided during that time as it is a "hurt" (2:222),[10] and the Prophet is known to have asked his wife Aisha to fetch his prayer mat from the mosque during her menstrual period, correcting her when she resisted by saying "Your menstruation is not in your hand!"[11] In fact two of Muhammad's widows, Aisha and Umm

[8] Brown, Jonathan. *Op. Cit.* (2015), 38.

[9] Abou El Fadl, Khaled. *Op. Cit.* (2003), 242.

[10] Some have taken the reference to menstruation as "a hurt" in 2:222 to refer to the discomfort it is known to cause women, but most have taken it to mean "uncleanness", probably influenced by pre-Islamic Arab customs. For more, see Nasr, Seyyed Hossein (editor-in-chief) et al. 2015. The Study Quran: A New Translation and Commentary. New York: HarperCollins Publishers, 97.

[11] le Gai Eaton, Charles. 2008. Chapter: "Purification" in The Book of Hadith: Sayings of the Prophet Muhammad, from the Mishkat al-Masabih. Watsonville, California; Bristol, England: The Book Foundation.

Salama, openly challenged one Companion's particularly insulting alleged *hadiths* on menstruation, telling him that they would often be lying in front of the Prophet or pass in front of him during their menstrual period while he was performing his prayers without issue, and numerous reports tell us that the Prophet urged menstruating women to join Eid celebrations at the mosque while others record that women attended prayers there even during menstruation.[12]

Historical Evidence and Medieval Jurist Support for Women as Leaders

All of these excuses aimed at preventing women from serving as *imams* ignore not only the absence of a Qur'anic restriction and the existence of some heavy-weight support for women *imams* from early and medieval scholars, but also the historical evidence from the Prophet's own time and earliest days of Islam, as recorded in multiple *hadiths* and later reports.

- **The Prophet himself in the seventh century had appointed a woman, Umm Waraqa, as an *imam* in Medina, and even assigned her a *muezzin*.**

  - To those who have argued that Umm Waraqa was instructed to lead the prayers only for members of her household, which consisted of herself and just two servants, one might respond by asking why would the Prophet have then bothered to assign her an old man as *muezzin* i.e. to perform the call to prayer that summons worshippers who are further afield.[13]
  - To those who have argued that Umm Waraqa was tasked with leading a women-only congregation in Medina, one might point out that according to the eighth-century scholar who is the source of this *hadith*, another five transmitters conveyed the same *hadith* without mention of a gender restriction[14].

[12] Abou El Fadl, Khaled. *Op. Cit.* (2003), 226 and 242.

[13] Reda, Nevin. 2005. Women Leading Congregational Prayers. Canadian Council of Muslim Women paper, 5 and Brown, Jonathan. *Op. Cit.* (2015), 194.

[14] Brown, Jonathan. *Op. Cit.* (2015), 194.

- After the Prophet's death and during the Umayyad caliphate (661–750), **a female warrior named Ghazala led her male fighters in prayer at the Kufa mosque they had just taken over.**[15]

Such a report, of a woman named Ghazala leading men in prayer so long ago, is not the kind we tend to hear about, any more than we hear about a woman warrior, Nusayba, who fought alongside the Prophet himself and of whom he is reported to have said:

> I did not turn right or left on the day of [the battle of] Uhud but saw her there fighting in my place.[16]

Umm Waraqa, who had originally asked the Prophet to join him in battle before he assigned her the role of *imam* instead, and **Ghazala** leading her men in prayers in Kufa (in today's Iraq) are not the only examples of women in leadership roles in the religious, political, literary and social spheres of early Islam. Nor was **Nusayba** the only example of a woman in combat from early Islam: there are reports of **Umm Fadl**, wife of the Prophet's uncle, attacking and ultimately causing the death of a leading enemy of Islam with a wooden post when she came to the aid of a Muslim slave he was beating,[17] and of **Asma bint Yazid** dispatching nine Byzantine enemy soldiers with nothing but her tent pole.[18]

In the religious as well as political realm, the leadership of **Aisha, wife of the Prophet,** can hardly be overstated. She is the fourth-largest source of *hadiths* (2,210 reports) however they may have been categorised, and:

> During her lifetime, she (Aisha) was also honoured for her expertise in medicine and Islamic law. Regarding the *hadith,* she had not only learnt a large volume of these from her husband, she also showed a critical appreciation of them, and corrected mistakes in understanding of many Companions [of

[15] Abou El Fadl, Khaled. *Op. Cit.* (2003), 230.

[16] Kahf, Mohja. 2000. Braiding the Stories: Women's Eloquence in the Early Islamic Era. In Windows of Faith: Muslim Women Scholar-Activists in North America, ed. Gisela Webb, 148. New York: Syracuse University Press.

[17] Lings, Martin. 1988. Muhammad: His Life based on the Earliest Sources. London: Unwin Hyman Limited, 153.

[18] Brown, Jonathan. *Op. Cit.* (2015), 198.

the Prophet]...even the most important Companions sought her advice on legal problems.[19]

Aisha's co-leadership of an armed uprising following the death of the caliph Omar, whether one sympathises with that rebellion or not, would surely have been impossible if the woman who was the Prophet's beloved and known to be so close to him had ever been told by her husband that God wanted women confined to their homes and playing no part in leading society.

In the religious realm, women as leading Islamic scholars and teachers of mixed-gender audiences flourished in significant numbers until the sixteenth century, as already discussed in Part I, when their numbers began to dwindle noticeably, likely due to multiple external pressures. Their names, those of their notable students, their own teachers and anecdotes from their lives, alongside their male peers', are documented in volume upon volume that form a part of the Islamic religious heritage.[20] Interestingly, it is known that in the first century of Islam, for example, the following four of the Prophet's wives and two of his female Companions became prominent religious teachers:

- Aisha taught 232 men and 67 women;
- Umm Salama (Hind) taught 78 men and 23 women;
- Umm Habiba (Ramla) taught 18 men and 2 women;
- Hafsa taught 17 men and 3 women.
- Asma bint Abu Bakr taught 19 men and 2 women;
- Asma bint Umays taught 11 men and 2 women.[21]

In fact, the oldest continuously operating institution of higher learning in the world, the **University of Qarawiyyin in Fez, Morocco, was founded in the year 859 by a woman, Fatima al-Fihri.**[22]

In the literary realm, too, women appear as admired personalities, right from the beginning of Islam, of that highest form of Arabic literature: poetry. "Early Islamic literature" i.e. of the first 40 years of the

[19] Siddiqi, Muhammad Zubayr. 1993. Hadith Literature: Its Origin, Development and Special Features. Cambridge, England: The Islamic Texts Society, 21.

[20] Ibid., Appendix I.

[21] Abou El Fadl, Khaled M. 2006. The Search for Beauty in Islam: A Conference of the Books. Maryland: Rowman & Littlefield Publishers, Inc., 292.

[22] The Economist. 2020. Bygone Civilisations: Secret gardens. February 1.

new religion, from the Prophet's migration to Medina in the year 622 up to the first four caliphs who succeeded him, includes the Qur'an, *hadith*, sermons by the Prophet and others, and poetry, with one female poet named **Khansa** included.[23] And several major literary works after that time point to the influence of women as poets: the renowned **anthology of poetry *Hamasa***, from the ninth century, contains some poems by women; ***The Eloquence of Women***, also from the ninth century, is an anthology of women's contributions in poetry as well as religion and history; ***The Poetry of Women*** from the tenth century is a collection of poems by women; and an anthology of poetry by women in the fifteenth century declares that it skips over the early Islamic periods because there is too much poetry by women from those times to cover, choosing to focus on the "modern age" only.[24]

Even in the commercial realm, the fact that Omar, who became caliph just two years after the Prophet's death, appointed a literate woman named Layla (also known as Al-Shifa' i.e. The Cure) as minister of trade and commerce, effectively, in charge of running the *souks* or commercial marketplaces, speaks volumes.[25]

And in the social realm, likewise, women were never invisible during those first ten centuries or so of Islam in particular, as so many historical documents attest—Hollywood depictions and current Muslim imagination to the contrary notwithstanding. But everyone's favourite story in this regard is the following: when the second caliph, Omar, tried to place a cap on the pre-marital gift the Qur'an had made obligatory for a man to offer his prospective wife for her personal use, **a woman interrupted Omar while he was addressing the congregation from the pulpit (yes, she and other women were present in the mosque and not cordoned off out of sight), challenging his premise for doing so and after a debate, Omar conceded his error and backed off.**[26]

In terms of Muslim women-rulers overall:

[23] Kahf, Mohja. *Op. Cit.,* 149.

[24] Ibid., 151–52.

[25] Al-Baleek, Imad. 2017. Meet the First Female Minister of Commerce in Islam (in Arabic). Al Arabiya news website www.alarabiya.net, October 19.

[26] al-Hibri, Azizah. 2000. An Introduction to Muslim Women's Rights. In Windows of Faith: Muslim Women Scholar-Activists in North America, ed. Gisela Webb, 59. New York: Syracuse University Press and Brown, Jonathan. *Op. Cit.* (2015), 198.

The best-known women rulers in the premodern era include Khayzuran, who governed the Muslim Empire under three Abbasid caliphs in the eighth century; Malika Asma bint Shihab al-Sulayhiyya and Malika Arwa bint Ahmad al-Sulayhiyya, who both held power in Yemen in the eleventh century; Sitt al-Mulk, a Fatimid queen of Egypt in the eleventh century; the Berber queen Zaynab al-Nafzawiyah (r. 1061–1107); two thirteenth-century Mamluk queens, Shajar al-Durr in Cairo and Radiyyah in Delhi; six Mongol queens, including Kutlugh Khatun (thirteenth century) and her daughter Padishah Khatun of the Kutlugh-Khanid dynasty; the fifteenth-century Andalusian queen Aishah al-Hurra, known by the Spaniards as Sultana Madre de Boabdil; Sayyida al-Hurra, governor of Tetouán in Morocco (r. 1510–1542); and four seventeenth-century Indonesian queens.[27]

Such reports depicting women as leaders in various spheres are part of our heritage, and it is time for us to reclaim them. It is time to push back against those minority but loud voices that would claim that a woman's very voice must not be heard, that it is something to be hidden away just as surely as her private parts are. Outrageous as this claim is, it exists in some corners of "modern" Islam: it was in fact in a BBC report just today, the 3rd of December, 2017 as I write, on conflicting views about a newly pious Middle Eastern female singer's decision to re-embrace her music, after a hiatus, by channelling it into devotional songs. Such a claim not only exists but passes itself along by asserting that God himself considers a woman's voice a *'awra*: at best, a private part to be hidden from detection and at worst, a flaw or defect. Give me medieval Islam any day, thank you!

In any case I was pleased to learn that despite the alleged *hadith* on women as inappropriate heads of state, **not all early interpreters had extended its questionable political application to also argue that women should never become judges or religious leaders either—including prayer leaders (*imams*)**:

- Many **jurists of the Maliki school** (there are 4 schools of jurisprudence in Sunni Islam) argued that women could become judges without restrictions[28]

[27] Oxford Islamic Studies Online. Women and Islam. Oxford University Press. www.oxfordislamicstudies.com/article/opr/t125/e2510#. Accessed November 2019.

[28] Abou El Fadl, Khaled. *Op. Cit.* (2003), 111.

- The founder of the Hanafi school of jurisprudence, **Abu Hanifa (d. 767)**, thought that women could serve as judges in commercial and civil cases but not in criminal and personal injury ones[29]
- The hugely respected Qur'anic commentator **Tabari (d. 923)** not only maintained that women could become judges without restrictions, but that women could also lead men in the communal prayers[30]
- **Two leading students of the founder of the Shafi'i school** in the ninth century had allowed women to lead the prayers[31]
- The towering **Ibn Arabi (d. 1240)**, who was a formidable jurist and *hadith* scholar and not only a great Sufi master, unequivocally affirmed women's right to lead the communal prayers by pointing to the absence of Qur'anic or even *hadith* proof to support the objection, citing women's roles as spiritual leaders and bearers of prophecy in history, and concluded that those who argue otherwise "should not be listened to"[32]

[29] Ibid., 111.
[30] Ibid., 111.
[31] Brown, Jonathan. *Op. Cit.* (2015), 192.
[32] Ibid., 190.

CHAPTER 9

When Men Deprive Women of Their Free Will, They Are Not Protecting Anyone: They Are Obstructing God's Plan

Qur'anic Verses on Free Will and Accountability

The notion that men deprive women of making their own decisions in many families—not just certain communities—in order to protect them from God's wrath is again adding insult to injury.

But arguably more seriously from a metaphysical perspective, interfering with women's freedom of choice throws a wrench in God's plan of creating human beings, giving them free will, sending them guidance, and then judging them by the choices they make and the degree of spiritual growth they achieve.

Because **if women cannot make their own decisions, what is God to judge them on? Women will certainly get no credit for a "good deed" that is forced upon them, nor grow spiritually from it**, any more than they will for or from any good their menfolk do. Meanwhile men will certainly be accountable for having prevented their womenfolk from spiritual growth through their own choices and good deeds—not a good deed by any measure! Both men and women are indeed set back.

It really seems to me as simple as that.

Those looking for explicit Qur'anic proof of this self-evident truth need only refer to the large number of verses scattered throughout the book on accountability and how **every single soul—whether male or**

L. El-Ali, *No Truth Without Beauty*, Sustainable Development Goals Series, https://doi.org/10.1007/978-3-030-83582-8_9

female—will ultimately face God individually. Here is a small sampling of such verses[1]:

> The House of *'Imran* (Joaquim, father of Mary), 3:195
> So their Lord responded [i.e. to their prayer]: I do not let an act [i.e. good deed] by any of you go to waste, whether male or female. You are of each other...
>
> Cattle, 6:164
> ...every soul earns only for its own account, and none bears the burden of another...
>
> The Bees, 16:97
> Whoever does a good deed and believes, whether male or female, We shall give them a good life and reward them according to the best that they had done.
>
> The Confederates, 33:35
> For submitting men (to God) and submitting women, believing men and believing women, devout men and devout women, truthful men and truthful women, patient men and patient women, humble men and humble women, charitable men and charitable women, fasting men and fasting women, chaste men and chaste women, men who remember God often and women who remember God often—for them God has prepared forgiveness, and a great reward.

The above was cited earlier as an example of God's response to specific requests or questions by women, and is repeated here as it is one of the clearest verses on every woman's, and not just every man's, individual freedom and accountability before God.

> The Confederates, 33:73
> That God may punish the hypocritical men and the hypocritical women, the idolatrous men and the idolatrous women, and that God may relent unto the believing men and the believing women. And God is ever-Forgiving, ever-Merciful.

[1]Yet other verses on individual responsibility and accountability include 4:124, 82:5, 99:7–8, 17:15, 39:7, among others.

Forgiver, 40:40
Whoever does a bad deed will only be repaid its equivalent, while whoever does a good deed and believes, whether male or female, shall enter the Garden where they will be rewarded without measure.

Kneeling, 45:22
And God created the heavens and the earth with truth, and so that each soul may be rewarded what it has earned. And they will not be wronged.

The Star, 53:38–40
That none shall bear the burden of another,
And that every human being shall have only what it strove for,
And that its endeavour shall be seen.

Finally, every soul will not only be **judged individually but also, in case there was any doubt, irrespective of whether that soul had been associated with a believing or non-believing, virtuous or unethical, devout or non-devout *spouse*.** This point is made in the Qur'an with regard to women who sought out the Prophet to pledge their allegiance independently of their husbands and families,[2] as well as in relation to three famous women from a previous era—two who go astray and one who chooses the right path—despite each of them being married to a man of the opposite character:

The Woman Tested, 60:12
Oh Prophet! When believing women come to you pledging not to associate anything with God, nor steal,...then accept their pledge and seek God's forgiveness for them...

Prohibiting, 66:10–11
God cites the example, for those who disbelieve, of the wife of Noah and the wife of Lot. They were under (the guidance/influence) of two of our righteous servants yet they betrayed them, and they (the husbands) did not avail them anything against God. And it was said to them both: Enter the Fire with those who enter.

[2] Nasr, Seyyed Hossein (editor-in-chief) et al. 2015. The Study Quran: A New Translation and Commentary. New York: HarperCollins Publishers, 1362–1363.

> And God cites the example, for those who believe, of the wife of Pharaoh when she said: My Lord, build me a house with You in the Garden and deliver me from Pharaoh and his deeds, and deliver me from wrong-doing people.

The Pushback of Alleged *Hadith* on Women Having Free Will: Not Just Immoral and Intellectually Lacking, But So as Not to Defy the Prophet!

The twin-anchors of all approaches that try to deprive women of their free will and prevent them from making their own decisions in life are the faux-*hadith* arguments denigrating women's moral nature and intellectual capacity as described above. Such arguments are not only intuitively and experientially preposterous but also counter-Qur'anic, often propping themselves up with additional questionable *hadiths* taking up the campaign indirectly. Some of the latter are positively shocking yet are included in the *hadith* compilations despite their dubious authenticity, not to mention their illogical content, such as alleged Prophetic *hadiths* that make a wife's access to heaven basically dependent on being in her husband's good graces (what if he is a despicable fellow?), or effectively place a wife's obedience to her husband on the same level as worshipping God several times a day and fasting during Ramadan![3] For those looking to justify their own chauvinism, such evidently unreliable *hadiths* trump many others that are shown to be unquestionably reliable, such as the reply of Omar's wife when arguing with her husband:

> You reproach me for answering you! Well, by God, the wives of the Prophet answer him, and one of them might even desert him from morning until night.[4]

[3] Abou El Fadl, Khaled M. 2003. Speaking in God's Name: Islamic Law, Authority and Women. Oxford: Oneworld Publications, 219–20.

[4] Ibid., 214–15.

CHAPTER 10

God Does Not Prefer Sons Over Daughters (!)

Qur'anic Verses on Gender Equality

It feels odd even having to deny this bizarre idea, but since apparently those who make this argument often reference certain Qur'anic verses taken out of context,[1] the idea warrants addressing.

- Yes, there are at least seven instances[2] in which the Qur'an denounces the idea of God having daughters. But this is in the context of criticising the pagan Meccans' worship of female deities whom they claimed were God's daughters, and also in response to certain tribes' belief that the angels were God's daughters.

These ideas are denounced outright in the Qur'an, which proceeds in several instances to also point out the idolaters' insolence in moreover ascribing to God what *they* deemed to be an undesirable gender to have as their own offspring. Such was the pagan Arabs' dislike of having daughters that they had a custom of burying alive unwelcome female babies, a practice vehemently condemned in the Qur'an repeatedly.

[1] Lang, Jeffrey. 1995. Struggling to Surrender: Some Impressions from an American Convert to Islam. Maryland: Amana Publications, 146–49.

[2] Verses denouncing the claim that God has daughters include 4:117, 16:57–59, 17:40, 37:149–53, 43:16, 52:39, 53:19–21. Overall, the Qur'an denounces the idea of God having children at all, insisting that angels and prophets and regular human beings are all essentially God's subjects, i.e. they are His creation, not offspring.

L. El-Ali, *No Truth Without Beauty*, Sustainable Development Goals Series, https://doi.org/10.1007/978-3-030-83582-8_10

Here is an example of this combination of rebukes:

The Bees, 16:57–59
And they assign to God daughters—glory be to Him!—while to themselves what they
desire.

And when one of them receives news of a female child, his face darkens, and he chokes
inwardly.

He hides from people on account of the bad news he has received: should he keep it in
humiliation, or bury it in the dust? How evil is their judgment!

- Yes, the Qur'an does say at one point that "…the male is not like the female…". But the context reveals it to be a factual statement relating to the Virgin Mary's birth—Mary, no less!—in a discourse involving Mary's mother Hannah, wife of Joaquim:[3]

The House of *'Imrān* (Joaquim, father of Mary), 3:35–37
Remember when the wife of *'Imrān* said: My Lord, I dedicate what is in my belly to you as a consecrated offering. So accept it from me. Truly you are the All-Hearing, the All-Knowing.

Then when she delivered her, she said: My Lord, I have delivered a female. And God knew well what she had delivered—the male is not like the female. And I have named her Mary, and I seek refuge in You for her and her progeny from Satan, the outcast.

And her Lord accepted her with a beautiful acceptance, and made her grow in a beautiful way, and entrusted Zacharia with her…

Ironically, if we were to set context aside altogether and look at the phrase "…the male is not like the female…" through a purely linguistic lens, we would have a stronger case for arguing that this verse is saying that the female is the superior being!

Anyway, the critical point here is this: When "…the male is not like the female…" is cited out of its natural context shown above, it is bound to

[3] See commentary on 3:35–36 in Nasr, Seyyed Hossein (editor-in-chief) et al. 2015. The Study Quran: A New Translation and Commentary. New York: HarperCollins Publishers, 141.

sound like a judgmental statement regarding the two sexes, one way or another. It is then also easy to miss the fact that though Hannah dedicated her unborn child to God before knowing its gender (while praying for a boy),[4] **God as Creator decided to make that child a *girl* and proceeded to not only accept her as an offering but to elevate her above all women (3:42) as well as above all men barring God's prophets, among whom Mary is listed as an equal in her own right and not only as the mother of Jesus**. This occurs in **a long flow of verses in the chapter in fact entitled "The Prophets"**, verses 21:48–92, which essentially tell us the following:

- That God gave **Moses** and **Aaron** the Criterion (of right and wrong), and a light and a reminder to the reverent
- And He gave **Abraham** his sound judgment (the Qur'an retells Abraham's story here at length, showing his courageous steadfastness in the face of the idolaters)
- And God additionally bestowed upon Abraham **Isaac** (his son) and **Jacob** (his grandson), and made them leaders (*imams*) in God's way
- And **Lot** was given judgment and knowledge, and was saved from the morally corrupt town
- And **Noah**'s prayer was answered and he was saved, alongside his family
- And God gave **David** and **Solomon** sound judgment and knowledge, and gave Solomon the power to command the wind towards the blessed land
- And **Job**'s prayer was answered and his affliction was lifted, and he was given his family and others like them in mercy and as a reminder to others
- And **Ishmael**, **Idriss** (either Enoch or Elias) and **Dhul-Kifl** (a prophet of disputed identity)[5] were all made to enter into God's mercy
- And he of the whale (**Jonah**), whose prayer was answered, was thus saved from grief
- And **Zacharia** had prayed for a child and so God healed his barren wife and bestowed **John** upon him
- "And she who preserved her chastity [**Mary**] and We breathed into her of Our Spirit, and made her and her son [Jesus] a sign for all the worlds" (21:91)

and finally, in exquisite conclusion to this particular listing of *some* of the prophets sent by God to humanity:

[4] Ibid.
[5] Ibid., 824.

- "This is your (pl.) community *(umma)*—a single community—and I am your Lord, so worship Me." (21:92)

In fact, such are the patriarchal influences on the interpretation of the Qur'an that they have even crept into Western Arabists' translation of the Qur'an in a number of ways. In one example, the word "children" is rendered "sons" in all but a couple of translations I have seen of the following verse, which was already cited earlier:

> The Bees, 16:72
> And God made for you (pl.) mates from your own souls, and made for you from your mates children [i.e. not just sons] and grandchildren, and provided you with good things.....

Meanwhile, other verses that speak of the two genders at the same time are completely ignored—notice how the order is reversed in the two mentions of gender here, almost as if to emphasise their interchangeability, or sameness:

> Consultation, 42:49–50
> And to God belong the heavens and the earth. He creates what He wills. He bestows upon whom He wills females, and He bestows upon whom He wills males.
>
> Or He pairs them, male and female, and makes whom He wills barren. For He is all-Knowing, all-Powerful.

In summary, **the two phrases sometimes plucked out of either their full verse or their accompanying verses to be cited as supposed proof that the male is superior to the female are**:

> and they assign to God daughters—glory be to Him!... (16:57)

and

> ...the male is not like the female... (3:36)

when in fact these two phrases are about something totally different:

Verse 16:57 is about the absurdity of the pagan worship of their female deities and the insolence of their assigning to God daughters when they considered baby girls to not be good enough for themselves, going so far as to bury them alive at times.

Verse 3:36 is about the birth of Mary even though her mother had prayed for a son to dedicate to God, and God's full acceptance of the offered daughter and His making of Mary and her son, Jesus, a sign for all the worlds.

This is straight from the Qur'an, and that truly is all we need. But I cannot resist asking, nonetheless, why if God truly favoured boys over girls, He would have allowed His beloved prophet Muhammad to enjoy only daughters—four in total—while letting his three sons die in infancy.

The Pushback of Alleged *Hadith* on Women Being Equal to Men: Morally and Intellectually Unworthy!

Finally, the same twin-arguments that try to deprive women of their free will also anchor the policies, laws and customs that prioritise men over women generally, treating them as unequal. Even when the so-to-speak "naturally immoral" and "intellectually deficient" arguments are implicit, as they often are, they are sown into the social psyche in some communities in an insidious manner that nonetheless enables such laws and customs to survive. Such beliefs or positions—because often they are in fact just cynical positions and not really beliefs by those who promote them—are intuitively, experientially, Qur'anically, and Prophetically unconvincing if one takes into account Muhammad's own example in this regard, which has been alluded to here and there but is not really the subject of this particular book.

AT A GLANCE: The Nature of Women

Reclaiming Women's Origin, Innocence, Morality, Capacity, Freedom and Equality

If we take a step back to look at the totality of the historical narrative undermining women's intrinsic worth, it becomes hard not to notice how comprehensive the philosophical approach to this effort has been.

By treating Qur'anic verses selectively and in accordance with cultural preferences, and by pointing to alleged *hadith* to support such curious interpretations despite them being utterly devoid of the Qur'anic spirit or vision for humankind, six essential characteristics of women are called into question. These are women's nature, innocence, morality, capacity, freedom and equality.

1. **Nature**—By picking and choosing bits and pieces from verse 4:1 and overlooking the fact that its topic is the creation of humankind, this foundational verse's messages as relating to the female human being end up either diluted or wholly overlooked. Recall also that this is the very first verse of the early and long chapter entitled "Women", laying the groundwork for all that follows. The verse's foundational messages are that:
   - Adam and Eve were created from the same soul (which was created with divine breath—15:28–29, 32:7–9, 38:72)
   - Adam and Eve were created as "mates", i.e. together forming a "pair"

- All men and all women emanate from Adam and Eve *together*, the first human pair
- All men and all women emanate from the same soul, which contains the divine breath
- Therefore all that comes out of the human womb must be reverenced, *or else…*

Here is the verse again, for its importance cannot be overemphasised, notwithstanding all the other supporting verses already detailed alongside it in Chap. 5:

Women, 4:1
Oh humankind: Reverence your Lord, who created you (pl.) from a single soul and from it created its mate, and from the two of them disseminated multitudes of men and women; and reverence God, Whose name you invoke to one another, and the wombs [i.e. the human creation]; for God is always watching you.

Once the above is sliced and diced so that its profundity and gravity are reduced to the false narrative that women were created "second" and only as "companions" to men, it is only a small step from there to concluding that women are inferior to men by divine decree. Coupled with the egregious "crooked as a rib" alleged *hadith*, such an approach unjustifiably undermines women's very nature.

2. **Innocence**—By choosing not to pay enough attention to the fact that the Qur'an repeatedly faults Adam and Eve *equally* for the Fall from the Garden (2:36, 7:20–24), preferring to adopt the "blame Eve" narrative already in circulation at the time among other religious communities, women's primordial guilt becomes the popular belief. Never mind that verse 4:1 tells us that all men and all women emanate equally from both Adam and Eve: suddenly, women become the "daughters of Eve" in popular parlance, somehow cut off from the primordial soul and its divine breath, and forever guilty by association to a faux-claim, to boot.

And once again, alleged *hadith* condemning Eve and making her solely responsible for the Fall is pulled out and embraced, never mind the fact that such reports *directly* contradict the Qur'anic version of events. Surely the choice could hardly be clearer for a believer.

3. **Morality**—By redefining what *fitna* means, away from its Qur'anic and regular Arabic meaning of social discord/divisiveness (2:217, 9:48, 29:10) or personal ordeal/affliction (8:25, 8:28, 22:53) and towards an obsessive view of women as a source of all sorts of social ills, women become a veritable danger to society that must be guarded against, if not countered. By this bizarre definition, women are naturally conniving and sexual temptresses as a matter of course, never mind that the Qur'an tells us that God created men and women of the same divine breath and, as we shall see in Part III, regards men and women as partners, each other's protectors, equally charged with representing God on earth and building good societies.

   An alleged *hadith* claiming that the Prophet had said that the majority of the inhabitants of Hell are women has seemingly frightened so many of us, causing us not only to suspend our thinking abilities and all we know of the Prophet's character and teachings, but even to forget what the Qur'an that we hold in our very hands tells us of how God created both women and men and entrusted them with the entire world.

4. **Capacity**—Arguments that attempt to undermine women's capabilities come at it from three angles.

   By re-defining and expanding the Qur'anic terms *hijab* and *fitna* to make them women-centric and women-critical, the resulting conclusion that gender segregation is a must for the good of society then automatically restricts women from full participation, not to mention from leadership roles. Whereas in reality, *hijab* simply meant curtain or screen (see Chap. 16's "What of *hijab*?" section), while *fitna* simply meant social discord or personal ordeal in the Qur'an (per Morality above). This angle is particularly insidious, as it leads many who would otherwise not object to women's full and unrestricted participation in society to feel that the matter is out of their hands—*if* they believe the myth that it is the Qur'an that actually says women must stay away.

   By pointing to an alleged *hadith* that the Prophet had supposedly said that no people led by a woman would succeed, again many of us who have been brought up to think that all *hadiths* are equally accurate and valid will feel that our hands are tied: *we* may not mind women in leadership positions, but our faith demands that we submit to God's will, so we accept the status quo. Never mind that such a claim runs contrary to the Qur'anic narrative of the creation of men and women as equals and God's entrusting of both with the wellbeing of the world. Never mind the example that the Qur'an itself gives of the excellent leadership of the Queen of Sheba, a woman (27:22–44). And never mind all we know of the Prophet's high regard for women and his counting several women in his life as close advisers.

Lastly, by grasping at the straws of circumstantial evidence (women generally lined up behind men for prayers in Muhammad's time), invoking the all-purpose concept of *fitna* (how could men possibly focus on their prayers with women in front of them?), and resuscitating the age-old boogey-man of menstruation that too many cultures have been guilty of (women are *sometimes* "impure" therefore cannot *fully* participate in the spiritual rites), the scales are tipped against women serving as prayer leaders, or *imams.* Never mind that men arriving late to prayers used to line up behind the women without fuss, or the fact that women do not menstruate every day of their lives. And never mind the evidence that the Prophet had a more relaxed view of menstruation and had encouraged women to come to the mosque even during their time of the month, which they did both for prayers and Eid celebrations.

5. **Freedom**—Once the creation and Fall-from-the-Garden narratives in the Qur'an are disregarded (i.e. on women's nature and innocence) and women's innate qualities are re-defined (by denigrating women's intrinsic morality and capacity), the ground becomes set for men seizing the reins as the alleged superior human beings.

   And this has indeed been done, both patronisingly—with some men depriving women of their free will *for their own good*—and "altruistically", with some men holding women back from decision-making *for the greater good* of society as a whole.

   Yet depriving women of their free will during their lives on earth, for whatever stated reason, conflicts very directly with the Qur'an's countless verses on how every soul will be accountable *individually* before God for its own choices in life, and on how no soul shall bear the burden or reap the reward for what another soul chooses to think or do (e.g. 3:195, 6:194, 45:22, 53:38–40 etc.). For is God not Just?

6. **Equality**—Finally, with regard to another minority claim that the Qur'an states that the male is better than the female—sons better than daughters—this is categorically false.

   The Qur'an expresses anger towards those among Meccan society who used to bury their unwanted new-born baby girls alive (16:58–59). The evident immorality of infanticide surely begged a response from the divine revelation that was unfolding at the time.

   The Qur'an also expresses outrage at the pagan Arabs' worship of female deities they claimed were God's daughters, and also at the claim by some tribes that the angels were God's daughters (4:117, 16:57, 17:40, 37:149–155, 43:16, 52:39, 53:19–21). The egregiousness of idolatry for an explicitly monotheistic religion such as Islam again requires no further comment. Overall, such a rebuke is fully in keeping with the Qur'an's insistence that God's angels, prophets, and human beings (among others) are all His creation—his subjects, as it were, whom He simply has to will into existence—and that He does not produce offspring as such.

   At the same time, the Qur'an tells us elsewhere of how the wife of the Hebrew prophet *'Imrān* (Joaquim) had prayed for a baby boy whom she promised to dedicate to God. Yet God granted her a girl who was named Mary instead, whom He fully received as the consecrated gift her mother Hannah intended her to be, and then elevated her to the level of prophethood (21:48–92), going beyond merely elevating her above all of womankind (3:42).

PART III

The Rights of Women

Introduction

We have seen in Part II how the human creation story in the Qur'an establishes men and women's natural and spiritual sameness,[1] with God further declaring that He will assess the actions of both by the same measure. And as already mentioned, this logically requires that every man and every woman be free to make their own choices in life, as we cannot be judged if said actions have been imposed on us, one way or another. God's justice is both complete *and* perfect, after all.

Moreover in the glorious verse 33:35 already cited twice, God could hardly be more explicit that a woman's belief (or not), devotion to God (or not), truthfulness (or not), forbearance (or not), humility (or not), charity (or not), fasting (or not), chastity (or not), and remembrance of God (or not)—the latter being both a specific act and an all-encompassing attitude in life—are all choices that she must make freely and voluntarily, as must every man.

So in reality, there should be no reason to speak of women's rights as such, as though they could naturally be any different from men's rights. But we must, for two reasons.

First, because we all know that while women have not been treated as equals to men in most societies, they are treated especially egregiously in

[1] Men and women's natural and spiritual sameness does not contradict the notion that men and women's general characteristics primarily reflect different aspects of God (while simultaneously containing the possibility of all the divine attributes). The ninety-nine Names of God in the Islamic tradition indeed consist of both feminine and masculine attributes.

many modern Muslim societies, including in the name of so-called Islamic law.

And second, because **in the course of its 23 years of gradual revelation during Muhammad's prophetic mission, the Qur'an responded to many social aspects of women's lives as they existed or arose,** yet many of these verses have been mis-used to undermine the same human creation story that the Qur'an itself articulates with regards to women's nature and stature. This is akin to revising the main argument of a book by constructing an entirely new and stand-alone narrative out of a series of unconnected sub-plots within that book. We will see below how various verses on **circumstantial topics such as inheritance, polygyny and testimony** (the latter to be discussed in Part IV) **in particular combine with agenda-driven interpretations of other verses on women's primordial innocence, morality and capacity** (already discussed in Part II) **to justify creating two classes of human beings**, so that women are subdued within the very fabric of alleged "Islamic" law.

CHAPTER 11

Women Were Not Meant to Be Subordinate to Men

Having recounted how men and women were created from the same ingredients using the same process, and having declared repeatedly that every man and every woman will be judged individually and by the same measure for their decisions in life, the Qur'an does not leave the matter there. It proceeds to spell out what this essential sameness means on a practical level, in terms of **human beings' foremost role: as God's viceroys (*khalifas*, aka caliphs) on earth** (2:30, 6:165, 10:14, 27:62, 43:60, among others).

Guardianship: The Qur'an Defines Women and Men as Mutual Protectors (*Walis*)

> Repentance, 9:71
> And believing men and believing women are each other's protectors/guardians...

The notion that men are *literal* guardians of women, in the way an adult may be the guardian of a minor, clearly does not come from the Qur'an, where **women and men are equally empowered as *mutual* benefactors** as this verse shows. Yet some nonetheless claim that the Qur'an instructs men to be the all-empowered guardians of women and in a handful of societies this view has even been turned into law, whereby a

L. El-Ali, *No Truth Without Beauty*, Sustainable Development Goals Series, https://doi.org/10.1007/978-3-030-83582-8_11

father (or in his absence, an uncle or brother) wields the power to grant or prevent a woman's education, marriage, divorce, work, or indeed travel outside the country or in extreme cases, even outside the home. Typically in this patriarchal view the role of guardian is transferred to the husband once a woman marries.

This is an extraordinary view to adopt as **it strips a woman of the means of serving God as His viceroy on earth**, a role for which men and women will be evaluated individually according to the Qur'an. **It moreover strips her of her God-given dignity, having been created from the soul of Adam and by extension, from the divine breath**, as already shown in Part II.

It is also extraordinary because the very *hadith* compilations discussed at length in Part I contain ample evidence of Muhammad having counted on his wives in major political and other decisions, even deferring to them at times—hardly the behaviour of an all-knowing "guardian" dictating every move of his "wards". For example it is reported that his first wife **Khadija**, who was 15 years his senior and his sole spouse for 25 years until her death, was consulted and deferred to on many occasions; and that one of his later wives **Umm Salama** helped defuse a tense situation when consulted by the Prophet about the Treaty of Hudaybiyya, when his followers who had marched with him from Medina initially resisted his orders around deferring the pilgrimage for one year as part of a peaceful settlement with the Meccan enemy.[1] Mutual protectors, indeed.

Nor does the harm stop there, at the spiritual level. If a man is thought of as the guardian of his wife, then by extension he becomes the *sole* guardian of his children, especially when a couple divorces. Upon divorce, it becomes an uphill if not impossible battle for a woman to retain custody of her children or even see them at times, no matter how young they are. Though a general rule adopted by most religious authorities is that the **children of divorced parents** must remain with their mother until puberty, a web of cultural and economic levers afforded men in patriarchal societies has ensured that this is the case only when an accommodating man is involved. As to why the traditional view in some places has, at least nominally, drawn the line at puberty, I believe it relates to the medieval norm whereby one became eligible for marriage at puberty, combined with the patriarchal norm whereby one's marriage prospects improved if the figure of a father was involved in the negotiations—as the all-empowered "guardian", naturally, in the case of a daughter in particular.

[1] Abou El Fadl, Khaled M. 2003. Speaking in God's Name: Islamic Law, Authority and Women. Oxford: Oneworld Publications, 229 and 254.

Participation: Women and Men Are Jointly Responsible for Shaping Society

So often with religion, we get sucked into specific and narrow questions about this or that, questions that often feel like a barrage of arrows shot from every direction by the well-meaning and less-so alike. It can be overwhelming for those who love their religion. We instinctively dodge this one, argue against that one, distance ourselves from yet another, and generally get worked up and defensive. I would like to suggest that instead, we try to make sure that the right question is asked and answered *first*.

The right question, to my mind, when it comes to women's full participation in society, is surely the following:

What does the Qur'an tell us is God's *purpose* in creating human beings and placing them on earth?

First, the Qur'an tells us, over and over again, that we human beings are **God's viceroys** or deputies on earth. An example:

> The Confederates, 33:72
> We offered this Trust to the heavens and the earth and the mountains, but they refused to bear it and were wary of it—yet humankind bore it: (but) it proved to be a foolish sinner.

Second, the Qur'an offers its followers a **core job description**, as it were, for the position of viceroys, to help us get it right:

> Repentance, 9:71
> And believing men and believing women are each other's protectors: they command with[2] kindness [i.e. *bil-maaroof*] and abstain[3] from the abominable, perform the prayer, give the alms, and obey God and His Messenger...

[2] Other translations of 9:71 include phrases such as "...*enjoin* what is right/just and *forbid* what is wrong/evil...", or "...*bid* to honour and *forbid* dishonour..." and so on. Firstly, rather than directing *others* to do what is kind and forbidding *others* from the distasteful, the Arabic can be heard to mean behaving with kindness and abstaining from the distasteful *ourselves* (such as in 24:21, where there can be no doubt of this phrase's reflexive meaning), which in fact makes more sense since the rest of the verse lists other things one can only do oneself, such as perform the prayers and give the alms, etc. Secondly, while "right" and "wrong" etc. are all good enough meanings, the Qur'anic Arabic here is in fact more specific than that: the actual words used are "kindness" (*maaroof*, whose root meaning points to "what is known or recognised as such") and the "abominable"(*munkar*, whose root meaning is "senseless"), clearly referring to what is gentle versus what is extremely distasteful, respectively.

[3] See the above footnote.

(notice that in the above God clearly expects women and not only men to command or lead), and

> The Spoils, 8:53
> ...God would never alter a grace He has bestowed upon a people unless they have first altered what is in their souls [i.e. hearts]; for God is all-Hearing, all-Knowing.

> Thunder, 13:11
> ...God does not change the condition of a people until they change what is in their souls [i.e. hearts]...

Third, the Qur'an speaks of our **compensation**, so to speak, if we serve as good viceroys. Many such verses have already been cited in Part II, but here are just a few of the many others for variety, and to underscore how **the Qur'an never tires of emphasising, over and over again, that all it is laying out applies to men and women equally and individually**:

> Women, 4:124
> Whoever does a good deed, whether male or female, and is a believer—those shall enter the Garden, and they shall not be wronged (the equivalent of) so much as a dent in a date-stone.

> Repentance, 9:72
> God has promised believing men and believing women gardens under which rivers flow—where they shall be immortal—and blessed dwellings in the Gardens of Eden. But God's goodly acceptance is greater by far—that is the mighty triumph!

> Iron, 57:18
> Men who give in charity and women who give in charity, and who (therefore) lend God a goodly loan—it shall be multiplied for them (in return), and theirs shall be a generous wage.

To summarise, **the Qur'an basically gives its followers a road-map**. If we:

- **spread kindness** and **eschew the morally distasteful**;
- **worship** God, and give in **charity**;

- **obey God** and His Messenger (Muhammad), and
- work on the contents of our hearts, or **inner selves**

then **we shall reap what we sow whether in this world or the next**, as no good deed goes unnoticed by God.

Now that we have answered the right question first through the lens of the Qur'an itself, surely—*surely*—there is no need to pick at this or that aspect of a woman's life, be it her education, marriage, work, appearance or anything else. One cannot possibly, neither religiously nor rationally, make the case that women can be prevented from full decision-making in their lives or full participation in the world around them. **To prevent women from full engagement in the world is, quite simply, to *dis*-obey the Qur'anic God**.

- **Education**

In the Qur'an, stretching the human mind to its fullest potential is so important a virtue that **the word *'ilm*—literally meaning both knowledge and science—is mentioned in its various derivatives no less than 854 times**.[4] Knowledge/science (*'ilm*) implies effort, search, and inquiry and is different from plain knowledge (*ma'rifah*), which means "having information or awareness" and is somewhat more static. It is unsurprising then that the sciences flourished in Muslim lands during the first eight centuries after the Qur'anic revelation, and that **Muslim societies have never found there to be a conflict between religion and science, always regarding the pursuit of science as a means of better understanding and therefore glorifying God's omnipotence and creativity**.

The word *'ilm* is also the Arabic word for learning, or education.

In the *hadith* compilations, likewise, we find memorable sayings and stories about the importance of pursuing *'ilm* that reflect the Prophet's understanding of education's central role in the new religion he was founding:

[4] Lang, Jeffrey. 1995. Struggling to Surrender: Some Impressions from an American Convert to Islam. Maryland: Amana Publications, 176.

Seeking knowledge/science/education is an obligation for every Muslim.[5]

It is also narrated that the Prophet once declared that all prisoners of battle who could read and write and were willing to teach his followers how to read and write would be set free with no strings attached, whether they were freepersons or bondpersons, i.e. slaves.[6] And it is reported that when Muhammad learnt of a woman in Medina who could read and write, he soon asked her to teach his wife Hafsa to do so.[7]

A fringe but notorious few today in a couple of countries argue that only scriptural knowledge is legitimate while all else is heretical. In this view all other subjects, whether the humanities or sciences, are a dangerous distraction. This view fails to grasp that to better understand God's message, every ounce of our intellectual capacity needs to be exercised to the best of our abilities, and not just our minimal powers of reading, memorising, and unreflective movements and utterances during ritual prayer. This view also misses the point of our existence, namely to participate constructively in life on earth as God's viceroys and in accordance with the profound roadmap provided by the Qur'an itself, as outlined above.

"God, grant me knowledge of the ultimate nature of things," prayed the Prophet.[8]

[5] Ibn Abdel Barr, Al-Hafedh. Sahih Jami' Bayan al-Ilm wa Fadlihi as compiled by Al-Zuhairy (in Arabic). Cairo: Maktabat Ibn Taymiyya, 8; and www.nabulsi.com/web/article/3791.

[6] For example see Al-Batyawi, Aziz. 1981. Sunan al-Umran al-Bashari fi al-Sira al-Nabawiyya (in Arabic). Amman: Al-Ma'had al-'Alami lil-fikr al-Islam, 524; and Al-Albani, Muhammad. 1400H. Al-Ajwiba al-Nafi'a 'an As'ilat Lajnat Masjid al-Jami'a (in Arabic). Beirut: Al-Maktab al-Islami, 47. Referenced on www.dorar.net—(both in Arabic).

[7] Rida, Muhammad Rashid. 1404H. Huquq al-Nisa' fil-Islam (in Arabic). Beirut: Al-Maktab al-Islami,

17. Referenced on www.dorar.net. The female teacher in question was none other than Layla or Al-Shifa' (i.e. The Cure), who was later placed in charge of running the *souks*, or commercial marketplaces, by the caliph Omar—see Chap. 8, footnote 25.

[8] Hassan, Riffat. 2000. Human Rights in the Qur'anic Perspective. In Windows of Faith: Muslim Women Scholar-Activists in North America, ed. Gisela Webb, 246. New York: Syracuse University Press.

- **Work**

If women are to participate fully in the world as God's viceroys by following the Qur'anic roadmap to divine representation and ultimate salvation, then it goes without saying that they are likely to engage in work of some sort at some point. I can almost hear a proud or otherwise resistant male voice somewhere in the world pushing back at this to say "not necessarily—if it's about doing good, a woman can always volunteer at a charity", which raises the question as to why it would bother anyone that a woman be paid for her efforts. It certainly did not bother the God of the Qur'an, who in fact deemed it only fair that women be paid for their contributions, and actually had strong words to say about it:

> Women, 4:32
> And do not covet what God has favoured some of you with over [i.e. at the expense of] others: for men is a share for what they have earned, and for women is a share for what they have earned. But ask God of His bounty, for God is the Knower of all things.

Stunningly, this verse was apparently revealed as a reprimand after men objected to the Qur'an granting women the right to inheritance, something utterly revolutionary at the time.[9] The verse makes reference to men and women both having *earned* a right to inheritance **by recognising women's in-kind contribution to society as work** after some women had lobbied for it to be so, which meant that they would henceforth also be able to inherit.[10] More will be said about the circumstances of this extraordinary verse in the next section entitled "Activism", but it must be mentioned here that the most repeated explanation for this verse has unfortunately been the exact opposite: we are told that God was reprimanding *women*, not men, for *their* objection to inheriting less than men, an issue I hope to address under Chap. 12, entitled Inheritance. I cannot begin to imagine women in seventh-century Arabia arguing for *more* inheritance when winning the right to inheritance at all must have surely been a seismic coup given what we know of the attitudes of the time and place. But I can easily imagine men objecting to this new arrangement, as

[9] Abou El Fadl, Khaled M. 2007. The Great Theft: Wrestling Islam from the Extremists. New York: HarperOne, 265–266.

[10] Ibid.

it is unequivocally recorded they actually did,[11] as from their perspective it meant a sudden loss of stature and wealth in favour of what had always been seen as a secondary class in their society.

Lastly, if women and men are mandated by God to pursue knowledge, science and education as we have already seen, surely it would be the height of selfishness for women to then keep all these treasures to themselves rather than put all they have learnt to good work, literally, for the benefit of their societies.

- **Activism**

I have often reflected on the verses that tell us that God does not change the condition of a people, to the better or worse, until or unless they have first changed what is in their hearts (8:53 and 13:11 shown above). Do we ever think about that as we consider the challenges we face in our societies and our world, before we translate our feelings into action? Perhaps we would choose more constructive and effective action if we internalised this higher notion of self-help a bit more.

Probably inspired and emboldened by the Qur'anic emphasis on fairness, women during Muhammad's time were inclined to act—by taking their grievances directly to the Prophet. But it was God Himself who often responded to their activism, which reminds me of the English saying, "Heaven helps those who help themselves."

- Thus when a group of women in seventh-century Medina felt that not only men but women also should inherit and took their case to the Prophet, **the Qur'an responded to their demand with revolutionary verses that established women as heiresses for the first time**—within an entirely new system of inheritance (4:7, 4:11, 4:12, 4:32, 4:33, 4:34, 4:176, 2:240). In tribal Arabia at the time only men who fought in battle were entitled to inheritance, and though some women were now also fighting at times, the men felt that this was a voluntary act on their part that no one expected or demanded of them, so nothing should change. When the women decided to petition the Prophet, they argued that even when they did not actually fight they contributed in a variety of critical ways to

[11] Nasr, Seyyed Hossein (editor-in-chief) et al. 2015. The Study Quran: A New Translation and Commentary. New York: HarperCollins Publishers, 193.

the wellbeing of the community that put men in a better position to fight. The Prophet told the women he did not have an immediate answer for them, and shortly afterwards the Qur'an addressed the women's concern by granting all women the right to inherit within a revamped system.[12]

- And when a woman named Khawla, whose husband had forsworn sexual relations with her in a fit of anger, pleaded most eloquently with the Prophet to find her and her husband a way out of necessarily keeping the oath, per custom, and ending the marriage (which neither wanted), **the Qur'an responded with a direct acknowledgement of Khawla's distress in a chapter named after her petition, and proceeded to ban the unfair custom and impose penalties on husbands who committed it**. For this was a practice that often left a wife stuck in a loveless marriage without the ability to move on and re-marry,[13] unlike her husband who could always take a second wife under certain conditions (polygyny will be discussed further down):

> The Woman who Disputes, 58:1–58:4
> God has heard the words of she who disputes with you (Muhammad) regarding her husband, she who complains to God. God hears the conversation between the two of you, for God is all-Hearing, all-Seeing.

Nor did Khawla's activism stop there:

> She then counters every penalty the verses impose on the man guilty of *zihar* [the foreswearing custom in question] with a convincing reason for excusing Aws [Khawla's husband] from it: He is too feeble to fast two months and too impoverished to feed dates to sixty poor people. Finally, the Prophet offers to donate half the dates. Khawla chips in with the other half, and between the two of them they get the sorry old fellow off the hook. Aws is reported to have said, 'But for Khawla, I would have been done for.'[14]

[12] Abou El Fadl, Khaled. *Op. Cit.* (2007), 265.

[13] Kahf, Mohja. 2000. Braiding the Stories: Women's Eloquence in the Early Islamic Era. In Windows of Faith: Muslim Women Scholar-Activists in North America, ed. Gisela Webb, 155–156. New York: Syracuse University Press.

[14] Ibid., 157.

- Finally, it is well worth repeating that when women questioned the Qur'anic usage of the generic masculine plural, **the Qur'an responded with the famous verse reiterating the distinct masculine and feminine plurals side by side** in some detail:

> The Confederates, 33:35
> For submitting men (to God) and submitting women, believing men and believing women, devout men and devout women, truthful men and truthful women, patient men and patient women, humble men and humble women, charitable men and charitable women, fasting men and fasting women, chaste men and chaste women, men who remember God often and women who remember God often—for them God has prepared forgiveness, and a great reward.

These Qur'anic verses that were revealed in response to proactive women's concerns show an intimate and moving degree of responsiveness and attention by God. There was no admonishment of these women for demanding formal entitlement, no upbraiding them for upending custom, no reprimand even for questioning Qur'anic formulations. **This is a very different picture of God from what some would have us believe** these days. Perhaps God looked into the petitioning women's hearts and liked what He saw. Perhaps God wanted to show us that things only change for the better when we strive to make them so through constructive means, or that all customs are open to debate. Indeed as a renowned expert and educator has put it:

> The thorough and fair-minded researcher will observe that behind every single Qur'anic revelation regarding women was an effort seeking to protect women from exploitative situations and from situations in which they are treated inequitably. In studying the Qur'an it becomes clear that the Qur'an is educating Muslims on how to make incremental but lasting improvements in the condition of women that can only be described as progressive for their time and place.[15]

One cannot but wonder what other topics the Qur'an might have addressed, that are not already covered by the holy book, if someone had posed the question at the time—whether man or woman.

[15] Abou El Fadl, Khaled. *Op. Cit.* (2007), 262.

Historical Evidence of Women's Full Participation

If we know the circumstances and context of the above verses, it is because they have come to us through the *hadith* compilations which, it must be remembered, also hold many accurate reflections of the Prophet's words and deeds. But positive *hadith* relating to women is not the kind that society has chosen to promote or educate us on, and 99.99% of us are probably unaware of the correlation between women's activism and the revelation of certain verses, such as the one that resulted in an overhaul of inheritance customs and the one that removed all doubt regarding the inclusion of women in all aspects of God's vision for humanity. I had no idea whatsoever myself, until one book led to another in a long chain over a period of many years. We must change that and make this common knowledge.

And there is a lot more in *hadith* that underscores quite how thoroughly engaged women were during Muhammad's reign as the deliverer of the Qur'an, as the prophet of Islam. But again, they are stories that we are not told.

Women would meet individually and privately with the Prophet to consult on matters of concern; as a group, women in Medina demanded to meet with him in weekly sessions dedicated just to them; women insisted on the right to join military campaigns, attend prayers in the mosque, and grant assurances of safe conduct to the enemy, all against apparent opposition from men.[16]

The Prophet reportedly raced one of his wives (Aisha) in public; women would watch sports in Medina; **men and women visited one another and exchanged gifts; and women would come up to Muhammad in the street and take him by the hand**, sit with him, chat with him.[17]

And we already know from earlier on in this book of specific women's participation as leaders of various sorts: Aisha, the religious and political leader; Nusayba, Asma bint Yazid and Umm Fadl, the valiant warriors or occasional fighters; and Umm Waraqa, the would-be warrior assigned by the Prophet to serve as *imam* or prayer leader instead.

We also learn interesting snippets from various historical records from the first eight centuries after the Prophet's death: that some of the greatest scholars would issue religious opinions (*fatwas*) with their learned wives'

[16] Abou El Fadl, Khaled. *Op. Cit.* (2003), 230.
[17] Ibid., 239.

or daughters' signatures attached in approval; and that the Hanafi school of Islamic jurisprudence had concluded from the outset in the eighth century that women did not need a male guardian's permission to marry.[18] And as already mentioned, one learned woman known as Al-Shifa' (i.e. The Cure) was even appointed by the caliph Omar as minister of trade and commerce, effectively, in charge of running the *souks*, or commercial marketplaces.[19]

The Alleged Pushback of the Qur'an on Guardianship and Participation: But Verses 4:34 and 2:228 Say Men Are Superior and Therefore in Charge!

This is the first of several mentions that will be made of verse 4:34, a long verse which consists of several sentences that have been seized upon to argue that the Qur'an itself calls for the subordination of women to men (and more), never mind all the other verses scattered throughout the holy book to the contrary. **Importantly, this verse comes immediately after two verses that speak of *all* men *and* women now having the right to inherit in varying degrees, so bearing this in mind is crucial**. Its first half says the following:

> ✓ Women, 4:34
> Men are upholders/maintainers *(qawwamūn)* of women with whatever God has favoured some [i.e. men] with over others [i.e. other men], and with whatever they spend of their wealth [i.e. on the women]. Therefore righteous women are devoutly pious *(qanitāt)*, keeping private what God has ordained be so-kept…

This first half of the above is utterly unsurprising if one is paying attention to the flow of verses within the Qur'anic chapters—a theme we now come back to—and given the historical context. Here are some observations:

[18] Brown, Jonathan. 2015. Misquoting Muhammad: The Challenge and Choices of Interpreting the Prophet's Legacy. London: Oneworld Publications, 198–199.

[19] See footnote 7 and also Al-Baleek, Imad. 2017. Meet the First Female Minister of Commerce in Islam (in Arabic). Al Arabiya news website www.alarabiya.net, October 19.

- Firstly, seventh-century Arabia, like most other societies then and now, was a society where men were the breadwinners who supported their families. So for the Qur'an to speak of men as the financial supporters of women is natural.
- About two dozen verses earlier in the same chapter, several verses (4:7, 4:11–12) had laid out the pillars of the division of inheritance.
- The two verses just before this one (4:32–33) come back to the question of inheritance allocations, specifically mentioning the fact that women as well as men would now indeed inherit—*for what they have earned*.
- And now the Qur'an pulls it all together: in this first part of 4:34, it takes what was the de facto custom of men supporting women and turns it into a man's *obligation*, so **although women would also now be eligible for inheritance, men would have a *duty* henceforth to support women**. Notice that the reference in 4:34 is to men and women generally not just to husbands and wives, with an implied and indeed socially accepted obligation in Muslim societies also towards sisters, mothers, and so on. Thus in 4:34, God converts a de facto custom into a de jure one, moving from description to prescription.

But most translations and indeed interpretations in Arabic of the first half of 4:34 have unfortunately conveyed a different meaning, rupturing it in no less than six different places:

> × Men are guardians/in charge of women because God has preferred the one (men) over the other (women), and because they spend of their wealth [on the women]; therefore righteous women are obedient, guarding in (their husbands') absence what God would guard…

The completely different meaning that this version transmits speaks for itself but for the benefit of those who will ask "how can this be?", here are a few facts that should be helpful:

- Several Arabic-speaking contemporary scholars have pointed out the error of translating *qawwamūn* as guardians/protectors rather than upholders/maintainers, not least given the context supplied by the rest of the sentence regarding financial support.

Moreover the same word is used elsewhere in the Qur'an both in the singular form, in reference to God upholding justice (3:18), and in the plural later in the same chapter, when the Qur'an speaks of human beings upholding justice:

> Women, 4:135
> Oh you who believe: Be upholders/maintainers *(qawwamīn)* of justice, witnesses for God even if it be against yourselves, or your parents and relatives, whether it be (a case of) someone rich or poor—for they both belong to God. So do not follow whims, lest you be unjust…

- As several scholars have pointed out, "to favour someone with more of something" is not to "prefer them", or in some translations "to cause them to excel", but simply to allocate to them more of something—more inheritance and wealth, in this case;[20] in fact besides 4:32 and 4:34 already discussed, another verse later on uses the same turn of phrase in a material context and not related to gender at all: "And God has favoured some of you over others in provision…" (16:71)
- Though it is clear in this verse that God is saying to men (not just husbands) that whether God favours them with plenty or little they must support women to the extent that their wealth (including inheritance) permits, interpretations that point out the above two biases still go along with the conventional view that the comparison here is between the inheritance God grants *any man* above and beyond what He grants *any woman*. **But this is utterly illogical in my view as not every man will inherit or have more wealth than every woman**, this being a function of the personal and family circumstances of each person. For instance with regard to inheritance alone and assuming the same total value of the two estates: if a woman dies leaving behind a husband and a daughter, the husband would get only 25% of her inheritance whereas her daughter would get 50% (with the balance going to other relatives as may exist); or if

[20] al-Hibri, Azizah. 2000. An Introduction to Muslim Women's Rights. In Windows of Faith: Muslim Women Scholar-Activists in North America, ed. Gisela Webb, 63–64. New York: Syracuse University; Abou El Fadl, Khaled. *Op. Cit.* (2007), 267; among others.

a man dies leaving behind a wife, mother, father and sister, the father would inherit less than each of the three women, specifically only 8%.

- Arabic-speaking scholars have also pointed out the misleading use of "because" in this verse, since the original word *bima* literally means "via" and so is better rendered here as "with whatever" or "to the extent that" or "in accordance with", though per the previous point made they often still relate that to the idea that every man receives more inheritance than every woman and *therefore* must financially support them.[21] I do not disagree with this principle, but I do believe the intent *here* was to say to each man that he must support the women of his family to the extent that he is able, or in accordance with what God has favoured him with ("Men are upholders of women with whatever God has favoured some (men) with over others", i.e. relative to other men).
- Most shockingly, a good Arabic speaker can readily point out that the word *qanitāt* means "devoutly pious" or voluntarily submitting *to God*, so to translate it as "obedient" in this context especially leaves many thinking that the Qur'an is demanding that women obey *men*[22]*...because God has preferred men over women*, to boot! A number of translations even insert mention of husbands in parentheses as shown above, which only exacerbates the problem, even though in some cases it is in fact unintentional: it results from understanding the phrase "keeping private" to mean (rather awkwardly) "guarding in absence", which then begs the question of *in whose absence*—hence the introduction of the husbands in parentheses as part of the translation. Whereas **having made it a duty for men to financially support women despite women now being able to inherit in their own right, the Qur'an is actually articulating God's expectation that righteous women be devout and do as God bids them, i.e. to be faithful to their husbands**.

It is not difficult to see how one can jump from an erroneous interpretation like this one of 4:34's first sentences to insisting that men are literal

[21] Ibid.

[22] Several scholars have pointed out the error of interpreting *qanitāt* as obedience to fellow humans rather than God. See some of the scholars cited in Barlas, Asma. 2015. Believing Women in Islam: Unreading Patriarchal Interpretations of the Qur'an. Texas: University of Texas Press, 187.

guardians of women, that they receive more inheritance because God prefers them to women, and that women should obey their men no matter what if they want to be in God's good graces. It is only a small step from there to saying women should not study or work or be socially active unless their men *allow* them to, otherwise they are being disobedient to the Qur'an itself. Except that this is not what the Qur'an says at all—far from it. **It is a monotheistic book, after all, uncompromising in its dictate that every human being submit to God and God alone, taking no other as his or her Lord**.

Some of us, even after hearing all the above arguments, will think of one other verse that is often cited to argue that men are better than women. But when that verse is read in full and in the context of its three preceding verses that condemn a certain kind of unfair divorce by husbands, it becomes clear that what it is saying is that **husbands bear a greater responsibility towards their wives than vice versa**, especially where a child is involved (more will be said about this verse and its context in Chap. 15, entitled Divorce):

> The Cow, 2:228
> Divorced women must wait alone [not re-marry] for three menstrual cycles, and it is not lawful for them to hide what God may have created in their wombs, if they believe in God and the Last Day. And their husbands [who had unfairly divorced them] would be more just (*ahaqq*) in taking them back in that case if they (the husbands) want to fix things (*islah*). Women are due the same as what they owe in kindness (*bil-maaroof*), and men (owe) a degree more than them. For God is Mighty, Wise.

CHAPTER 12

Inheritance: No, Women Did Not Get the Short End of the Stick

Overview of the Eleven Inheritance Verses

This chapter and Chaps. 13, 14 and 15 will cover women's socio-economic rights in the Qur'an. We begin with the subject of inheritance, which may appear a strange place to start rather than the more obvious topics of marriage or divorce, for example. But in building a socio-economic identity for women, the Qur'an introduces their right to inherit as a pillar of its vision for a just society, so it is a good place to start.

There are several critical things to understand about the **eleven Qur'anic verses** dealing with the subject of inheritance:

- The introduction of new inheritance rules **occurs upfront in the chapter entitled "Women", and expands the pre-existing pool of beneficiaries from adult men only to now include women and children**.
- It is **woven into an impassioned defence of orphans** (4:2–4:12) which begins immediately after the very first verse 4:1 on the creation and nature of women, regarding which I argued earlier that reference to "the wombs" must refer to *all* human beings and not just blood ties (an understanding that is reinforced by this ensuing emphasis on orphans).
- The three verses referencing inheritance allocations (4:7, 4:11, 4:12) that are interspersed within this defence of **orphans—who were understood to be women who lacked supporting menfolk,**

L. El-Ali, *No Truth Without Beauty*, Sustainable Development Goals Series, https://doi.org/10.1007/978-3-030-83582-8_12

widows as well as bereaved children—make reference to the following groups of beneficiaries, facts and behaviours:

- men and women, parents and kinsfolk, sons and daughters, **orphans** and **the needy**, husbands and wives, brothers and sisters
- **allocations** to the official beneficiaries, i.e. close blood relatives and spouses
- **charity** and **kindness**
- **usurpers of orphans' rightful inheritances**
- **special bequests** and **debts**

- Another three verses refer to the morality and etiquette that God expects at the distribution of an inheritance (4:8, 4:9, 4:10) and are also interspersed within this same defence of orphans, including **an instruction to offer some of one's inheritance to non-inheriting relatives, orphans and the needy who may be present at the division, accompanied by appropriate words of kindness addressed to them.**
- Yet another three verses (4:32, 4:33, 4:34) a little later on in the same chapter, some of which I have already touched upon, speak of the principle of fairness behind the new inheritance rules and specifically about **men inheriting more so long as they (continue to) support their womenfolk, establishing a clear conditionality for the 2:1 ratio for sons-to-daughters** laid out earlier in 4:11.
- A tenth verse on inheritance (4:176) comes as the very last verse in the chapter "Women", and speaks of specific allocations in additional scenarios, including mention of a 2:1 ratio for brothers-to-sisters when they are eligible for inheritance.
- Finally, a verse (2:240) that appears in the middle of a lengthy discussion of divorce in a different chapter specifies what a widow must receive as a minimum, namely one year's maintenance and a residence until she re-marries.

So 10 of these 11 verses on inheritance appear in the fourth chapter of the Qur'an, entitled "Women".

Below are excerpts from these verses on inheritance just cited that touch upon the non-numerical aspects, namely the **Qur'anic morality behind the inheritance system**:

> Women, 4:7
> Unto men is a share of what parents and kinsfolk leave, and unto women a share of what parents and kinsfolk leave, be it little or much—a share ordained.

In yet another example of God's attentiveness in the Qur'an to injustices suffered by women, it is recorded that verse 4:7 was revealed in connection to a widow with three daughters who had been left destitute by her husband's male heirs under the pre-Qur'anic inheritance laws.[1]

> Women, 4:8–10
> And when kinsfolk and orphans and the needy are present at the division, make provision for them from it, and speak to them kind (*maaroof*) words.
>
> And let those who may leave behind them weak offspring fear that they may have (reason) to fear for them; so let them reverence God, and speak justly.
>
> (For) Those who consume the wealth of orphans unjustly are only consuming fire in their bellies, and will endure a blazing flame.

Incidentally, **adopted children inherit the same as biological children**, in case there is any doubt. First, because the Prophet had proclaimed loudly of his adopted son Zayd, a former slave: "All ye who are present, bear witness that Zayd is my son; I am his heir and he is mine."[2] And second, because the Qur'an's pronouncement on adoption many years later was simply that the surname of an adoptee not be changed so that their lineage can be known for the purpose of licit marriage, but no other change in prevailing custom was decreed (more on this in Chap. 14, in the section "Muhammad's Marriages").

[1] Nasr, Seyyed Hossein (editor-in-chief) et al. 2015. The Study Quran: A New Translation and Commentary. New York: HarperCollins Publishers, 192. Typically, pre-Islamic Arabia practised primogeniture—restricting inheritance to the eldest son—which "concentrated wealth in a limited number of enormous estates", which the Qur'an now flatly outlawed—see Smith, Huston. 2001. Islam: A Concise Introduction. New York: HarperOne, 61.

[2] Lings, Martin. 1988. Muhammad: His Life based on the Earliest Sources. London: Unwin Hyman Limited, 38.

Women, 4:11–12
[a long section listing specific allocations]...after paying any bequest he may have bequeathed or any debt...

[another long section listing further specific allocations]...after paying any bequest they (women) may have bequeathed ... after paying any bequest you (men) may have bequeathed ... after paying any bequest he may have bequeathed or any harmless debt...

Regarding 4:11 above, which first mentioned the inclusion of women as heiresses: "When the verse was first revealed, there was much resistance to it among the Prophet's followers, who were stunned that women and minor children, who could not fight and were not entitled to shares of booty obtained in battle, should inherit a significant portion from their husbands and fathers."[3]

The Qur'an itself does not give further guidelines or mention any limitations on bequests and debts beyond mentioning them in 4:11 and 4:12. However it is said that the Prophet instructed the following: (a) that a deceased person's legitimate debt to another (but that is not overly burdensome to their heirs) be paid first from their estate; (b) that special bequests never exceed one-third of what remains after debt; and (c) that bequests not be made to someone who is already guaranteed a legal share, e.g. a favourite child, for example.[4]

Women, 4:32
And do not covet what God has favoured some of you with over [at the expense of] others: for men is a share for what they have earned, and for women is a share for what they have earned. But ask God of His bounty, for God is the Knower of all things.

Verse 4:32 was already cited in Chap. 11's sections "Work" and "Activism", when **the Qur'an recognised women's contributions to the survival and wellbeing of the community as work after they lobbied for it to be so**, which meant that they would henceforth also be able to inherit.

Women, 4:33–34
...Those to whom you have given your oath, give them their share, for God is a witness over everything.

[3] Nasr et al. *Op. Cit.*, 193.
[4] Ibid., 194–5.

> Men are upholders/maintainers *(qawwamūn)* of women with whatever God has favoured some with over others [other men], and with whatever they spend of their wealth [on them]...

And finally **to round off the substantive inheritance references in this chapter comes verse 4:34 above, which leaves no doubt that this verse relates to inheritance allocations and corresponding responsibilities and not to men's "guardianship" over women** because they are "preferred" or "better", as previously pointed out. The tenth verse on inheritance in this chapter is the last verse, 4:176, and simply lists further specific allocations relating to siblings.

As a matter of fact, elsewhere in the Qur'an **a verse on parenting after divorce reinforces the point made in 4:34, namely that inheritance allocations correspond directly to family responsibilities** and not to any favouritism on the part of God of one gender over another:

> The Cow, 2:233
> And mothers may nurse their children for two whole years, for those who wish to complete the nursing; and it is incumbent on the father to provide for them [the mothers] and clothe them in a kindly *(maaroof)* manner...And what was incumbent (upon the father) is incumbent upon the heir...

which means that if the father dies, his primary male heir/s has/have a duty to provide for his still-nursing ex-wife. For example, if the father leaves behind one son as primary heir, then he would be responsible for the upkeep even of his father's nursing ex-wife, i.e. his ex-stepmother and half-sibling.

But perhaps most interestingly and tellingly, **the Qur'an allocates no financial responsibilities to women the way it does to men—even as it assures them, like men, of an independent economic identity with multiple potential sources of inheritance income**.

The eleventh verse on inheritance which can be found in another chapter addresses the minimum that a widow must receive, with her total potential inheritance being a function of applying the inheritance verses above:

> The Cow, 2:240
> And (for) those of you who die leaving behind wives, a bestowal to their wives of provision for a year and (there is to be) no expulsion [from the dead husband's property]. But if they move out [i.e. re-marry], there is no blame

upon you (pl.) in whatever they may do with themselves honourably. For God is Mighty, Wise.

Unfortunately some have interpreted the above to mean that a widow's residence in her late husband's home is also capped at one year,[5] not just the maintenance she is entitled to while she remains single, despite the wording.

The Big "Why"

For nearly three weeks as I contemplated the inheritance topic as laid out in the Qur'an, determined to understand mathematically the three verses that specify allocations (4:11, 4:12, 4:176), my questions only mounted. I am a huge fan of Excel spreadsheets and love financial modelling of all kinds, but this exercise was doing my head in. Eventually I got it, and was relieved to find that my understanding of how to allocate an inheritance converged more or less with how it appears to be done in practice in my admittedly limited experience. I also got why it is said that: "The specificity of these Quranic injunctions led to a whole science called the 'science of inheritance' and played an important role in the development of the science of algebra by Muslim mathematicians",[6] and marvelled at the kind of mind that can visualise the whole without the help of Excel!

But understanding "how" to divvy up an inheritance is not the same as understanding "why" the rules were drawn up as they were. Too many questions swirled in my head:

- Why do the prescribed allocations often not seem to add up to 100%, either overshooting or undershooting?
- Why is there a mention of bequests, when the rules are telling us exactly who is eligible for inheritance and how much they should get?
- Why is the allocation to a deceased person's mother, but not father, specified in six scenarios, with only one scenario mentioning both parents, basically to say that they would inherit equally in that case?

In other words while I had come to understand how the rules are to be implemented—and that there is room for society to decide on *how* to

[5] Ibid., 105.
[6] Ibid., 194.

implement them in some instances to be discussed further on—I still did not truly understand **why the complexity within seemingly finite boundaries, precision within apparent elasticity, or the special attention to mothers** when daughters, on the face of it at least, did not get much.

As mentioned in the Preface, the process of writing this book has been a spiritual journey for me, one filled with joyful surprises. Sometimes new insights would develop gradually as my investigation progressed and then climaxed in an overwhelming sense of grateful certainty. Sometimes confirmation of a verse's meaning would come suddenly with startling clarity of thought, or with a novel angle that underscored and refined the track I was on. And at other times, a thought would come in what would feel like a direct message planted in my head out of nowhere, like a lightning bolt shot through my mind as I sat in silent invocation, asking for help in understanding something.

The word "pagoda" was one of those lightning bolts. After days of agonising over the "why" of the Qur'anic inheritance system and yearning to understand it more fully, I knew exactly what was meant when I sensed the word suddenly light up in my mind. I knew what a pagoda was, and I remembered reading an interesting article about Japanese pagodas and earthquakes in *The Economist* magazine once, though I had not thought of them since. So I went online and searched *The Economist*'s website and found the article: to my amazement, I realised that I had read it over 20 years ago.

The article begins by asking how Japan's approximately 500 and very tall wooden pagodas could have remained intact for centuries in the face of the typhoons and earthquakes that plague its lands. After arriving from China in the sixth century, apparently the Japanese extended the eaves significantly away from the building so that heavy rainfall would not wash down the walls and into the ground below, softening it and eventually weakening the pagoda's foundation. There is a pillar in the centre called a *shinbashira* and despite appearances, it is not like the trunk of a tall tree that flexes with the elements to avoid snapping in two, but carries no weight at all: in fact, it is often suspended from above and may not even touch the ground, for the entire building is supported by sturdy pillars forming two concentric squares, a large outer square and a smaller inner one. Meanwhile since pagodas are multi-storey and are shaped somewhat like pyramids, a lower floor has a greater surface area than the floor above it so the sturdy pillars at the base that carry the weight of the building do not connect with their corresponding pillar above, no matter how many storeys there are! Nor are the individual storeys attached to one another, but are simply stacked on top of each other with nothing more than loose wooden brackets for joints to allow the floors to glide around.

So the question that arises is why the *shinbashira* is there in the first place if it has no structural role to play. If a massive force were to hit the pagoda from one side, the loosely stacked storeys would glide around independently of one another, with each floor moving in the opposite direction to the floors just above and below it, as if the building were doing a snake dance. What this massive column running through a hole in the centre of the building does is prevent each storey from swinging too far in one direction as it bangs up against the *shinbashira's* steadying force, which additionally then absorbs some of that kinetic energy and disperses it safely into the ground. The extra-wide and heavily tiled eaves that extend out on all sides, meanwhile, allow the pagoda to maintain its balance in the face of a violent thrust, through a gentle swaying. As the article concludes:

> ...So the secret of the Japanese pagoda's enduring strength and stability is out. It is in effect the sum of three mutually reinforcing factors: the inertia of its extra wide eaves, the freedom of the loosely-stacked storeys to slither to and fro independent of one another, and, above all, the energy-absorbing capacity of the ingenious *shinbashira*.[7]*

As I re-read this article after more than two decades, I felt that I understood the fundamental "whys" of the Qur'anic inheritance rules. Simply put, it is **a system designed to distribute wealth** (rather than energy) in a manner that ultimately:

- **benefits every member of society irrespective of gender and age**, by including both the vertical beneficiaries, i.e. children and parents, as well the horizontal beneficiaries, i.e. spouses and siblings (the wide eaves)
- **confers a measure of economic freedom and security** upon a deceased person's relatives, in accordance with their relationship to the deceased *and* their socially accepted familial responsibilities (the loosely stacked storeys)

[7] The Economist. 1997. An Engineering Mystery: Why pagodas don't fall down. December 18.

– **promotes stability** by narrowing economic differences within society across gender and age (the stabilising *shinbashira*)

The Technical "Whys"

If the pagoda analogy is one way of understanding the fundamental "whys" of the inheritance system, where does that leave the technical "whys" that had swirled in my head, especially the three questions I mentioned earlier? With the image of a pagoda now in mind, consisting of **verticality and horizontality, fluidity and stability**, I could begin to imagine why inheritance instructions may have been framed the way they were.

- **On allocations not adding up to 100%**
  When the specified allocations to legal heirs fall short of 100%, they open up **room for human agency** to determine what to do. For example in the early days the balance went to the surviving father of the deceased, who was still regarded as the primary heir, on top of his legal share, but there are other possibilities: the Shiite view and a minority Sunni one is typically in favour of an only daughter as the primary heir rather than the father (assuming both are in play), who would then receive the balance on top of whatever her legal share is.[8] This is just one scenario to show the kind of complex decision-making involved.

  When the specified allocations to legal heirs exceed 100%, again human agency must come into play and the way this has typically been done is to decide whose allocation gets calculated first, so that the rest follows as a proportion of the reduced estate that remains. The early view and typical Sunni approach has been to prioritise the calculation for spouses and then parents, while the typical Shiite one has been to prioritise surviving mothers, then spouses, then fathers.[9] (The Qur'an has children receiving their portions only after spouses and parents have received their specified allocations, which is clearly indicative of its moral hierarchy.)

[8] Nasr et al. *Op. Cit.*, 193.
[9] Ibid., 193.

All these approaches have merits and make sense to me at some level, though my initial thought was that a pro rata approach to make everything add up to 100% would have been the most straightforward. But even so, the question would still be "why": why such specific allocations if they don't settle the distribution once and for all?

I believe the specified allocations to legal heirs are meant to serve as both minimums and maximums, so that when the distribution falls short of 100% we as heirs are nudged to **redirect any balance remaining towards those who seemed uppermost in God's mind as He revealed in those verses on inheritance: the orphans, the needy, and non-inheriting relatives who could use a hand.**

It is this explanation that speaks to my heart, because it would mean **taking into consideration the totality of what the inheritance verses convey, namely the morality behind them and not only the allocations to the legal heirs indicated.**

I also believe that God left us room to adapt the rules to the situation of our time and place and perhaps even our particular family, so that when the allocations *exceed* 100% we can prioritise as we deem appropriate, so that it is up to us to decide whose portion to calculate first, spouse's or parent's. Perhaps it is a matter of culture, or the age of the parents. The point is, room for interpretation could not have accidentally been built into these allocation verses and must have been intentional.

Lastly, I believe that by not limiting the number of heirs to a narrow few such as spouses, parents and children but making others contingent heirs, such as siblings when there are no children[10] and grandchildren,

[10] For references to when siblings inherit, see 4:12 and 4:176. In both verses, siblings inherit only when the deceased has no children. In 4:12, brothers and sisters inherit equally, but in 4:176, brothers and sisters inherit in a 2:1 ratio, as with sons and daughters. Early/classical commentators took 4:12 to refer to half-siblings (probably since it specifically cites the absence of direct heirs), and 4:176 to refer to full siblings (see Asad, Muhammad. 2003. The Message of the Qur'an. Bristol, England: The Book Foundation, 120). Others, however, say that 4:12 is *replaced* by 4:176 on this issue (see Nasr et al., *Op. Cit.*, 194), i.e. that part of it is abrogated or cancelled so that brothers always inherit twice as much as sisters whether "full" or "half", a concept I am personally uncomfortable with as I believe every word in the Qur'an has its rightful place, and because the context of 4:12 of there being no direct heirs implies that half-siblings only inherit if there are no full siblings (who would constitute direct/blood heirs). This question of abrogation, i.e. of one verse supposedly cancelling out another, will be revisited with regard to another, more controversial topic in Part V, namely the question of sex outside marriage.

in the customary view, when there is no direct heir in the vertical line,[11] we are deliberately left with a non-finite system that can stretch when needed to ensure that an inheritance is not concentrated in the hands of a mere few.

- **Bequests**
  And what of bequests? I could understand right away the Qur'anic instruction to honour a deceased person's debt from their estate as the very first step, so long as it is not overly burdensome or too infringing upon the estate so as to disadvantage the heirs too severely. But with such an extended and seemingly elastic family entitled to an official share in any inheritance, is there room really for bequests by the deceased to an unrelated stranger, typically through a will, by up to as much as a third of the estate?

  Once again, to my mind **this points to the value system that the Qur'an tries to promote even as it guarantees rightful creditors and heirs their due**. Perhaps one wants to say "thank you" to a friend who had stood by one in a time of need by leaving that friend a gift. Perhaps one empathises with a neighbour's challenges in life and would like to make a contribution from their estate to ease things for them. Or perhaps one wants to leave a donation to an organisation that does good work in tackling a social problem close to one's heart. By formally including personal bequests in the Qur'anic vision for the division of an inheritance, it is as if **every human being is called upon to continue to exercise their free will and choose their own legacy in the final act of their life on earth**.
- **Mothers**
  Verse 4:11 is striking in that it mentions that the parents of a deceased person each inherit one-sixth of the estate if the deceased also leaves behind children; but that the *mother's* share doubles to one-third if there are no children, though if there are no children but there are siblings her share remains at one sixth—*without mention of the father in either case*. What this means in practice (when combined with siblings'

[11] The Qur'an does not make reference to grandchildren as heirs. If there are no children or other direct heirs, it does however make reference to siblings or half-siblings then inheriting. But custom has interpreted the absence of a "direct heir" in 4:12 to refer to the vertical line of ascendants and descendants only, i.e. excluding siblings, which can then open the way to a grandchild also inheriting in lieu of their deceased parent and great-grandparent, although I did not come across a reference that clarified the portion they would then receive or if that then left any siblings out altogether.

shares per 4:176) is that when there are no children a father's share is calculated as a balance or remainder *after* the mother and/or mother-plus-siblings (and of course spouse) have been allocated their share, with the mathematical result being that **a surviving father may receive the *same* as the surviving mother, *twice* as much, or *half* as much**.

What this manner of formulating the share of parents conveys to me is **a clear desire by God to secure a bereaved mother first, over and above a bereaved father—a remarkably symbolic gesture and acknowledgement of the special place that motherhood holds in creation** that cannot possibly be overlooked. Of course, it also underscores women's independent financial identity in the Qur'anic worldview by not lumping both parents into a single inheriting entity.

How Fairness Turns to Injustice Over Time When We Overlook Just One Verse

If I were to take stock of what I have learnt from looking into the question of inheritance in the Qur'an, I would say this: that the entire system of inheritance is constructed so as to sway while keeping society stable, **by allowing for human agency within a pragmatic framework meant to reduce poverty/income inequality and support one's responsibilities, while weaving women deliberately and specifically into every single pronouncement on allocations**.

Even a preliminary review by the reader, if they are willing to play around with pen and paper or Excel a bit, of the specific allocation verses will show that **there are occasions when women would receive the same or more than men, despite the headline instruction that a daughter receive only half of a son's inheritance (within a particular social construct where men support women—verse 4:34, which is reconfirmed in 2:233)**. The instructions readily point to scenarios where surviving parents would receive the same inheritance, a bereaved mother would receive more than the father, a lone sister would receive the same as what a lone brother would, and where inheriting brothers and sisters receive the same thing.

The Qur'anic system of inheritance, in other words, is somewhat fairer and certainly more progressive than the headline "daughter gets half the son's share" would have us believe. There is no question that it is a system that has served a huge swathe of humanity well over the centuries, men and women alike.

But we have a huge number of instances where **women today do contribute to the welfare of their families, community and society in a direct, monetary way and not only in-kind, as had been the case at the time** of the Qur'anic revelation.

A **daughter** today may literally be contributing financially to support her parents' household or to educate a younger sibling or support an unemployed one, for example. In such a context, surely the Qur'anic paradigm of linking inheritance shares to family responsibilities (4:34) itself requires that her share be at least the same as her brother's. Likewise for a **sister**, when there are no children and siblings inherit in their place (though in the case of half-siblings when there are neither children nor full-siblings, half-sisters and half-brothers already receive an equal share—see footnote 149).

Likewise a **wife** today may be a contributor to household income alongside her husband. In such a context, surely the Qur'anic paradigm of linking inheritance shares to family responsibilities (4:34) again itself requires that her share as a widow be the same as her husband's as a widower, i.e. 50% of her husband's estate, and not just 25% (4:12).

It is my personal view that religious authorities responsible for divvying up inheritances should consider the particular case of the family in question to ensure that inheritance shares to men and women broadly correlate with the heirs' responsibilities, so as to determine if the 2:1 ratio should apply or if indeed a 1:1 ratio in the case of daughters and sons, for example, would be more compatible with the Qur'anic message. I believe this is a necessary step at this time for any society that genuinely cares about complying with the Qur'anic directive on inheritance.

It really is as simple as that. **Just as there is no body without soul, there is no scripture without morality, and the Qur'an actually spells out its moral and values system for us with regard to inheritance**: it relates to sharing our good fortune with orphans, the needy, and hard-up relatives; it is about charity and kindness; it is about safeguarding the property of defenceless orphans; it is about honouring our debts and the freedom to make bequests only after we have done so; **and it is about understanding that we receive less or more inheritance in a manner that corresponds to a) our relationship to the deceased and b) whether or not we find ourselves supporting our family members**.

CHAPTER 13

Nuptials: Women Do Have the Right to Choose Their Own Spouse, and How the Qur'anic Nuptial Agreement Advocates for the Bride

Qur'anic Verses on Women's Nuptial Rights

> Women, 4:19
> Oh you who believe: it is not lawful for you to inherit women against their will, nor to constrain them [i.e. from re-marrying] so that you can take away some of what you (pl.) had given them…

The above verse abolished the pre-Qur'anic Arabian custom of men inheriting the wives of their deceased relatives as spouses. Having established that women have a right to their own property, the Qur'an also abolishes the earlier custom of forcing widows into marriage (in a bid to take over the deceased husband's property), while also condemning the alternative approach of preventing them from re-marrying (so that the relatives of the widow's husband can retain some access to that property through leverage). In effect, **this combination of Qur'anic actions established women as the *subjects* and not *objects* of inheritance**.

Needless to say, the principle that the Qur'an defends in this verse is the right of a woman to choose when and whom to marry (and what to do with her property or wealth).

L. El-Ali, *No Truth Without Beauty*, Sustainable Development Goals Series, https://doi.org/10.1007/978-3-030-83582-8_13

Women, 4:4
And give the women their (bridal) gifts without conditions. But if they voluntarily offer you any part of it, then you are welcome to consume and enjoy it.

Women, 4:24
...And those (women) whom you seek to enjoy (in marriage), give them their dues [i.e. bridal gifts] as a duty. And there is no blame on either of you for whatever you may mutually agree after the duty (has been done). For God is all-Knowing, Wise.

Verses 4:4 and 4:24 established the legal requirement henceforth that the groom provide a bridal gift (*mahr*) directly to the woman he is marrying, and makes it crystal clear that this is an unconditional gift that is to be treated as her property alone. In so doing, the Qur'an essentially introduces yet another source of income for women, alongside inheritance income and the right to earn discussed earlier in Chap. 11's section entitled "Participation". **The word often used to refer to bridal gifts is "dues" or "wages", which serves to underscore that God views it as an *entitlement* of the bride's, not a charitable gift**.

The Confederates, 33:50
Oh Prophet: We have made lawful for you your wives whom you have given their dues [bridal gift]...

Nor was the Prophet exempt from providing the bridal gift, as this verse shows, although there is an exception to this if he marries one of his own slaves or prisoners per verse 33:50, which will be discussed under Chap. 14's section "Muhammad's Marriages".

The bridal gift is of the utmost importance in a social context where women may have limited access to an independent source of income like work or sufficient inheritance. Among the more affluent today the bridal gift is often a symbolic one, typically a beautifully decorated copy of the Qur'an together with a solitaire ring or jewellery set. The point of the bridal gift appears to have been to ensure commitment on the part of a prospective husband in a social context where men often acquired and discarded women on a whim, or at least without sufficient consideration to their wellbeing. This concern on the part of God in the Qur'an is made clear in several verses on divorce guidelines, to be discussed a bit later in Chap. 15, entitled Divorce.

Crucially, the decision as to what constitutes a suitable bridal gift (*mahr*) was always the bride's, starting from the Prophet's time, and marriage did not merge a woman's economic identity with that of her husband:

> In a patriarchal society, even a general declaration of equal rights is not sufficient to protect women. Consequently, divine wisdom gave women further protections. Paramount among these protections is the ability of a Muslim woman to negotiate her marriage contract and place in it any conditions that do not contradict its purpose. For example, she could place in her marriage contract…a condition requiring him to support her in the pursuit of her education after marriage. She could also use the marriage contract to ensure that her marriage would foster, rather than destroy, her financial independence. This goal is usually achieved by requiring a substantial *mahr* [bridal gift].
>
> …One woman may prefer cash, another property, depending on her relative needs or even taste…A woman of meager means may prefer to ask for capital that she could immediately invest in a business. Her husband would have no access to either the capital or income from that business even if he were in need because legally, her *mahr* belongs to her alone.
>
> …Sometimes women resort to the custom of dividing the *mahr* into two amounts: advanced and deferred. The advanced *mahr* is usually small and merely symbolic. It is due by the time of the marriage ceremony. The deferred *mahr* is usually a substantial lump-sum payment. Unless otherwise specified, it becomes due only in case of death or divorce. If the husband dies, the deferred *mahr* becomes an outstanding senior debt against his estate (not to be confused with the woman's share/inheritance in the estate of her husband). If the couple divorce, the husband must pay the deferred *mahr* at the dissolution of the marriage. Thus the concept of deferred *mahr* is somewhat analogous to that of lump-sum alimony in the United States.[1]

Most demonstratively, the importance of non-coercion in marriage and the bridal gift (*mahr*)—as well as universal gender equality—are combined in a verse about marrying bondwomen (slavery was still prevalent in seventh-century Arabia). The Qur'an addressed the case of men who

[1] al-Hibri, Azizah. 2000. An Introduction to Muslim Women's Rights. In Windows of Faith: Muslim Women Scholar-Activists in North America, ed. Gisela Webb, 58–60. New York: Syracuse University.

could not afford to marry a free and believing woman, but who would be able to marry a servant-slave:

> Women, 4:25
> And those among you who cannot afford to marry chaste, believing (free) women then (let them marry) the believing maids you (pl.) rightfully possess. God knows best your faith. You are from one another, so marry them with permission of their folk and give them their dues [bridal gifts] with kindness (*bil-maaroof*), as married women and not as debauched women or illicit lovers…

This is an extraordinary verse on many counts. The same, "you are from one another" used in the Qur'an to describe the universal male and female is applied here contextually to equate a freeman with a bondwoman united in belief, while **ensuring that a woman's slave status is not regarded as license to force her to marry, skip the bridal gift, behave unkindly towards her or with a lesser courtesy than would be extended to a freewoman**. More will be said about the institution of slavery and how it appears to have functioned at the time in seventh-century Arabia in Chap. 14's section on monogamy.

The Alleged Pushback of the Qur'an on a Woman Choosing Her Own Spouse: But It Is for Her "Guardian" to Decide!

Once verse 4:34 discussed above is misinterpreted to mean that men are literal guardians rather than now obligated financial supporters of women, it becomes easy to strip a woman of her ability to marry without a "guardian" not only to authorise her marriage but to speak for her, quite literally, during the ceremony itself. As a reminder here is that section of the verse again compared with how it is usually interpreted/translated:

> ✓ Women, 4:34
> Men are upholders/maintainers *(qawwamūn)* of women with whatever God has favoured some [i.e. men] with over others [i.e. other men], and with whatever they spend of their wealth [i.e. on the women]. Therefore righteous women are devoutly pious *(qanitāt)*, keeping private what God has ordained be so-kept…

× Men are guardians/in charge of women because God has preferred the one (men) over the other (women), and because they spend of their wealth (on the women); therefore righteous women are obedient, guarding in (their husbands') absence what God would guard...

It is a disturbing manifestation of this type of patriarchy when a woman is asked by the presiding officiant at her own nuptial service who her (male) guardian is who will act on her behalf—literally who her "deputy" or "representative" is, as though she were totally absent from the imminent proceedings!

Yet this is what happens in most cases with few but growing exceptions, with officiants often priding themselves on being diligent enough to even ask the bride who will represent her (rather than taking any present man's word for it, I suppose).

As for the claim that a woman cannot disobey her parents with regard to marriage in particular, this is false. The Qur'an commands respect and *kindness to parents, not obedience, from both men and women*:

Women, 4:36
And worship God and do not ascribe any partner to Him. And be good to parents...

The Night Journey, 17:23
And your Lord has decreed that you worship none but Him, and to be good to parents. If one or both of them reach old age, do not (even) say "Uff!" to them nor chide them, but speak to them a gracious word.

Nor does the Qur'an ever single out the father as deserving more respect or having more authority than the mother, whereas it does make special mention of mothers:

The Sand Dunes, 46:15
And We have charged every human being with being good to its parents; its mother bore it in discomfort and gave birth to it in discomfort...

And as for the claim that marriage is incumbent on everyone, it is also false and there is no evidence for it in the Qur'an. There is an alleged and disputed *hadith* that says "marriage is half of religion",[2] which is often used to pressure people into marriage in many parts. But **classical and early jurists themselves always maintained that while marriage is advantageous it is not a requirement**, and in fact many a conservative and highly recognised religious personality are known to have never married.[3]

The Pushback of Society on the Nuptial Agreement: Don't Be Greedy, Woman!

As for the bridal gift and any special requests or conditions that a bride may want to include in her nuptial agreement to safeguard her rights or interests, it has become a largely neglected mechanism that has almost totally fallen out of use. A bride and her family may feel that the marriage would no longer take place if there were an attempt to utilise this tool to protect the bride, fearing they would cause offence to the groom and his family. And in some societies the culture of the dowry continues to dominate, whereby it is the bride who makes the traditional payment to her new husband or his family.

Patriarchal attitudes have basically turned the Qur'anic means of protecting women after marriage into a targeted accusation of materialism and bad faith. This is **a travesty of Qur'anic justice especially in poor or conservative societies** where women may have few independent resources or alternative avenues for independent decision-making.

Historical Evidence of Women Exercising Their Nuptial Rights

- It was interesting to learn that the Prophet had proposed marriage to several women with whom a marriage contract was ultimately not concluded; and that several women had offered themselves as wives

[2] Abou El Fadl, Khaled M. 2006. The Search for Beauty in Islam: A Conference of the Books. Maryland: Rowman & Littlefield Publishers, Inc., 170.

[3] Abou El Fadl, Khaled M. 2003. Speaking in God's Name: Islamic Law, Authority and Women. Oxford: Oneworld Publications, 195.

to the Prophet directly, reportedly waiving their right to a bridal gift as they "negotiated" their own nuptial agreement.[4]

- I particularly enjoyed reading about one feisty and articulate **Umm Aban, a widow who appears to have been proposed to at one time or another by both Omar and Ali (among others)—only to turn them down and eventually go for Talha, one of the Prophet's other Companions**:

> Omar proposed to Um Aban...after her husband, Yazid bin Abi Sufyan, died, and she said, 'He does not enter but scowling and he does not leave but scowling; he closes the doors and minimizes his bounty.' Then Zubair proposed to her, and she said, 'He has one hand on my temples and one hand on the whip.' Then Ali proposed to her, and she said, 'Women get no luck from him except that he sits among their four parts; they do not get anything else from him.' Then Talha proposed to her, and she was responsive and he married her. So Ali...visited her and said, 'You rejected whom you rejected, and you accepted the son of the daughter of a ...[southern Arab]!' She said, 'Decree and destiny.' He said, 'Now then, truly you have married he among us who is most beautiful of face, most generous of hand, and the greatest in bounty to his family.[5]

And in another version, which also shows that **mingling between men and women had been considered natural in the Prophet's day and that women were empowered to decide on proposals for themselves**:

> Then Talha proposed to her...she said, 'I am well aware of his dispositions. When he enters, he enters laughing, and when he leaves, he leaves smiling. When I ask, he gives; when I am silent, he initiates; when I work, he thanks; and when I do wrong, he forgives.' So after he had dwelled with her, Ali said, ...'Peace be unto you, oh woman dear to herself.' She said, 'And unto you peace.' He said, 'The Commander of the Faithful [Omar] proposed to you and you rejected him?' She said, 'It was so.' He said, 'And I proposed to you and you rejected me although I am from the Messenger of God? [i.e. of the Prophet's household]" She said, 'It was so.'[6]

[4] Stowasser, Barbara Freyer. 1994. Women in the Qur'an, Traditions, and Interpretation. New York: Oxford University Press Inc, 87.

[5] Kahf, Mohja. 2000. Braiding the Stories: Women's Eloquence in the Early Islamic Era. In Windows of Faith: Muslim Women Scholar-Activists in North America, ed. Gisela Webb, 160. New York: Syracuse University Press.

[6] Ibid.

- And as previously mentioned in Part II, when Omar as caliph attempted to cap the amount of the bridal gift in his time, a woman rose up and interrupted him while he was addressing the congregation from the pulpit, challenging his right to take away from women what the Qur'an had granted them as a nuptial right. The noble Omar conceded he had been mistaken, withdrawing his proposal.[7]
- As importantly, when a woman named Khansa complained to the Prophet that her father had forced her to marry someone against her wishes, he annulled her marriage.[8]
- Nor could the Prophet's own intercession in favour of a marriage outweigh a woman's right to choose her own destiny:

> … there was a woman named Barira who was married to a man who loved her madly, named Mughith. But Barira did not love Mughith and divorced him. Mughith would follow Barira around crying—with his tears flowing down his beard. The Prophet felt sorry for the love-struck fellow and asked Barira if she would take him back. Barira asked the Prophet if this was a Divine command, and the Prophet said no, it was simply a personal appeal. Consequently, Barira refused to take Mughith back.[9]

- Finally, though the pre-Qur'anic custom of women marrying through a male guardian or appointed male representative persisted despite the absence of a religious mandate for it, it is notable that the Hanafi school of (Sunni) jurisprudence has always maintained that no guardian is necessary, and a woman can execute her own nuptials in a Hanafi court.[10]

[7] al-Hibri, Azizah. *Op. Cit.*, 59 and Brown, Jonathan. 2015. Misquoting Muhammad: The Challenge and Choices of Interpreting the Prophet's Legacy. London: Oneworld Publications, 198.

[8] Abou El Fadl, Khaled. *Op. Cit.* (2006), 172.

[9] Ibid., See also le Gai Eaton, Charles. 2008. The Book of Hadith: Sayings of the Prophet Muhammad, from the Mishkat al-Masabih. Watsonville, California; Bristol, England: The Book Foundation, 85.

[10] Brown, Jonathan. *Op. Cit.* (2015), 51 and Abou El Fadl, Khaled. *Op. Cit.* (2003), 150.

CHAPTER 14

Marriage: A Sublime Institution, Not Mere Social Contract

Qur'anic Verses on Marriage

The many beautiful verses in the Qur'an about the nature and intended relationship between the male and the female, which were cited at length in Part II, are certainly the bedrock of the Qur'anic view of marriage. But rather than repeat them all, I will re-mention just a couple after first introducing other verses that highlight marriage as a sacred institution and a sublime human experience.

> The Cow, 2:102
> And they followed what the devils recounted against Solomon's kingdom. Solomon did not disbelieve but the devils disbelieved, teaching people sorcery…And they would learn from them how to come between a man and his wife…

In the first mention of Solomon in the Qur'an, it is interesting that a denunciation of his satanic enemies references the fact that they would not hesitate to use magic to separate a man from his wife. The very fact that this is the example of evil given in this verse underscores the sanctity of the relationship between a husband and his wife in the Qur'anic worldview.

> The Cow, 2:187
> It is made lawful for you (pl.), on the nights of the fast, to go unto your wives; they are clothing for you, and you are clothing for them. God is aware

L. El-Ali, *No Truth Without Beauty*, Sustainable Development Goals Series, https://doi.org/10.1007/978-3-030-83582-8_14

> that you defraud yourselves in this respect, so He turned to you in mercy and pardoned you. So now lie with them and seek what God has ordained for you, and eat and drink until you can discern the white streak from the black streak of dawn, then complete [i.e. resume] the fast till nightfall…

For me, this is a most tender portrayal of marriage in the Qur'an. The "clothing" metaphor conjures up intimate closeness as well as enveloping comfort between husbands and wives. Before this verse was revealed, people thought they had to abstain from sexual relations throughout the fasting month of Ramadan and not only during the daylight fasting hours as such, which resulted in making those who did indulge in sex after sunset feel guilty because they thought they had cheated.

> The Cattle, 6:98
> And it is He who produced you (pl.) from a single soul, thus a dwelling-place and a repository [i.e. for you in one another]. We have spelt out the verses/signs clearly for those who understand.

> The Byzantines, 30:21
> And among His signs is that He created mates for you (pl.) from your own souls so that you may find tranquillity in them, and established between you love and compassion. In this there are signs for people who reflect.

Finally, a brief word on the contractual aspect of the Qur'anic marriage. From the start in the seventh century, legal marriage was executed as a social contract, unsurprising given the rights and protections that the Qur'an established for women, including and especially with regard to divorce (more on this later in Chap. 15, entitled Divorce). It is interesting to note that marriage did not become contractual meanwhile in Europe till the fourteenth century, and the inclusion of divorce terms did not occur there till the nineteenth century.[1] Yet **today, with Muslims mostly using their marriage contract to the *minimum* of its capacity either wilfully (patriarchally) or bashfully (due to social pressure/custom), it is usually in European and generally Western marriage contracts that Muslim women are able to protect themselves**.

[1] Barlas, Asma. 2015. Believing Women in Islam: Unreading Patriarchal Interpretations of the Qur'an. Texas: University of Texas Press, 230.

How Monogamy Is the Norm in the Qur'an (as in Reality)

As with the male-female relationship overall, many of the verses that underscore the centrality of mates—literally "two", as in two souls forming a human unit (not three or four or five souls), have been covered in Part II. So I will only re-mention a couple of them here, after introducing some very interesting and again, overlooked verses.

> Women, 4:20
> And if you wish to exchange one wife for another and you had given one of the two a significant treasure, do not take a thing from it...

The allusion to having to divorce one's wife in order to marry another woman is a clear indication that monogamy is the norm in the Qur'anic worldview[2] despite the allowance it makes for polygyny in certain cases, as will be shortly discussed.

> Light, 24:32
> And marry the single (*ayāma*) among you, and the righteous among your male and female slaves and handmaids [i.e. domestic servants]. If they be poor, God will enrich them from His bounty. For God is all-Embracing, all-Knowing.

In this doubly emancipatory yet conspicuously overlooked verse, which is partially reminiscent of 4:25 in the earlier Chap. 13, entitled Nuptials, in its encouragement of marriage to slaves, there are two additional gems regarding women as spouses.

First, the Qur'an here explicitly instructs marriage to unmarried *men* and not only to unmarried women, which unquestionably establishes monogamous marriage as the norm in its worldview.

Second, the Qur'an also instructs marriage to *male* as well as female slaves and servants (not just freepersons) who are virtuous, **which indicates that women were also being encouraged and empowered to marry a bondman and not only the other way round** as was the case in 4:25. In addition, in 4:25 what the freeman and bondmaid had in common was "belief", whereas here what unites the freeperson and

[2] Asad, Muhammad. 2003. The Message of the Qur'an. Bristol, England: The Book Foundation, 123.

bondperson whom the Qur'an is encouraging to marry is the broader concept of "righteousness", or virtue.

Lastly, the Qur'anic reference to slaves and bondservants possibly being poor no doubt sounds strange to us today. Most of us think of slavery exclusively through the lens of the African American experience (or white European practice), and therefore expect slavery anytime anywhere to have been a) racist and b) systematically brutal, whereas this was not always the case. For example, we would expect that slaves at that time would not have been allowed to own anything to begin with and so would have been poor by definition. But like its approach to women in general, the Qur'anic verses on slavery reflect a process of regulation and limitation of unjust customs that had until then been unrestricted. Thus **the Qur'anic revelation comes along and proceeds to deal with the already existing institution of slavery by introducing incentives to mitigate its inherent injustice and eventually mandating, after Muhammad and his followers had triumphed over their enemies, a mechanism for its elimination altogether**:

- By encouraging mixed (free-bonded) marriage, as we have seen (4:25, 24:32)
- By equating the free and the enslaved in God's eyes, judged solely by the quality of their souls (4:25) even as *God halved the punishment for a slave for the same crime committed by a freeperson* (second part of 4:25)
- By requiring the same kindness towards slaves as that required towards parents, relatives, neighbours and strangers (4:36)
- By instituting the freeing of a slave as an act of atonement, an even more desirable act of charity (*zakat*) than feeding 60 needy persons (58:3)
- By accepting the freeing of a slave as atonement for breaking a sincere oath (5:89)
- By stipulating the freeing of a slave as atonement for inadvertently killing a fellow believer (4:92)
- By defining the freeing of a slave as an act of "belief, perseverance and compassion" and equating it with providing food amid famine to an orphan, relative, the needy and the wretched, all of which are acts carried out by the "righteous" who choose the "steeper" or higher path (90:8–18)

- By mandating that prisoners of war be released either through a voluntary act of grace or through ransom *until peace is restored*—which means that once peace is restored all remaining prisoners must be released unconditionally (47:4)
- By banning the acquisition of slaves by distinguishing it from those who are naturally captured in the course of battle as prisoners of war (8:67)
- By ordering the allocation of community funds to purchase the freedom of slaves after the new religion was victorious and became the law of the land[3] (9:60)

It is interesting to note that **Muhammad's earliest followers tended to be slaves and freed slaves, and young men and women with little influence.**[4] Thus it is particularly disappointing despite this and all of the above—the last two verses cited in particular (8:67 and 9:60)—that Muslim societies would not so easily relinquish slavery in the 13 centuries following the Qur'anic revelation, with formal abolition only beginning to take place in the nineteenth century.[5] That said, it is quite true that slaves within those systems were not drawn from a particular race and that they could hold different positions within these societies—mostly within the military, as civil servants (including as Grand Vizier), and as domestic workers—and for the most part could intermarry and produce offspring who were not slaves.[6]

He Frowned, 80:33–7
So when the piercing trumpet sounds [for the resurrection]
On a day when a man will flee his brother,
And his mother and father,

[3] Lang, Jeffrey. 1995. Struggling to Surrender: Some Impressions from an American Convert to Islam. Maryland: Amana Publications, 89 and Lings, Martin. 1988. Muhammad: His Life based on the Earliest Sources. London: Unwin Hyman Limited, 310–314.

[4] Lings, Martin. Ibid., 65.

[5] For example, see Dar al-Iftaa Al-Missriyyah. 2013. Fatwa No. 4607. www.dar-alifta.org.eg/AR/ViewFatwa.aspx?ID=14761&LangID=1&MuftiType=0 *(in Arabic)*. June 11.

[6] See The BBC. 2009. Slavery in Islam. www.bbc.co.uk/religion/religions/islam/history/slavery_1.shtml. September 7; Brown, Jonathan, and Ali, Abdullah Hamid. 2017. Slavery and Islam: What is Slavery? www.yaqeeninstitute.org/jonathan-brown/slavery-and-islam-what-is-slavery/#ftnt1. February 7; and Sherwood, Marika. Britain, slavery and the trade in enslaved Africans. https://archives.history.ac.uk/history-in-focus/Slavery/articles/sherwood.html#5.

> And his wife and children:
> Every one of them that day will have enough concern of their own.

In the above verse depicting people's state of mind on the Day of Judgment, where the Qur'an takes the example of a typical man with typical relatives, it is notable that the normative reference is to a man having a single "wife", not "wives".

> Creator, 35:11
> And God created you (pl.) from dust, then from a drop, then He made you into pairs...

> Consultation, 42:11
> Creator of the heavens and the earth, He has made for you (pl.) mates from your own souls...

> The Tiding, 78:8
> And we created you (pl.) in pairs.

The Pushback of Myth: But Any Man Can Have Four Wives!

The institutions of polygyny—where a man can have multiple wives—and slavery have two things in common.

First, they were both widely practised in seventh-century Arabia (as in many parts of the world) *before* Muhammad's prophethood and preaching began.

Second, the Qur'an proceeded to deal with both these already-existing institutions by introducing rules to limit them alongside incentives to do away with them, with a final instruction on how to use state funds to eliminate slavery altogether.

Qur'anic scholars actually agree that polygyny was a solution to a particular problem at a particular time, namely the shortage of men as spouses, due to war.[7] They point out that before the Qur'an men in Arabia could in fact marry any number of women, and that the Qur'anic

[7] Lang, Jeffrey. *Op. Cit.*, 163.

revelation restricted it to four wives at most *and* made fairness a condition henceforth to polygyny *and* proclaimed that it would be impossible for a man to be fair if he had multiple wives. But until recently, scholars stopped there and did not point out another condition for polygyny besides fairness, which we will now discuss.

The view that argues that a man can have up to four wives at a time, period, without conditions is one that results from considering one part of verse 4:3 while ignoring the rest, and ignoring verse 4:129 of the Qur'an altogether. See what follows below, where I also show both of these verses' neighbouring verses to give context. Once again, we see a Qur'anic concern for orphans—whether children or women lacking a provider—and in fact verse 4:3 is one of the verses in the impassioned defence of orphans (4:2–4:12) already cited in Chap. 12, entitled Inheritance:

> <u>Women, 4:2–4</u>
> Give (pl.) orphans their wealth, and do not substitute the corrupt [i.e. what is yours] for the good [i.e. what is theirs]; and do not absorb their wealth into your own wealth, for that is a great crime.
>
> ✓ And if you (pl.) fear being unfair to the orphans, then marry those women who <u>are lawful for you</u>—two, three or four; <u>but if you fear being unjust then (only) one, or whom you rightfully possess [i.e. are already married to]—this way it is more likely that you will not be unjust</u>. (4:3)
>
> And give the women their bridal gifts without conditions. But if they voluntarily offer you any part of it, then you are welcome to consume and enjoy it.

Thus while verse 4:2 speaks generally of not wronging orphans by withholding or manipulating what is their rightful property, the next verse 4:3 speaks of orphaned women, i.e. who have lost their husbands and are now dependent on others: the Qur'an exhorts believing men to marry those women who are lawful for them, i.e. those not inappropriately related to them by blood or marriage or foster-nursing and who are not sisters to one another (per 4:22–23), even as it emphasises that marriage to more than one, as was common, is unlikely to result in fairness, which it makes clear is important. The subsequent verse 4:4 then makes it crystal clear that though some of these men may be caretakers of the properties of these women, they must still offer them upon marriage the obligatory bridal gift from their own means, which is not to be merged back into the men's own wealth after the marriage is consummated. **This is an extraordinary example of the detail God was prepared to go into in the**

Qur'an to protect women's property both from their (male) wealth managers as well as any prospective husbands.

Unfortunately, verse 4:3 is usually translated (and interpreted) to flat out contradict two of the verse's own injunctions at once: first, that polygyny is a pragmatic solution to a social problem (not a mechanism through which men could indulge themselves) and second, that the fair practice is to have only one wife:

> × Women, 4:3
> And if you (pl.) fear being unfair to the orphans, then marry those women who (seem) good to you—two, three or four; but if you fear being unjust then (only) one, or whom you rightfully possess (from your slaves and prisoners of war)—this way it is more likely that you will not be unjust.

Nor are the pre-conditions for polygyny or its unfairness to women issues of fleeting concern in the Qur'an, which comes back to the subject later in the same chapter: in this second iteration **we are sternly reminded of the pre-conditions for polygyny (and the centrality of the bridal gift) and told bluntly that God's view is that polygyny is inherently unfair**, even as He offers possible solutions for those who find themselves in polygynous marriages:

> Women, 4:127, 4:129, 4:130
> They consult you about women. Say: God instructs you about them, and what is recited to you in the Book regarding the orphaned women—whom you do not give what has been decreed as their rightful due yet whom you desire to marry—and the helpless among the children: that you should uphold justice for the orphans…
>
> You will not be able to deal justly between women, however much you wish to. But do not turn away from one altogether so as to leave her suspended [i.e. in limbo, neither happily married nor free to move on]; and if you come to an agreement and are reverent, God is Forgiving, Merciful. (4:129)
>
> But if they separate, God will compensate each of them from His abundance. For God is all-Embracing, Wise.

What is striking in the above iteration of multiple marriages to orphaned, i.e. widowed, women is not only the renewed emphasis on equal treatment for all wives but also God's encouragement of a man, together with whichever wife he is not close to, to come to some sort of arrangement that both can live with, in which case God promises to look more favourably on the situation. Even more striking, **the Qur'an goes on to say that if the two decide to separate, then God will enrich both of them, which to me sounds like a reward to the man for choosing to separate rather than be unfair, and a reassurance to the woman that God will provide for her** and she will not become destitute—the two key issues God seems concerned about here.

Many subscribe to a view on polygyny that is somewhere between the Qur'anic whole, which is values-driven and conditional as we have seen, and the heavily patriarchal "no-conditions" position. This quite common view argues that a man can have up to four wives at a time as long as he can provide equally for all and spend an equal amount of time with all. Yet even this view is unsupported by the Qur'an as it completely overlooks the three explicit divine pronouncements in the above verses regarding polygyny:

- **that polygyny be considered specifically in the case of widowed women** (4:3, 4:127),
- **that it is more just in God's eyes to have only one wife** (4:3),
- **that God states that a man will never be able to treat multiple wives equally** however ardently he tries (4:129),

and indeed in a later chapter, in a verse unrelated to polygyny but which touches upon a number of personal relationships, the Qur'an begins by first stating a fundamental, universal fact that is nonetheless relevant here:

- "God has not given any man two hearts within his breast..." (33:4)

Muhammad's Marriages[8]

Mention must be made of the Prophet's own marriages and how all the above marriage guidelines actually played out in his case.

Muhammad received a marriage proposal from his employer in Mecca, via a female friend of hers, when he was 25 years old and she was 40.

[8] Unless otherwise indicated, all the information, descriptions, and quotations cited here regarding Muhammad's wives and other women are from Lings, Martin. *Op. Cit.*, 34–39, 96, 105–106, 132–133, 164–165, 201, 206, 211–214, 233, 241–242, 259–260, 268–272, 277, 280–286, 317, 326–327, 342–344, 347. The analysis and opinions, on the other hand, are the author's.

Already twice-married, Khadija was a beautiful and rich merchant who had hired The Trustworthy One (*al-amin*), as Muhammad was then known, to take her merchandise from Arabia to Syria following the death of her second husband. This was 15 years before Muhammad received the first verses of the Qur'an from the archangel Gabriel that would launch his mission, which occurred when he himself was 40 years old.

Though Khadija was rich while Muhammad was of very modest means, it was agreed that his bridal gift to her (an already existing custom which the Qur'an would later make mandatory) would be 20 she-camels. On the day of his marriage the Prophet set free an enslaved woman named Baraka, later also known as Umm Ayman, whom he had inherited from his father. She would remain very close to the Prophet till the end of his life. At the same time he received from his bride a fifteen-year-old male slave named Zayd, who would soon choose to remain with the Prophet as a slave rather than return to his noble people and the loving family that had finally found him after he had been snatched from them years earlier and sold into slavery. Moved by Zayd's decision, the Prophet set him free and formally adopted him. Muhammad and Khadija had six children together: the first and last were sons who died in infancy (Qassem and Abdallah), and the four who survived into adulthood were all daughters, namely Zaynab, the exceptionally beautiful Ruqayya, Umm Kulthum, and Fatima, who would go on to marry the Prophet's cousin, Ali.

> In the year AD 619,...the Prophet suffered a great loss in the death of his wife Khadijah. She was about sixty-five years old and he was nearing fifty. They had lived together in profound harmony for twenty-five years, and she had been not only his wife but also his intimate friend, his wise counsellor, and mother to his whole household including 'Ali [his cousin, whom he had taken in to ease his uncle's financial hardship] and Zayd [his adopted son]. His four daughters were overcome with grief, but he was able to comfort them by telling them that Gabriel had once come to him and told him to give Khadijah greetings of Peace from her Lord and to tell her that He had prepared for her an abode in Paradise.[9]

So Muhammad remained in a monogamous marriage with Khadija for 25 years until she died when she was 65 and he was 50, even though polygyny was a common practice then. He would certainly have been able to afford more than one wife during his long marriage to

[9] See previous footnote.

Khadija: the Qur'an had not yet come along to separate a woman's property from her husband's for it was only the last 10 years of their marriage that overlapped with the gradual unfolding of the Qur'anic revelation, which would continue for another 13 years or so after her death. I am not sure at what point during the 23 years that the Qur'an established the separate economic identity of women, but it is unlikely to have been in the first 10 years while the Prophet was still in Mecca and married to Khadija, which were more focused on spiritual rather than social issues.

The era of polygyny technically began for Muhammad in the year that followed Khadija's death, while he was still in Mecca and before the migration to Medina to escape persecution. A woman named Khawla who had taken it upon herself to look after the Prophet's household after Khadija's death suggested he consider re-marrying, and when he asked her whom he should marry, she had two ideas: a 30-year-old widow named Sawda (whose name means "she who is black", and who was said to be dark-skinned and had five or six children[10]), or the daughter of his closest friend Abu Bakr, named Aisha. The Prophet had earlier had two strange dreams where first a man, then an angel had indicated to him that Aisha, though still a small child then, would be his wife, so Khawla's suggestion now seemed like a third sign and he instructed her to proceed with arranging both marriages. Sawda accepted the Prophet's proposal and they were soon married. As for Aisha, she was already betrothed to someone else but her father would easily undo that arrangement and contractually marry her to the Prophet himself (without Aisha being present) some months later, though she would remain in her parents' house for a few more years due to her young age. Some months after Aisha's betrothal to Muhammad, Abu Bakr and others fled to Medina leaving behind their families. Two years after that the Prophet sent for Sawda while Abu Bakr sent for his family, and it was then that a simple wedding (a bowl of milk rather than the customary feast) took place when Aisha is said to have been nine (or 10 in other early accounts). However, it is hard to know exactly how old Aisha was when her marriage was actually consummated, for several reasons:

- **The *hadith* reports from three centuries later indicate that several years passed after Aisha's marriage before it was**

[10] www.islamweb.net/ar/fatwa/115147 and www.dar-alifta.org/ar/Viewstatement.aspx?sec=new&ID=5144 (both in Arabic).

consummated. The conventional wisdom has taken this to mean a few years after the betrothal effected by Aisha's father in Mecca and soon after the wedding in Medina at age nine (or 10). However, this may well have meant a few years after the wedding in Medina, which would make her closer to or in her teens.

- ***Hadith* reports also say that at her marriage, Aisha had "good knowledge of Ancient Arabic poetry and genealogy" and "pronounced the fundamental rules of Arabic Islamic ethics"**.[11] This is highly unlikely of a nine-year-old girl. In fact prominent and widely recognised religious leaders today have made the argument that Aisha must have been at least 13 and possibly a few years older at consummation—an opinion which gels with these reports—based on their review of other (non-*hadith*) early documents that provide detail of the Prophet's life, the migration to Medina, and her sister Asma's age.[12]
- **My own view is that Aisha must have been close to or in her early teens when her marriage was consummated, for a combination of reasons:**

  - **First**, because there is no evidence from Aisha's sometimes surprisingly explicit accounts of her personal life with the Prophet to suggest any difficulty or trauma in their early years together—quite the opposite, in fact.
  - **Second**, because the records imply that Aisha had been around in Medina long enough to have made friends there *before* moving to the apartment built for her by the Prophet (see quotation below), which indicates that she may have been older than nine even at the time of the wedding itself.
  - **Third**, because what we know of the early part of their cohabitation, including from Aisha herself, tells us that the marriage was not consummated for some time after the wedding:

For the last three years scarcely a day had passed without one or more of 'Aishah's friends coming to play with her in the courtyard adjoining her father's house. Her removal to the Prophet's house changed nothing in this

[11] Barlas, Asma. *Op. Cit.*, 126.

[12] Ibid., and see also Brown, Jonathan. 2015. Misquoting Muhammad: The Challenge and Choices of Interpreting the Prophet's Legacy. London: Oneworld Publications, 147.

> respect. Friends now came every day to visit her in her own apartment—new friends made since her arrival in Medina and also some of the old ones whose parents, like hers, had emigrated. 'I would be playing…with the girls who were my friends, and the Prophet would come in and they would steal out of the house and he would go out after them and bring them back, for he was pleased for my sake to have them there.' Sometimes he would say 'Stay where ye are' before they had time to move. He would also join in the games sometimes… 'One day,' said 'Aishah, 'the Prophet came in…and he said: 'Oh 'Aishah, whatever game is this?' I said: 'It is Solomon's horses', and he laughed. But sometimes as he came in he would simply screen himself with his cloak so as not to disturb them.[13]

Aisha would go on to become the Prophet's other great love, after Khadija, and we have already heard about her pivotal role as one of the greatest religious scholars and teachers after his death, and as a political leader. The two women were, on the face of it, very different: the one significantly older than Muhammad, twice-married already, mature and wise; the other significantly younger, inexperienced in every way, independent-minded, and quick to "perceive and react". But both were exceptionally close to Muhammad. Aisha would later recount how she was most jealous of Khadija's memory on account of what she had observed of her enduring effect on the Prophet, often feistily telling him, "It is as if there had never been any other woman in the world, save only Khadijah."

The Prophet would nonetheless go on to marry several other women while married to Sawda and Aisha during his time in Medina, where he now became a head of state and political leader.

He would marry the 18-year-old and recently widowed Hafsa, daughter of Omar. Sawda, Aisha and Hafsa had their own, separate yet adjacent apartments but formed part of one household, with Aisha reportedly pleased to have a companion closer to her age and with Sawda, then 38, extending her maternal kindness to the new member of the family. The Prophet would later marry another widow named Zaynab, aged around 30,[14] a year after her husband died in a key battle, though she herself would die just eight months later. Soon after Zaynab's death one of the Prophet's cousins died of a battle-wound and some months later he would marry his widow and mother of his now-orphaned children, the 29-year old and beautiful Umm Salama, who is said to have initially resisted the

[13] See footnote 8.

[14] www.islamqa.info/ar/answers/311718 (in Arabic).

proposal as she confessed to having a jealous nature unsuited to being one of several wives, and because she was concerned for the welfare of her now-orphaned children, though the Prophet's assurances on both counts comforted her and she would soon settle into Zaynab's vacated apartment. The Prophet had no room of his own and would move every evening into the apartment of the wife whose turn it was to give him a home for the next 24 hours.

Thus Muhammad's polygynous phase, which began technically in the year after Khadija's death but practically some years later, took shape when he was in his 50s. He married the widow and mother of five or six children Sawda, Aisha, the widow Hafsa, and the widow Zaynab "mother of the poor", with the widow and mother of several children, Umm Salama, becoming the fourth wife after Zaynab's premature death.

The verses on marrying up to four "orphaned" women (widows) had already been revealed at that time and with these four wives in total, of which three were widows, Muhammad had no reason to believe he would be marrying anyone else.

But prophets are not ordinary men even as they are ultimately human, and the Qur'an would go on to make this point in a number of ways, including with regard to marital issues. A verse would soon sanction the marriage of Muhammad to a fifth woman, his 40-year-old and extremely pious and beautiful cousin Zaynab, a widow whose marriage he had arranged years earlier to his adopted son Zayd, but which had been an unhappy one from the start and which had recently ended in divorce. The Qur'an would even say *"…We have married her to you…"* (33:37), so no formal wedding would take place. There had been a mutual attraction some months ago but marriage to Zaynab had been out of the question not just because Muhammad already had four wives but also because Zaynab was the ex-wife of his adopted son: the Qur'an had earlier made clear that marriage to the former spouse of a son *"sprung from the loins"* was unlawful, and among the Arabs "it was a strong social principle not to distinguish between sons by birth and sons by adoption". But the verses would make a distinction between the two types of sons for marital purposes (only) and effectively instruct that in future, adopted persons' surnames—the "son/daughter of" *(bin/bint)* configuration—not be changed so that their lineage can be known, and so Zayd bin Muhammad would revert to being known as Zayd bin Haritha 35 years after his adoption by the Prophet (33:5, 33:37, 33:40).

But this change did not annul his adoption as such, nor did it affect in any way the love and the intimacy between the adopter and the adopted, who were now nearing their sixtieth and fiftieth years. It was merely a reminder that there was no blood relationship; and in this sense the Revelation continued: '*Muhammad is not the father of any man amongst you, but he is the Messenger of God and the Seal (last) of the Prophets*'.

At the same time other Revelations [verses] stressed the great difference between the Prophet and his followers. The permission which God had given him, in virtue of his new marriage, to have more than four wives, was for him alone, and not for the rest of the community. Moreover his wives were given the title of "the mothers of the faithful", and their status was such that it would be an enormity in the eyes of God if, having been married to the Prophet, they should ever be given in marriage to another man.[15] (33:50, 33:6, 33:53)

The two verses immediately following the one on the heavenly and unconventional marriage of Zaynab to the Prophet then pull us back from the trees to give a glimpse of the forest, by making clear that God's prophets are not to be regarded like other men:

The Confederates, 33:38–39
There should be no discomfort for the Prophet in what God has ordained for him. That was God's way with those who passed before—and God's command is an assured destiny—

those (prophets) who deliver God's messages and fear Him, and fear none but God. And God suffices as a reckoner.

These verses reassure the Prophet that he should not be concerned with what people think but solely with what God almighty has ordained, and tell us that God had bestowed privileges on previous prophets, too. But they also serve to remind us that we err when we measure prophets by the same yardstick as other human beings: **prophets are human, yes, but ones tasked with a divine mission that *a priori* renders their very souls, and lives and responsibilities, anything but normal**. As I read these verses I cannot but think of other prophets, like Abraham and Solomon. Without knowing enough about what would have been customary in their time and place versus what was divine privilege in their

[15] See footnote 8.

case, I think of Abraham having had a son with his wife's bondmaid Hagar, his eldest son Ishmael from whom Muhammad is descended (Moses and Jesus being descendants of his second son Isaac, born of his wife Sarah); and I wonder about the Bible's claim that Solomon had 700 wives and 300 consorts, about how many of those may have been a reflection of his human nature, a question of custom, or even policy instruments, i.e. a bid to form certain bonds or alliances, as opposed to divine privilege. I do not know the answers to these questions, but it seems to me that the lives of God's prophets have never been ordinary.

A few verses later, the Qur'an makes clear that what is ordained for the Prophet is different from what is allowed other men:

> The Confederates, 33:50
> Oh Prophet: We have made lawful for you your wives whom you have given their dues [bridal gift] and those whom you rightfully possess that God has given you [i.e. if you marry one of your own prisoners of war or slaves then the bridal gift is not due][16]...and any believing woman if she offers herself to the Prophet and if the Prophet wishes to marry her—for you only, not for the (rest of the) believers. We know well what we have instructed them regarding their wives and those they rightfully possess, so that there be no discomfort upon thee. And God is ever-Forgiving, Merciful.

The story of a sixth wife, the 20-year-old[17] widow Juwayriya, is one I find particularly interesting. It was standard practice at the time for prisoners of war to be divided up between the victors, who would offer to free them in return for a ransom[18] or otherwise become responsible for their upkeep as de facto servant-slaves. Following the Prophet's victory in one battle, the daughter of the defeated clan's chief became a prisoner of war of one of his men, who placed a high price for her ransom. Juwayriya the captive visited the Prophet that day while he was at Aisha's apartment, introducing herself as "the daughter of Harith, the lord of his people", and asked him for help in the matter of her ransom. The Prophet offered to pay her ransom and to marry her, which she readily accepted, although

[16] Asad, Muhammad. *Op. Cit.*, 727. In this verse 33:50, where the privileges bestowed on the Prophet that do not apply to other men are listed, the Qur'an appears to waive the bridal gift requirement for Muhammad if he marries one of his own prisoners of war and slaves.

[17] Abdul Rahman, Aisha (aka Bint al-Shate'). 1979. The Wives of the Prophet (in Arabic). Beirut: Dar al-Kitab al-Arabi, 175.

[18] The practice of freeing prisoners of war in return for a ransom was so common in pre-Qur'anic Arabia that people often expressed their devotion to someone by declaring to them, "May my mother and father be your ransom!".

her father arrived before any marriage had taken place to ransom her himself (with some camels), and the Prophet thus restored her to her family. However during the exchange, a certain conversation led the father, along with two of his sons, to embrace Islam, and soon Juwayriya herself would do the same. The Prophet then asked the father for his daughter's hand in marriage, which was granted, and an apartment was soon built for her, as with the other wives.

> When it became known that the Bani Mustaliq [the defeated clan] were now the Prophet's kinsmen by marriage, the Emigrants [Meccans] and Helpers [Medinans] set free their captives who had not yet been ransomed. About a hundred families were released. 'I know of no woman,' said 'Aishah, referring to Juwayriyah, 'who was a greater blessing to her people than she.'[19]

Juwayriya's story, and the Prophet's decision to propose to her, is one that reminds me of something that many of us have heard growing up, which is that **several of the Prophet's marriages were strategic or political in nature, intended to build bridges, forge alliances or promote stability**. Indeed it cannot be coincidental that Muhammad also married the daughters of two of his four closest Companions while arranging the marriage of two of his own daughters to the other two Companions: he married the daughter of Abu Bakr, Aisha; and the daughter of Omar, Hafsa; while his own daughters Ruqayya and Fatima were married to Othman and Ali, respectively. Abu Bakr, Omar, Othman and Ali would become the four so-called "rightly guided" caliphs after Muhammad's death, in that order.

A little while later, the Prophet heard that his cousin and brother-in-law (Zaynab's brother) had died in Abyssinia, where he and a small group of Muslims had been instructed years earlier to emigrate from Mecca to escape local persecution and even torture of followers of the new religion. The Prophet had correctly predicted that the Christian ruler there, the Negus, would welcome his followers once he learned of the Qur'an's reverence for Jesus and Mary. Four months after the death of his cousin, Muhammad sent a message to the Negus asking if he would stand in proxy for him and ratify his marriage to his cousin's widow, Umm Habiba, if she would accept him, which she did. Not long afterwards the Prophet sent word inviting this small group of Muslims, whom he had sent away for

[19] See footnote 8.

their safety 13 years earlier, to join him in a new life with the rest of the community in Medina, and so Umm Habiba, who was around 35 then and had a daughter,[20] soon joined the Prophet's household as a seventh wife, in her own apartment. In doing so, Umm Habiba was reunited with several of her old friends from Mecca but also from her early days in Abyssinia, such as fellow wives Sawda and Umm Salama.

The Prophet would take an eighth wife, a young widow and Jewess named Safiyya aged 17, after her father and husband, enemies of the Prophet, had been killed in battle. She originally fell to the lot of one of his men as war booty, in the custom described earlier where prisoners of war could be ransomed. However when she was brought before the Prophet and he saw a bruise (or wound) on her face and asked her about it, she recounted that her deceased husband had struck her after she had told him of a dream she had about the Prophet that was positive and which also implied that he would be victorious against them. On hearing this, the Prophet sent instruction to the man who had been promised Safiyya to take another prisoner of war as his share of booty instead, and offered to set Safiyya free. At the same time he offered her a choice of either returning to her people as a free Jewess, or embracing Islam and becoming his wife. She replied, "I choose God and His Messenger," and they were married at the first halt on their march back to Medina. By the time they arrived back home, the Abyssinian friends had already arrived and Umm Habiba was already there, and Safiyya would be temporarily lodged in the house of a hospitable and generous man named Haritha. Many consider Muhammad's marriage to Safiyya another one of his strategic moves, intended to forge bonds with her defeated Jewish tribe.

Then there was Mariya (age unknown), the beautiful, Coptic Christian enslaved woman who was a gift from the ruler of Egypt to the Prophet, along with her sister Sirine and much gold and fine cloth, among other things. The Prophet made a gift of Sirine to another but found first temporary then permanent lodging for Mariya, whom he would visit often, developing a strong affection for her. It would be Mariya who would bear Muhammad a child, the only other woman to do so besides his first wife, Khadija. The people of Medina had long wanted the Prophet to have a child born in their city, further cementing his ties to them, and they were delighted with the news of her pregnancy. Mariya would give birth to a son, whom the Prophet named Ibrahim (Abraham) after the name of his

[20] Abdul Rahman, Aisha. *Op. Cit.*, 128.

"father", he told the people. But the much-loved child would die as a toddler when Muhammad was 60 and around two years or so before his own death, once again plunging him into the unique sorrow of losing a small child. It is sometimes assumed that since Mariya was a slave given to the Prophet as a gift, he would have had sexual relations with her outside of marriage,[21] but that is out of the question: **it is unthinkable that Muhammad would have disregarded God's command that bondwomen/slaves not be treated as concubines, but be honoured through mutually agreed marriage before sexual relations took place**. Recall the following verses:

> Women, 4:25
> And those among you who cannot afford to marry chaste, believing (free) women then (let them marry) the believing maids whom you (pl.) rightfully possess. God knows best your faith. You are from one another, so marry them with permission of their folk and give them their wages [bridal gifts] with kindness *(bil-maaroof)*, as married women and not as debauched women or illicit lovers...
>
> Light, 24:32–33
> And marry the single *(ayāma)* among you, and the righteous among your male and female slaves and handmaids [i.e. domestic servants]. If they be poor, God will enrich them from His bounty. For God is all-Embracing, all-Knowing.

promptly followed by:

> And let those (men) who are unable to marry remain chaste until God enriches them from His bounty. And if those (men and women) whom you rightfully possess desire the (marriage) contract, then contract with them if you know them to be good and give them from the wealth God has given you, and do not force your slave-girls into fornication if they desire chastity (or marriage) as you seek enjoyment of the worldly life. And he who forces them (the slave-girls)—then surely God will be, for their having been forced, all-Forgiving, all-Merciful [i.e. towards the women].

It must be said however that the last verse above (24:33) is never interpreted, much less translated, as I understand and translate it, the

[21] Differences of opinion as to whether Muhammad married Mariya or not abound, such as in the following commentary: http://www.dar-alifta.org/ar/Viewstatement.aspx?sec=new&ID=5142 (in Arabic).

divergence in meaning stemming from the two words I have underlined as shown. I find this odd as 24:33 continues the theme of male and female chastity found in the three preceding verses i.e. 24:30–32 and indeed begun seven verses before that, so it seems obvious to me that the contract in question is the marriage contract and not that of emancipation, by which a slave could agree a price for his or her freedom with their owner and work their way towards meeting that sum with the owner's financial contribution as an act of charity. The conventional interpretation[22] of this verse is that it warns slave owners against forcing their women slaves into <u>prostitution</u> to cover the cost of <u>emancipation</u> (rather than against forcing women slaves into fornication instead of marrying them honourably), which is undoubtedly a noble intervention except that once again, since the point here is to encourage marriage to slaves, surely the warning is against forcing them into fornication with the owners themselves. **The interpretation that relates this verse to an emancipatory rather than a marriage contract is unfortunate because here we have the most direct condemnation by God of the pre-Qur'anic treatment of enslaved women (and un-ransomed prisoners of war by extension) as concubines, even as He once again encourages believers to marry their righteous slaves**. But as with the institution of slavery overall, Muslim societies would not completely let go of the institution of concubinage either, with the most recent and perhaps most colourful example being the Ottoman empire's legendary imperial harem which included female slaves as concubines alongside the sultan's multiple wives, female relatives, and other female slaves and servants.

Many months later Muhammad and his followers made their first Lesser Pilgrimage[23] (*'umra*) to a vacated Mecca, in accordance with a treaty signed a year earlier with the Meccan enemy, spending three days there. His uncle Abbas, who had embraced Islam but remained in Mecca, came down from the hills and spent these days with him. It was then that Abbas offered the Prophet his widowed sister-in-law, Maymuna (age 26[24]), in marriage, and the Prophet accepted and would now have a tenth wife.

[22] See Asad, Muhammad. *Op. Cit.*, 602 and Nasr, Seyyed Hossein (editor-in-chief) et al. 2015. The Study Quran: A New Translation and Commentary. New York: HarperCollins Publishers, 877.

[23] The Lesser Pilgrimage (*'umra*) is a shorter and simpler (voluntary) rite than the Greater Pilgrimage (*hajj*), the latter also being an at-least-once-in-a-lifetime *duty* for those who are able.

[24] Abdul Rahman, Aisha. *Op. Cit.*, 233.

This new alliance established another link with the Meccan enemy, as events would show.

Thus between the age of 25 and 50 the Prophet had only one wife, namely the twice-widowed Khadija, who fell ill and died when he was 50 and she was 65. She bore him four girls and two boys, but only the four daughters survived into adulthood.

After Khadija's death he went on to marry 11 more times (up to 10 wives at the same time), when he was between the ages of 50 and 59. He died in the year 632 when he was around 63.

In total, 10 of the 12 women Muhammad married were widows (their ages appear to have ranged from 17 to 40 at the time of their marriage to him), **one of whom was also a divorcee and three of whom had children from their previous marriages** (Sawda, Umm Salama and Umm Habiba). Only one wife, Aisha, was previously unmarried and was also the youngest (probably an early teen) at the time that the marriage was consummated, while little is known about another, Mariya the Copt, who was a gift from the ruler of Egypt. **Remarkably, only one of these post-Khadija 11 wives (Mariya) bore him any children, namely one son (Ibrahim)**. Muhammad died in Aisha's arms at around 63, leaving 10 widows. He was buried right where he died, in a grave dug into the floor of Aisha's small rooms.

One other woman deserves mention in recounting Muhammad's private life.

The widow Rayhana (age unknown) was a battle captive from a Jewish tribe whose menfolk had been decimated and who became part of the Prophet's share of war booty. Muhammad placed her in the care of his aunt Salma, where she came under the influence of some young converts to the new religion and soon embraced Islam herself. When the Prophet heard the good news, he waited until enough months had passed to cover the mourning and pregnancy-check waiting periods (per Qur'anic guidelines), then offered to free her and to marry her. Her response was "Oh Messenger of God, leave me in thy power; that will be easier for me and for thee." As I reflect on this response, I can imagine how if Rayhana had not wanted to marry the Prophet for whatever reason yet had no one left from her tribe to provide for and protect her as a freewoman, this may have been her best option in the circumstances of the day. And perhaps she also understood, per her remark, that the Prophet did some things out of a sense of duty ("..easier for me *and for thee*"). Rayhana would thus remain the Prophet's slave until she died five years later.

It is usually assumed that the Prophet would have had intimate relations with Rayhana as a consort, but surely this account of their exchange points to the opposite conclusion. Besides, **those who maintain that sexual relations with one's prisoners of war and slaves was licit and normal are completely disregarding verses 4:25 and 24:32–33 as already explained above, where God insists that sexual relations with slaves be undertaken only after an honourable marriage** has taken place. Moreover, **if Muhammad had deemed it to be Qur'anically sanctioned to have sexual relations with a prisoner of war in his rightful possession, why would he have even bothered to propose marriage to Rayhana? This also again underlines the fact that the Prophet must have married Mariya, the Coptic enslaved woman who bore him Ibrahim, for why would he have proposed marriage to one slave he wished to have a relationship with (Rayhana) but not to the other (Mariya)?** Surely the verses just cited as well as this logic are sufficient to lay to rest the bizarre notion that sex with one's domestic servant-slave or prisoner of war was alright in God's eyes outside of (consensual) marriage.

And finally for the record and further clarity, the phrase **"those whom you rightfully possess" which appears several times in the Qur'an does not always mean slaves or prisoners of war as some imagine but also means spouses you *are already rightfully married to*:**[25]

- Such as in verse 4:3—otherwise God would be telling men He prefers them to have only one wife but that they can have as many concubines they want from among the slaves and prisoners of war they own!
  ("...marry those women who are lawful for you—two, three or four; but if you fear being unjust then (only) one, or whom you rightfully possess—this way it is more likely that you will not be unjust.")
- Such as in verse 4:24—otherwise God would be telling men to marry their female slaves and prisoners of war even if these women are already married[26] to other men!
  ("And married women (are forbidden to you) except for those you rightfully possess...)

[25] On "those you rightfully possess" often being a reference to legal spouses such as in verses 4:3, 4:24 and 23:6, see Asad, Muhammad. *Op. Cit.*, 123–124 on the similar views of leading classical commentators Razi and Tabari. See also verse 33:52 where it cannot mean anything else, per footnote 28.

[26] Stunningly, there are claims that verse 4:24 justified marriage to female prisoners of war even if these women were already married! See Nasr et al. *Op. Cit.*, 201.

– Such as 23:6—otherwise God would be telling ***men and women*** to save their chastity for their spouses, their slaves ***and*** their prisoners of war, which hardly leaves anyone out for either gender! It must also be recalled that "or" sometimes means "that is":

> The Believers, 23:5–6
> And those [i.e. believers] who guard their chastity
> Except from their spouses, or those they rightfully possess—then they are not blameworthy.

The incident with Rayhana took place before Muhammad's marriage to his sixth wife, Juwayriya.

Long after verse 33:50 had been revealed regarding Zaynab as a fifth wife and after the Prophet had married the subsequent women just mentioned, **the Qur'an moved to limit the Prophet to the wives he had at that point, and to forbid him from marrying others in their place should he divorce any of them,**[27] in a verse that is also interesting in that it reminds us that women were not made to hide their beauty in the Prophet's time, as many today believe:

> The Confederates, 33:52
> Women are not lawful for you (Muhammad) henceforth, nor to exchange them for other wives even if you admire their beauty, save those you (already[28]) rightfully possess. And God watches all things.

In closing something must be said, however briefly, of Muhammad's interactions with his wives. According to ***hadith*** and other reports about the Prophet and his wives—mostly relayed by the women themselves—**Muhammad was an exceptionally emancipated, egalitarian, and easy-going husband**. He would do housework and mend his own clothes. He consulted his wives and asked others to consult them in his absence. They were outspoken and anything but meek and subdued in their relationship with him, to the shock of many Meccans in particular, especially Omar.

[27] The Prophet was also entitled to divorce, like other men, as made clear in verses 33:28–29.

[28] Asad, Muhammad. *Op. Cit.*, 729. In fact this verse reinforces the argument already made that "those you rightfully possess" sometimes refers to existing wives.

The Prophet's wives felt so confident in their relationship with him that they once caused him not insignificant grief when they started demanding a less frugal life, now that victory was bringing in more war booty and everyone around them was living more comfortably; and when his affection for the young foreigner, Mariya the Copt, became apparent, they mounted a minor mutiny. They loved him deeply and were conscious of their unique status and privilege in being married to a prophet of God. Aisha appears to have been prone to jealousy over newcomers, but neither that nor her feisty nature derailed her special relationship with the Prophet, who appreciated her strong-mindedness and mischievous humour. My favourite anecdote is about how he apparently once told her that he always knew whether she was upset with him or pleased with him and when she asked him how, he replied that when she was pleased with him she would swear "by the Lord of Muhammad!" but when she was upset with him, she would swear "by the Lord of Abraham!"

> **"The believers who show the most perfect faith are those who have the best behaviour, and the best of you are those who are the best to their wives"**,[29] said the Prophet.
>
> He also said **"The best of you is he who is best to his family, and I am the best among you to my family."**[30]

Interfaith Marriage—If Everyone Agrees That Muslim Men Can, Why Can't Muslim Women?

Even our patriarchal religious authorities have always conceded that Muslim men can marry Jewish or Christian women, *i.e. without these women needing to become Muslim themselves*, because the Qur'an repeatedly identifies Jews and Christians, alongside Muslims, as being among the "People of the Book", and goes on to say the following:

> The Banquet (i.e. The Last Supper), 5:5
> On this day, all good things are permitted to you [i.e. followers of Muhammad]. And the food of those who have received the Book before

[29] al-Tirmidhi compilation, no. 1162 on https://sunnah.com/tirmidhi/12/17. See commentary on it also in www.nabulsi.com/web/article/10260 (in Arabic).

[30] al-Tirmidhi compilation, no. 4269: www.sunnah.com/urn/637830 and Ibn Majah compilation, no. 2053: www.sunnah.com/urn/1262960. See commentary also on www.dar-alifta.org/AR/Viewstatement.aspx?sec=&ID=5656 (in Arabic).

> you is permitted to you, and your food is permitted to them. And so are the chaste women among the believers [Muhammad's followers] and the chaste women among those who have received the Book before you, when you give them their dues [bridal gifts] in wedlock—not as fornicators, nor as secret lovers...

But many cultures and families nevertheless resist the message of this Qur'anic verse and object to their sons marrying any non-Muslim woman unless she converts. Perhaps some are simply unaware of it.

Or perhaps they are also aware of another verse that forbade Muhammad's followers from marrying *polytheists*, a reference in the Qur'an to the Arab *idolaters* of Mecca from whom Muhammad was to wrench the *Kaaba* that Abraham and Ishmael had built and dedicated to the one true God, *and are somehow conflating polytheists/idolaters with all non-Muslims.* In that verse, 2:221, once again the Qur'an takes pains to articulate that what applies to men also applies to women, obvious as that should already be from dozens of other verses:

> The Cow, 2:221
> And do not marry polytheistic/idolatrous women until they believe; a believing bondwoman is better than a polytheistic (free) woman, even if you find her attractive. And do not marry your women to polytheistic men until they believe; a believing bondman is better than a polytheistic (free) man even if you find him attractive...

Lest some readers be thinking it, Christians can in no way be considered polytheists because of the doctrine of the Trinity, which was already fully developed at the time of the Prophet yet did not stop God from issuing verse 5:5 above encouraging marriage to our Christian cousins (among others). The Prophet even had occasion to enter into a theological debate with a Christian delegation once, which ended with some disagreements concerning the person of Jesus, yet **he still invited them—60 Christian delegates in all—to perform their (Trinitarian) rites in the mosque in Medina when their prayer time came, which they did.**[31]

However even the officially inclusive view of interfaith marriage based on verse 5:5 still falls short in two respects.

First, this open-mindedness towards mixed marriages is extended by the authorities to Muslim men only, not to Muslim women. The usual

[31] Lings, Martin. *Op. Cit.*, 326.

argument is that the Qur'an here appears to be addressing men but is *silent* on whether women can marry from among the People of the Book too, so it must mean that they cannot.

This is a disappointing conclusion, to say the least, but quite in keeping with our societies' patriarchal approach to scripture on all matters. It is also in keeping with the tendency of far too many of us to zoom in on the letter of the holy book rather than on its spirit—one tree rather than the whole forest again.

Can it not be that God was simply seizing upon a reality on the ground as **a teachable moment to introduce the idea of interfaith coexistence *within families* to complement the Qur'anic theme of interfaith brotherhood *between communities*?** Besides talk of interfaith marriage, notice the reference to being able to consume each other's foods,[32] which further underlines the intent of this verse to bring the interfaith experience into one's very home by giving it God's blessing. **Must God repeat every single utterance addressed to humankind in both gender forms for the message to sink in that He is always necessarily applying His divine wisdom and mercy to both men and women?**

Furthermore, **since God encouraged Muslim women to marry their male slaves if they were "righteous", without insistence on them being "believers" as we saw under Marriage above in verse 24:32, why would He forbid them from marrying from among His other People of the Book**, such as Christians and Jews? It would make no sense.

Second, it has long been understood that the Qur'an's many references to the People of the Book is a reference to Jews and Christians (alongside Muslims). After all, the Torah, Gospel and Psalms are mentioned in the Qur'an 18, 12 and 3 times, respectively—always favourably—and described as "a guidance and light" to humankind, while as previously mentioned Moses (*Moussa*) is mentioned no less than 136 times and Jesus (*'Issa*) is mentioned 24 times including by titles such the Messiah, Word of/from God, Spirit from God, and Son of Mary.[33]

But the Qur'an hints at other religions too, and speaks of God having sent many more prophets than those we relate to the three Abrahamic religions. Indeed only 25 prophets are mentioned by name, the vast

[32] This implies that Christians at that time in Arabia still followed Judaic law and did not consume pork, which is also explicitly forbidden to followers of the Qur'an (2:173, 5:3, 6:145, 16:115).

[33] See Preface, footnote 2.

majority of whom were already known through Judaism and Christianity. But then **the Qur'an goes so far as to say that while God has spoken to us of some prophets in this holy book, He has not spoken to us of others** (40:78), **and declares that every nation throughout history has necessarily been sent a messenger** (16:36)—**for how could a just God judge people if He has not sent them guidance first?**

But we have always overlooked such verses as a community, to some extent understandably since it is only in recent times that access to information about other religions, and direct contact with almost anyone anywhere, have become so widespread. But we should never have overlooked how the Prophet's closest Companions themselves seem to have understood the phrase People of the Book so soon after his death, with no other than the famously strict Omar himself reportedly having included the Zoroastrians of Persia, for example, in the definition of People of the Book and regarded their scripture as divinely revealed when he was caliph[34] (though this did not ultimately soften his policies towards what he saw as a redundant religion at best, quite in keeping with what we know of his sometimes over-zealous nature even during the Prophet's days, which Muhammad often sought to temper). One cannot but wonder what other religious groups the Companions might have considered People of the Book, i.e. people whom God had sent their own messenger, had they but come across them.

The Pushback of Patriarchal Views on Muslim Women Marrying "Out": But the Children Wouldn't Be Muslim Then!

To oppose Muslim women's marriage to men from a different faith, religious authorities and our societies by extension have thrown, everything they can think of, at the idea. Besides the unconvincing argument that verse 5:5 does not mention women explicitly, they also argue that the children of any mixed marriage *must* be Muslim and that this is only possible if the *father* is Muslim, since the father is the "head" of the household.

There are two problems with this argument.

Firstly, if God tells us that the religions of the People of the Book were sent by Him, and that the followers of these religions are good

[34] Khutab, Mahmoud. 1965. Leaders of the Conquest of Persia (in Arabic). Beirut: Dar al-Fath, 31.

enough for us to marry, why aren't these religions good enough for our children too?

Secondly, is it not more likely that the children of mixed marriages will be Muslim—truly Muslim, in their hearts and not just by name—if their mother and main caregiver is Muslim, rather than their father? Surely this line of argument would be more effective in opposing Muslim *men's* marriage to women from another faith, rather than the other way round!

I draw attention to the shortcomings of these two ubiquitous arguments simply to highlight that it is obvious that the decision to bar Muslim women from marrying, say, Christians or Jews, was taken by society first, and then arguments to support that decision were found to prop it up. When families have allowed it, it has usually been only if the man agrees to formally embrace Islam, which no longer makes it an interfaith marriage at all.

Of course, most Muslims everywhere prefer to keep things simple anyway and have both their sons and daughters marry only from within the faith. That is perfectly understandable, and most opportunities for marriage generally arise within a given community anyway in most of the world. In fact, I had initially decided not to include a section on interfaith marriage in this book, but ultimately realised that it would be a glaring omission. In this day and age as we increasingly come into contact with other faiths one way or another, when we can no longer hide behind dogmatic answers or quash the questions that arise in our God-given minds, it is important to begin to face these unconvincing man-made arguments and look deeper into our divinely transmitted heritage.

CHAPTER 15

Divorce: Men Do Not Hold all the Cards—The Qur'an Actually Levels the Playing Field Through Mandated Process and Etiquette

Qur'anic Verses on Divorce

Divorce is a huge topic of concern for God in the Qur'an, which devotes a significant number of consecutive verses to it in its Chap. 2 as well as the first several verses of its chapters 58 and 65, alongside a handful of other scattered verses. Even as He makes clear that it is His least-favourable solution to marital discord and even as He counsels a period of reflection and even recommends mediation, God makes explicit His commandment that the divorce process be kind and fair in contrast to the then-prevailing customs, reflecting a clear preoccupation with protecting those whom He saw as the underdogs in the equation: women.

The discourse begins by addressing the pre-Qur'anic custom where a man would swear off sexual relations with his wife yet not divorce her, leaving her in limbo, often for years:[1]

> The Cow, 2:224–228
> Do not use God as an excuse in your oaths for not being good and reverent and making peace between people; for God is all-Hearing, all-Knowing.
>
> God will not take you to task for oaths uttered without thought, but He will take you to task for what your hearts have earned. For God is all-Forgiving, Clement.

[1] Nasr, Seyyed Hossein (editor-in-chief) et al. 2015. The Study Quran: A New Translation and Commentary. New York: HarperCollins Publishers, 98.

L. El-Ali, *No Truth Without Beauty*, Sustainable Development Goals Series, https://doi.org/10.1007/978-3-030-83582-8_15

Those who forswear their wives must wait four months, and if they go back (on their oath), truly God is all-Forgiving, ever-Merciful.

But if they decide upon divorce, truly God is all-Hearing, all-Knowing.

✓ Divorced women must wait alone [i.e. not re-marry] for three menstrual cycles, and it is not lawful for them to hide what God may have created in their wombs, if they believe in God and the Last Day. And their husbands would be more just (*ahaqq*) in taking them back in that case if they (the husbands) want to fix things (*islah*). Women are due the same as what they owe in kindness (*bil-maaroof*), and men a degree more than them. For God is Mighty, Wise. (2:228)

Bizarrely, the last verse above, 2:228, is the second most-cited verse by those arguing that the Qur'an itself says that men are superior to women (the most cited verse being 4:34 as already discussed under Guardianship and Participation and which we will come back to in Part V). The reason is that **even in Arabic, this verse can be understood completely differently *if* it is read in isolation from its neighbouring verses *and* with a pre-disposition to think that men are more important than women in God's eyes**. The penultimate sentence in particular is of issue here, though the other three I have also underlined above also play a part, depending on the interpretation or translation, which typically conveys the following:

× The Cow, 2:228
Divorced women must wait alone for three menstrual cycles, and it is not lawful for them to hide what God has created in their wombs, if they believe in God and the Last Day. And their husbands have the better right to take them back in that case if they (the husbands) desire reconciliation. Women have similar rights to the rights against them according to what is equitable/reasonable, and men *are* a degree *above* them. For God is Mighty, Wise.

This usual interpretation is unconvincing in my view if only because it completely breaks away from the direction in which the four preceding verses appear to be heading:

- **First**, remember that the two verses just before this one speak of situations where men abstain from their wives *unfairly*, and counsel a period of reflection (four months) before a final decision must be made, so that 2:228 is actually telling us what should *then* happen if the husband chooses divorce.

- **Second**, notice the difference in nuance between "would be more just" and "have the better right" (*ahaqq*), between "fix things" and "desire reconciliation" (*islah*): since this group of verses seeks redress *for wives* against an unfair abandonment practice by husbands at the time, doesn't the first interpretation offering men a path back to justice make a lot more sense than the second (usual) interpretation that appears to suddenly extend men preferential rights of first-refusal in this very matter where they have acted cruelly?!
- **Third**, there is a world of difference between acting "kindly" (*bil-maaroof*) as opposed to the common translation "equitably/ reasonably".
- **Fourth**, with regard to the penultimate and most critical sentence which is literally equivalent to "though men a degree more than women", I simply ask the reader to reflect on which is the more likely meaning in the context of the flow of the argument God is making here over these five verses, where He is seeking to redress the imbalance of a custom that left wives vulnerable (while acknowledging that husbands still had the free will to choose divorce), going so far as to spell out that women's rights are the same as men's rights in marriage: **why would God suddenly capsize His own argument by declaring, after all this advocacy, that husbands "are above" wives rather than that "they owe more kindness" since they are the providers and because of the additional burden carried by women *just mentioned in 2:228 itself, namely pregnancy and all that comes with and after it?***
- **Lastly**, it must be said by way of a general observation that the traditionally patriarchal interpretations appear to steer the spousal relationship towards the transactional realm, whereas **there is nothing transactional in the concept of doing something with kindness and/or honourably (with *maaroof*) by definition, a word repeatedly deployed by God in the Qur'an when speaking of divorce**. Like so much else in the Qur'an, divorce is addressed in values-driven language, if we can but hear it once again.

And the flow continues:

The Cow, 2:229
Divorce is [revocable] twice [i.e. during the waiting period], after which (a wife) must be maintained in honour or released in a goodly manner. And it

> is not lawful for you (men) to take away any of what you had given them (the women) save when both fear not abiding by God's boundaries [i.e. of companionship, intimacy, fidelity and no abuse].[2] So if you (the community) have reason to fear that the two of them will not abide by God's boundaries, then there is no blame on either of them if she offers something to free herself...

In 2:229 above, the Qur'an is safeguarding against husbands declaring divorce lightly or flippantly, proclaiming divorce and then changing their minds too frequently, thereby subjecting wives to endless cycles of pregnancy-check waiting terms that prevent them from moving on.[3] Importantly, **a husband cannot reclaim the bridal gift when he divorces his wife, and if it is the wife that wants a divorce, basically *if he is resistant* she can get her divorce *unilaterally* (*khul'*) by giving him back his bridal gift in full, if a partial offer does not do the trick**. In modern times, this would be the equivalent of returning the solitaire ring or bridal jewellery set, for example.

> <u>The Cow, 2:230–2:233</u>
> So if he divorces her [permanently, by re-confirming his intention at the end of the term], then she is no longer lawful for him (to re-marry) until she has (first) taken another man as husband. Then if he [the latter] divorces her, there is no blame on either of them if they get back together, if they both think they can abide by God's boundaries...
>
> And when you divorce women and they have reached their waiting term, then either retain them honourably or release them honourably. But do not retain them in order to cause harm and transgress, and he who does that will have wronged [or sinned against] himself...
>
> And when you divorce women and they have reached their waiting term, do not prevent them from (re)marrying their husbands if they have reconciled with one another with kindness (*bil-maaroof*). This is a warning for him who believes in God and the Last Day. That is more virtuous for you (pl.), and purer, for God knows and you (pl.) know not.
>
> And (divorced) mothers may nurse their children for two whole years, for those who wish to complete the nursing period, and it is for the father to provide for them (the women) and clothe them, with kindness (*bil-maaroof*). No soul is tasked beyond its capacity. A mother must not be harmed on

[2] Ibid., 100.
[3] Ibid., 101.

> account of her child, nor a father on account of his child. And the same duty [of support] is incumbent upon the (father's) heir. And if they both wish to wean (the child) by mutual consent and consultation, there is no blame on either of them. And if you (pl.) wish to entrust your children to foster-nurses, there is no blame on you so long as you hand over what you bring with kindness (*bil-maaroof*)...

In 2:233 just above, the Qur'an moves on to what should happen when the divorcing parents have infant children, spelling out the father's *minimum* alimony contributions towards his ex-wife (up to weaning of the infant): alimony to an ex-wife that is unrelated to children is formally established later in 2:241 (see below) but not specified quantitatively, which is why **it is important for a bride and her family to bear in mind that in the Qur'anic system, the bridal gift can consist of a pre- and a post-marriage gift within the marriage contract, which I highly recommend for avoidance of future conflict**. As for the mention of foster-nursing, this is not surprising: it was common among the great families of Arab towns at the time to send their new-born sons into the desert to be nursed and raised (up to around eight years) by foster-mothers among the nomadic Arabs, or Bedouins, where they could acquire the desired qualities of nobility and freedom through "fresh air for the breast, pure Arabic for the tongue, freedom for the soul".[4]

The Qur'an never addresses the question of custody of the children as such, but various verses make clear that providing for the children remains the father's responsibility regardless. I grew up with the understanding that children of divorced parents remain with their mother only until puberty, which I always assumed must have come from the seventh-century custom of considering puberty to be the eligible age for marriage, so that good marriages can be effected by the father, who would have been viewed as the more capable power-broker. Unfortunately most traditional jurists also maintained that the mother would automatically lose custody of the children if she re-married, although some thought that after a certain age the child should choose which parent to live with regardless.[5] In any case **this *pre*-Qur'anic custom surrounding puberty, if it made sense back then, certainly makes no sense now**, when puberty represents a very young age and corresponds to middle school for most. In any

[4] Lings, Martin. 1988. Muhammad: His Life based on the Earliest Sources. London: Unwin Hyman Limited, 23.

[5] Nasr et al. *Op. Cit.*, 103.

case I know of only a handful of cases, personally, where a divorced and still-single mother has succeeded in keeping her children even up to puberty, with all kinds of pressures being brought to bear on her and her family by the husband to hand them over upon divorce.

> The Cow, 2:234
> And those of you who die leaving behind wives, let them (the widows) remain alone [i.e. not re-marry] for four months and ten days. Then if they reach their waiting term, there is no blame upon you (pl.) in whatever they may do with themselves honourably…

Verse 2:234 above now turns the discourse from divorcees to widows, and their right to re-marry. The phrase "there is no blame", which appears often in the Qur'an and can also be translated as "no sin is incurred", always seemed curious to me. But I have come to appreciate this phrase more and more over time, and here it seems to be telling the community at large that it is not their responsibility (or business) whom these widows decide to go on to marry. As to the waiting period of four months and 10 days, this no doubt corresponds to the three menstrual cycles that divorcees also must wait out to ensure any forthcoming baby's father is not in doubt, and the additional 40 days represent the mourning period, which overturned the pre-Qur'anic custom that had often required widows to wait a full year while complying with harsh customs such as wearing the worst clothes and not bathing during that time.[6]

> The Cow, 2:235–2:236
> And there is no blame upon you (pl.) for what you have intimated to [widowed or divorced] women or hidden in your hearts. God knows that you intend to propose to them. However do not pledge yourself to them in secret, but speak in an honourable way. And do not resolve on (tying) the wedding-knot until the prescribed waiting term is complete…
>
> There is no blame upon you (pl.) if you divorce women you have not yet touched nor settled on a bridal gift for [the marriage contract is not complete till the bridal gift is specified]. Provide for (these) women—the affluent according to his means, the impoverished according to his means—an honourable provision, a duty of justice (*haqqan*) for those who would do good.

[6] Ibid.

Verse 2:236 above is extraordinary because it seems to say that **a man who enters into a marriage and then does not consummate the marriage will still owe alimony to the bride he leaves at the aisle, so to speak, even if they had not yet settled on a bridal gift—in accordance with the man's means**. Notice that this relates to an unconsummated marriage where there are no infants to be cared for either, yet alimony is still owed to the wife, which tallies with God's concern in previous verses over men approaching marriage and divorce flippantly. Yet I have never come across any commentary on how magnanimous that eye-popping second half of 2:236 is.

> The Cow, 2:237
> And if you (pl.) divorce them (the women) before you have touched them but you had (already) settled on a bridal gift for them, then (you are liable for) half of what you had agreed on unless they (the women) forgo it or he who holds the wedding-knot [the husband, in this case] forgoes his claim [i.e. offers the full gift]. And to forgo is nearer to reverence. And do not forget (the) generosity (*fadl*) between you, for God sees all you do.

Verse 2:237 above offers a concrete example of what acting with ***maaroof*, that combination of kindness and what is considered honourable (depending on how it is used) that the Qur'an is so insistent on**, can look like, and goes on to declare that acting as such is its own reward as it brings us closer to God. In the example above both the wife and the husband are encouraged to forgo their rightful half of the bridal gift when a marriage is not consummated, which becomes a mathematical impossibility if both of them choose the higher ground: if she forgoes her half then she is the more reverent one and gets zero, and if he forgoes his half then he is the more reverent one and is left with zero. So where does that leave the bridal gift, since it cannot disappear into thin air? This is one of those moments where I fall in love with the Qur'an all over again, because I do not think it is incidental that God ends this sequence with a phrase that can serve as both an instruction to be generous but also as a reminder to the couple not to overlook any generous acts between them, as though urging them to reflect and nudging back towards one another when this is the case. God in this sequence is taking the time to act as marriage counsellor, which I find a moving gesture of care and closeness. As He tells us himself: "...and We[7] are nearer to it (the human being) than its jugular

[7] "We" in the Qur'an is akin to the "royal we", or majestic plural.

vein" (50:16). (More will be said about the "wedding-knot" in the next section.)

> The Cow, 2:240–2:242
> And (for) those of you who die leaving behind wives, a bestowal to their wives of provision for a year and (there is to be) no expulsion [from the dead husband's property]. But if they move out [i.e. re-marry], there is no blame upon you (pl.) in whatever they may do with themselves honourably. For God is Mighty, Wise.
>
> And to divorced women (is due) a provision with kindness (*bil-maaroof*), a duty of justice (*haqqan*) for the reverent.
>
> In this way God makes His signs/messages clear to you (pl.), so that you may come to (use) your good sense (*taaquloon*).

The middle verse 2:241 above and its subject of alimony discussed in the previous commentary on 2:236 are important in that they actually established the concept of **alimony to an ex-wife irrespective of whether there are children or not, until she re-marries** (the latter is implied in a number of verses). Obviously alimony cannot be detailed as its amount and nature will depend on the husband's capacity, the time and the place. God here is encouraging **a "provision in kindness" to ex-wives irrespective of who divorced whom** (*"to divorced women is due…"*) and not only when it is the husband initiating the divorce, as patriarchal convention has always maintained: **recall that in 2:229 we are told that when the wife wants a divorce but the husband is uncooperative, she can divorce him unilaterally by giving back her bridal gift in full *if need be*, so it is clear that a woman can initiate divorce and that God is safeguarding her right to do so by establishing the unilateral divorce (*khul'*) *as a tool of last resort*** if the husband will not agree to it. That a unilateral divorce by a wife of her husband is to be an act of last resort, i.e. that ideally husbands and wives would come to an agreement on the terms of the divorce, is made clear from **the slew of references in the divorce verses to kindness, honourable behaviour, doing no harm, not transgressing, sacrifice, and generosity**. It is generally understood that alimony would not apply in extreme cases such as proven gross abuse or infidelity by the wife.[8]

[8] See such verses as 4:19–4:20 which effectively imply the same and commentary in Asad, Muhammad. 2003. The Message of the Qur'an. Bristol, England: The Book Foundation, 65.

The lengthy discourse on divorce in the Qur'an's second (and longest) chapter is then brought to a close with verse 2:242, which **literally urges us to "come to (use) your good sense" (*taaquloon*)**, something that the Qur'an repeats at least a dozen times and which is usually translated merely as "understanding". I point out the distinction here as there are many other words for "understanding" that do not reference the mind or reason or good sense, yet this word is undoubtedly the Qur'anic favourite.

> Women, 4:20–4:21
> And if you (pl.) wish to exchange one wife for another and you had given one of them a significant treasure, do not take a thing from it: (or) would you take it through slander and evident sin?
>
> And how could you (pl.) take it (back) after you have given yourselves to one another, and they (the wives) have received from you a solemn covenant?

In the above verses from the fourth chapter (the first of which affirms monogamy as the norm, as previously pointed out), God appeals to both honour and past intimacy between husband and wife to warn against a man being miserly or short-changing his wife upon divorcing her. He also reminds us that the marriage oath is a most serious one and uses the same expression ("solemn covenant") usually deployed in the Qur'an to refer to God's covenant with the Children of Israel (4:154) and with the prophets (33:7).[9]

> Women, 4:35
> And if you (pl.) fear a breach between the two of them [i.e. a married couple], then send an arbiter from his folk and an arbiter from her folk. If they wish to fix things, God will make the two of them reach agreement. For God is all-Knowing, all-Aware.

> Women, 4:128
> And if a woman fears rebellion (*nushooz*) from her husband or desertion, there is no blame upon the two of them should they make amends between them in reconciliation. And reconciliation is better, for souls are prone to greed...

[9] Abou El Fadl, Khaled M. 2006. The Search for Beauty in Islam: A Conference of the Books. Maryland: Rowman & Littlefield Publishers, Inc.,170.

In two examples of how divorce is an accepted but not encouraged solution to marital discord God recommends, to put it in modern terms, calling in mediators if necessary for a conflict resolution session. Reconciliation is urged even in the case of the above two cases, where in one case the wife (based on a previous verse) and in the other case the husband has acted with rebellion (*nushooz*) against the other (to be further discussed in Part V).

> The Confederates, 33:49
> Oh you who believe: if you marry believing women then divorce them before you have touched them, you have no (waiting) term to calculate and claim from them, so give them cause to be pleased [per 2:236–237 on their bridal gifts] and release them in a beautiful way.

And then, about half-way through the Qur'an, comes something to remind us that the plight of every individual is of concern to God, not just the wellbeing of the community as a collective, something that many of our societies have overlooked over time:

> The Woman who Disputes, 58:1–58:4
> God has heard the words of she who disputes with you [Muhammad] regarding her husband, she who complains to God. God hears the conversation between the two of you, for God is all-Hearing, all-Seeing.
>
> Those of you who swear off their wives by likening them to their own mothers: they are not their mothers, their mothers are those who gave birth to them. Truly they utter a senseless (*munkar*[10]) proclamation, and a falsehood. Yet God is all-Pardoning, all-Forgiving.
> And those who swear off their wives by likening them to their mothers and then retract what they have said must free a slave [i.e. in atonement] before the two of them [i.e. the husband and wife] touch one another (again). This is what you (pl.) are counselled, and God is aware of all you do.
>
> And he who does not have the means (to do so) must fast two consecutive months (instead) before the two of them touch one another (again). And he

[10] The original meaning of the often-repeated word *munkar* is "something that the mind/reason rejects", yet another example (alongside *taaquloon*) of the emphasis the Qur'an places on using our minds. But the usual translations are *indecent, dishonourable, wrong, iniquitous,* which do not change the meaning materially but do sever the link with reason as such. See Asad, Muhammad. *Op. Cit.*, 456 for this definition.

who is unable (to do that) must feed sixty needy persons. This is so you may believe in God and His Messenger [i.e. Muhammad]. And these are God's boundaries...

The above opening to chapter 58 shows how seriously God takes the act of hurting a wife's feelings by making her feel undesirable, in this case through invoking an ancient oath that likened her to her mother-in-law. Apparently this was the case with a woman named Khawla (already mentioned under Chap. 11's section entitled "Activism") who took her grievance to the Prophet. After the archangel Gabriel delivered the above four verses to Muhammad in response, he told Khawla that her husband must free a slave but she replied that he could not afford it, so he counselled that he fast the indicated two consecutive months. But she replied that her husband was too old to keep the fast, so the Prophet instructed that he feed 60 needy people instead. Again Khawla replied that her husband had nothing to give in alms. In the end the Prophet contributed a basket of dates he would soon receive as a gift and Khawla offered to contribute the same amount from her own pocket, and she was counselled to go feed 60 people on her husband's behalf so they may be reunited, which is what they both desired. (Notice that the required atonement when the wife's feelings are hurt through a verbal utterance appears tougher than it was in the very beginning of this chapter in verse 2:226, where the offence was simply swearing off touching a wife for whatever reason and the punishment was a four-month wait, period.) I tell this story[11] because in allowing the intervention of others when the husband could not atone for his sin directly, **the Prophet effectively placed justice for the wronged wife ahead of punishment of the offending husband, no doubt reflecting his understanding of divine justice's own priorities**.

Lastly, another set of opening verses in a short chapter actually entitled "Divorce" and devoted entirely to the subject revisits the key themes already discussed, specifically with regard to when husbands initiate divorce:

<u>Divorce, 65:1–7</u>
Oh Prophet: if you (pl.) divorce women, divorce them (with a view) to their waiting terms [i.e. for pregnancy-check] and keep good track of the term. And reverence God. Do not expel them from their homes [i.e. during the waiting term], nor shall they leave unless they have committed a <u>proven</u>

[11] Asad, Muhammad. *Op. Cit.*, 959 and Nasr et al. *Op. Cit.*, 1342.

indecency (*fahisha mubayyina*). Those are God's boundaries...You never know: perhaps God will cause after that something new to happen.

So when they (the women) have reached their terms, either you (pl.) retain them honourably or separate from them honourably. And call to witness two just people from among you, and bear witness before God [regarding what you have decided]. Whoever believes in God and the Last Day is thus counselled, and whoever reverences God, He will find them a way out (of distress),

and provide for them from where they do not expect. For whoever puts their trust in God, He will suffice them...

As for those of your women who no longer expect menstruation, if you (pl.) are unsure, then their waiting period is three months, the same as for those who have not menstruated [the condition amenorrhea, which can still result in pregnancy]. And for those who are pregnant, their waiting term lasts until they have given birth. And whoever reverences God, He will ease their situation.

That is God's command, which He has sent down to you (pl.). And whoever reverences God, He will absolve them of their bad deeds and make their reward great.

And let them [your wives awaiting divorce] dwell as and where you dwell in accordance with your means. And do not harass them so as to make things tight for them. And if they are pregnant then spend on them until they give birth, and if they nurse your children then give them what is owed to them [per 2:233]. And consult with one another honourably, but if you make difficulties for one another, then let another woman do the nursing for him [i.e. the mother is not obliged to nurse and the father is financially responsible for the cost of foster-nursing].

Let him who has abundance spend from his abundance, and let him whose means are limited spend from what God has given him. God does not charge a soul except with what He has given it. God will (surely) grant ease after hardship.

The above introduces a new concept in the very first verse 65:1: of not kicking a wife out of the house immediately after announcing the intention to divorce her (obviously assuming the house is provided by the husband to begin with), so that the waiting term post-divorce announcement is spent in the marital home. God here is trying to give compassion and reconciliation a chance, as the last sentence of 65:1 makes indisputable (*"You never know: perhaps God will cause after that something new to happen"*). The only time God instructs that a wife is to leave the marital home during the waiting period is when she has committed a proven indecency. I have underlined this phrase because it is usually translated as "flagrant indecency"—which is not incorrect—but since another reference to indecency (*fahisha*) requires four eye-witnesses (verse 4:15), I think "*proven* indecency" is a more appropriate term, not to mention that the actual adjective used here implies "visibility" (*mubayyina*). Notice how **verse 65:1 does not seem to expect any kind of private punishment by the husband of the wife's proven indecency beyond the wife leaving the marital home** (to be further discussed in Part V).

Otherwise with regard to the curious mention in 65:4 of married women who have never menstruated but may still be pregnant and so also need to observe the pregnancy-check waiting period, I find it odd that several translations insert "yet" so that the phrase becomes "those who have not *yet* menstruated" (the Arabic original certainly does not include "yet"). This may give the impression that men were allowed to consummate marriage with young girls prior to menstruation—which we know was not the case for various reasons, including from Muhammad's own wait for Aisha to come of age and arguably even longer than that. The only logical meaning of this phrase is that it refers to a condition where a woman does not menstruate,[12] called primary amenorrhea, yet who might be pregnant. This actually happened to a woman I know who never thought she could get pregnant because of never having had a period in her life, yet was surprised when she went on to bear a beautiful, healthy daughter when she was in her 30s.

The Pushback of Patriarchy on Women Initiating Divorce, and on Custody Issues

The usual claim by religious authorities is that women cannot seek a divorce, and that only a man can, for two reasons.

First, because when the Qur'an in 2:235 speaks of men wishing to marry divorced or widowed women whose waiting terms are not up yet, it tells these *men* not to resolve on tying the wedding-knot until they are; and when the Qur'an in 2:237 speaks of the wedding-knot, it implies that

[12] See also Asad, Muhammad. *Op. Cit.*, 995.

it is held by the *husband*. **In both examples the husband is the one seeking both the marriage and the divorce, respectively, so of course it is the husband who holds the key to making or breaking the marriage!** In other words, surely **the Qur'an is *describing* how it was and not necessarily *prescribing* how it should be**.

What more proof do we need beyond the great lengths God goes to in ensuring justice for wives in verse after verse after verse, including by granting wives a tool of last resort when the husband will not cooperate, namely the unilateral divorce (*khulʿ*), despite its Qur'anically admitted economic injustice to the woman (2:229)? In an extraordinary demonstration of how far the Prophet would go to comply with women's right to divorce under *any* circumstance, he is known to have ruled on a divorce in a somewhat unusual and extreme case, when a woman named **Jamila** came to him regarding her husband to say:

> By God! I do not dislike him for any fault in his character or faith, but I dislike his ugliness. By God, if I had no fear of God, I would have spat in his face when he came to me. O Messenger of God! You see how beautiful I am and that Thabit is an ugly man. I don't blame him for his faith or character, but I fear becoming [a bad believer].[13]

Even in this case that had no other grounds but personal dislike of physical looks which was moreover expressed most cruelly and certainly without a trace of kindness or *maaroof* by the woman, the Prophet still granted Jamila her divorce, although given the circumstances I am not surprised that he first asked her if she would give the man back the garden he had given her, so that it was effectively a unilateral divorce not requiring negotiation with Thabit. When Jamila responded that she was prepared to give more than that, the Prophet responded no, just the garden. He then, as de facto jurist, ordered Thabit to accept both the unilateral divorce and its settlement.[14]

Yet most of us grow up hearing that the "wedding-knot" (*ʿisma*) is a right to divorce that is held by the husband alone, and not a figure of speech, and that it means he can execute a divorce easily *with or without cause*. Whereas **a woman with an uncooperative husband cannot usually initiate a divorce unless**:

[13] Lang, Jeffrey. 1995. Struggling to Surrender: Some Impressions from an American Convert to Islam. Maryland: Amana Publications, 159.

[14] Ibid.

- She throws herself at the religious courts' mercy by making a good case for wanting the divorce (recall that a man seeking divorce is not even asked to provide a cause)—a gruelling process and true Pandora's box depending on the country, culture, school of jurisprudence, and presiding jurist. For example, verbal abuse or preventing a woman from studying or working may not be considered serious enough by a court depending on the where, how, why or who of the judicial process.
- She invokes verse 2:229 to obtain a unilateral divorce (*khul'*) by giving up her bridal gift in full[15] as well as her Qur'anically mandated right to alimony, thereby immediately dissolving the marriage—a process that could possibly complicate any custody negotiations. However, even the less-than-just (in most cases) unilateral divorce mechanism has been "edited" for the worse by religious authorities, with most Muslim-majority countries now requiring a wife to obtain her husband's *permission* for her "unilateral" divorce to take effect![16]
- She is knowledgeable, brave, and strong enough to have insisted on being designated **co-holder of the wedding-knot (*'isma*) in the marriage contract, to get round the surreal transformation of a Qur'anic description of an observed situation** (where men had mostly made the divorce decision) **into a permanent legal fixture in an Islamic marriage contract**.

The simple and quite obvious solution to all of the above is to stop assuming that the wedding-knot is held by the husband alone by default. But given how prevalent this belief and custom is, the only way to do it now would be to **write into the very structure of every Islamic marriage contract an explicit clarification that both parties jointly hold the wedding-knot (*'isma*) so that either of them can initiate divorce**, so that the unilateral divorce that the Qur'an grants women goes back to being a tool of last resort as originally intended, as opposed to the only way for a woman to free herself when she is the one who wants out. This is the only fair way forward, which ensures that all related considerations

[15] al-Hibri, Azizah. 2000. An Introduction to Muslim Women's Rights. In Windows of Faith: Muslim Women Scholar-Activists in North America, ed. Gisela Webb, 70. New York: Syracuse University.

[16] Ibid., 71.

of bridal gift, alimony and possibly even custody can be processed through the proper Qur'anic methods we have been given.

As for the question of custody and visitation rights when there are children involved, there can be no whitewashing how awful and even cruel so many societies have been in denying divorced mothers custody of their children to some degree or other, often also limiting their visitation rights. **There can be only one protection against this within a Qur'anic marriage: that custody and visitation rights of the children in case of divorce be stipulated upfront in the marriage contract**. After all that's what these nuptial contracts are for, and we have had them at our disposal longer than any other community on the planet. If this turns out to be an issue for the prospective groom, then the prospective bride will at least know before it is too late whether they have enough values in common to proceed with the marriage or not.

Second, because all the divorce narratives in the Qur'an revolve around the case where men are initiating the divorce, and there is no narrative outlining what should happen when it is the women initiating it. In other words as with interfaith marriage, **the claim is that the Qur'an is *silent* about women initiating divorce and therefore it must mean that they cannot**. Even verse 2:229 which speaks of women divorcing unilaterally is dismissed as a specific instruction for a particular case where the husband had initiated (an unfair) divorce to begin with! This is a vivid example of downright refusing to absorb the message while scurrying about to fulfil instructions unthinkingly. **As with the case of interfaith marriage, could it not be that God was simply focusing on the problem at hand, in this case that of husbands mistreating their wives through abandonment and unfair or recurring divorces?** The sheer number of verses on the topic of divorce and the creative variety of unfair practices we are treated to surely speak for themselves—or do we need every one of those verses *also* articulated in reverse gender roles in a wildly hypothetical set of scenarios where the wives are the ones doing the abandoning and divorcing of their husbands unfairly and repeatedly, to get the point that whatever *principle* applies to one human being necessarily also applies to the other? Once again a single tree reigns supreme, never mind the forest or the entire message.

The Pushback of Dogma When Men Initiate Divorce: Three Months for You, But Just Three Words for Me!

We have seen how the divorce verses make frequent reference to the waiting term required of wives after a divorce is announced to ensure the identity of an unborn child is not thrown in doubt, and that this term is defined as three menstrual cycles in 2:228. So if a wife already has in mind marrying someone else, for example, it can only happen after this term is honoured.

We have also seen that **when a man announces that he is divorcing his wife, he is not to expel his wife immediately (assuming the property is his to begin with) and must also maintain her as before until the waiting term is up** and in accordance with his finances, as detailed in 65:1 and 65:6.

If the husband changes his mind during this waiting period and revokes his divorce announcement, then all is well. If he changes his mind again however, and announces his intent to divorce a second time, then he only has one last chance to keep his wife (respectfully) because if he were to announce divorce a third time, which **would be effective at the end of the waiting period, then that would be final** per 2:229–230. After that any thought of revoking his stance is out of the question and he only becomes eligible to marry her again if she has meanwhile married and divorced another man (2:230), as though to teach the whimsical man a lesson!

So basically **the initial expression of wanting to divorce is equivalent to the modern "separation" phase, except that the Qur'an instructs that the couple continue to live together for at least three menstrual cycles afterwards** while abstaining from sexual relations, probably to encourage the rethinking of things while limiting the potential for conflict over parentage should the woman turn out to be pregnant. During this time (typically three months) there is room for a change of heart by the husband, but up to a point: there is a clear intention here by God to limit flippancy and abuse by husbands of the divorce and waiting mechanism, as we have seen.

So what happens in reality?

First, there is a tendency to completely ignore the Qur'an on living together for three months to let things settle, whether biologically or emotionally, **even as the three months' waiting period is imposed on**

the wife but not on the husband, who is regarded as free to go off and get married to someone else right away! This is justified by arguing that the Qur'an references the waiting term in relation to the wife for biological/pregnancy reasons, but not the husband, though no one ever mentions the very opening of the chapter entitled "Divorce" that tells the divorcing husband not to expel his wife from their home for the duration of the waiting period while not harassing or pressuring her. Or are we to believe it would be alright for him to marry another woman and bring her into the same house, that this would not constitute harassment and pressure? Nor would a husband be off the hook if he had a second home and could afford to maintain his wife as before even as he moved on with his life with another woman, for that is surely missing the point of verses 65:1 and 65:6 with regard to a cooling-off period.

Second, and more curious, has been the inversion of a Qur'anic divorce guideline. **The Qur'an never told husbands that they must declare their intention to divorce three times for it to take effect: declaring it just once, and not going back on that declaration at the end of the three-month waiting period, would be sufficient**. God told them, **rather, that they could change their minds about a divorce they have initiated only twice during the waiting term/cooling off period**, a clear bid to make them behave responsibly. In any case **the result is that a husband seeking a divorce usually rushes to utter the divorce proclamation as fast as possible three times in a row, taking no more than three seconds probably, without feeling the need to honour the three months because he has already been absolved from it anyway through the argument that it is a women's thing**, as just mentioned. I vividly remember a scene from one of the many excellent Egyptian films I watched growing up, when I was about 10 or 11: a troubled married couple is in a heated exchange and the man then declares "You are divorced!", and the music takes a dramatic turn for a few seconds as the woman is stunned and begins trembling and pleading "No!", followed by another "Divorced!" and the music is raised a notch and the woman is now besides herself and in tears, and then the final blow comes as the man utters for the third time the word: "Divorced!"—and both the music and wife are now at their most excruciating expressions of distress… all within less than a minute or so.

AT A GLANCE: The Rights of Women

A Frequent Clash between the Qur'an and Patriarchal Preferences

We have seen in Part III how the Qur'an sought to address the skewed status of women in seventh-century Arabia by granting them the social and economic identities and rights they had been lacking. As mentioned in the Preface, one gets a distinct sense of divine advocacy on behalf of women from reading the Qur'an attentively, specifically an apparent bid by God to recognise, protect, include and promote women within society.

No core subject affecting women's lives at the time is deemed too insignificant: from women's foundational role as God's viceroys (aka caliphs) on earth alongside men and their necessary participation in society that this entails all the way through to women's rights in inheritance, marriage contracts, marital relations and divorce—all these are addressed explicitly, to a remarkable degree.

Yet on every single one of these social issues that the Qur'an addressed with concern, empathy and fairness, we appear today to have fallen short collectively, albeit by varying degrees depending on the issue and the place, or culture.

How the Qur'an Institutionalises Women's Socio-economic Identities and Rights

The section "Participation" in Chap. 11, Chap. 12 entitled "Inheritance" and Chap. 13 entitled "Nuptials" together outlined how the Qur'an also ensures that **the independent economic identity granted women is fed by three to four streams of income established by the Qur'an itself: work (4:32), inheritance from multiple sources (4:7, 4:11, 4:12, 4:176), and the bridal gift (such as 4:4, 4:24, 33:50)—with alimony playing an additional part in the case of divorce (2:233, 2:236, 2:241)**. Men on the other hand have only two sources of income, work and inheritance from multiple sources, although their usually larger share of inheritance in return for supporting their wives and dependent female relatives ultimately keeps the "pagoda" fair and stable *when all other Qur'anic conditions are honoured equally.*

This is why it is no exaggeration to say that the Qur'an institutionalises women's freedom and independence by granting them **a viable economic identity, one that moreover does not merge with the husband's upon marriage. In fact Muslim women never used to take their husbands' surnames** but keep their own, which reflected their lineage as well as independent identity, although in many Muslim societies today the Western custom of adopting a husband's surname has become the norm. Among the more educated, it has become increasingly common in the past 15 years or so to join the relatively recent Anglo-Saxon trend of adding the husband's surname after the wife's (i.e. inserting the wife's surname in the middle, after an earlier complete adoption of the husband's name), such as in the relatively early example of Hillary *Rodham* Clinton.

These same chapters, combined with those on marriage and divorce, also show how **women's contribution to a better world, right to self-determination, and right to dignified treatment are all inseparable from the Qur'anic worldview**. The emphasis on tenderness and partnership in marriage is evident in verses too numerous to re-list (such as 2:187, 30:21, 42:11, 75:39), just as the emphasis on kindness and generosity in divorce on the part of the husband in particular is evident in numerous verses (such as 2:228, 2:231, 2:237, 65:7)—and safeguarded within the pragmatic framework of a legalised nuptial contract.

Lastly, I must mention how striking I find it that God seems to address societal offences against women with equal outrage irrespective of whether the impact is morally and practically catastrophic or rather limited in scope.

From the beginning, the Qur'anic revelation condemned the custom of burying alive unwanted new-born baby girls (6:140, 16:58–59, 81:8–9), a fundamentally abhorrent act that requires no further comment. But we also come across condemnation of the curious habit of men saving good meat for themselves and denying it to their wives, allowing them to share in the meat only when the animal is stillborn (6:139). It seems that the God of the Qur'an was not about to let any unfair or disrespectful act aimed at women go unaddressed.

PART IV

Some Inconvenient Truths

Introduction

We have seen in Parts II and III how various Qur'anic teachings on the nature and socio-economic rights of women have sometimes been either denied or ignored. Now we turn to those Qur'anic teachings relating to women that are stretched out of shape, so to speak, so as to end up looking nothing like their original selves.

CHAPTER 16

Clothing: There Is No Dress Code for Women Beyond Covering their Private Parts, as with Men

Qur'anic Verses that Mention Clothing

Most of us grow up assuming that the Qur'an stipulates that women must cover their hair and wear clothing that covers all skin except for the face, hands and feet. Even in cultural environments or families where this is not expected and modern clothing is the norm, the underlying belief of most people is still that the Qur'an does mandate such a dress code, but that the intent must have been for women to dress modestly, i.e. conservatively, and so what is today considered "modest" is naturally very different from what was the case in seventh-century Arabia.

Here are the verses in the Qur'an that mention clothing in one way or another, in the order in which they appear. The first cluster of verses on this topic is extraordinary in that hardly anyone ever mentions what the Qur'an tells us about the nature and purpose of clothing, which I find highly relevant and instructive.

> <u>Group 1: The Heights, 7:26, 7:31–33</u>
>
> <u>The Heights, 7:26</u>
> Oh Children of Adam: We have bestowed upon you clothing to cover your shaming parts, and <u>as a thing of beauty</u> [literally feathers, a metaphor]. <u>Yet the clothing of reverence—that is best of all</u>. This is one of God's signs [or messages], that they [i.e. humankind] may remember.

L. El-Ali, *No Truth Without Beauty*, Sustainable Development Goals Series, https://doi.org/10.1007/978-3-030-83582-8_16

The above verse clearly addresses all men and women, and comes in the middle of a description of the fall of Adam and Eve from Paradise and the lessons their descendants must learn from that. The phrase I underline above tells us that **an *attitude* of piety and God-consciousness counts for more with God than any outer act of *dressing* piously**.

"Yet the clothing of reverence—that is best of all" is such a powerful and unambiguous phrase that it is no wonder that one of the greatest of the classical Qur'anic commentators (Razi) had declared:

> that the private parts of believers are always covered, even when they are naked, while those of the profligate are always 'uncovered', even when they are clothed.[1]

> ...continued in 7:31
> Oh Children of Adam: bring your adornment [i.e. beautiful attire] to every act[2] of worship, and eat and drink, but do not be profligate. Truly He does not love the profligate.

In verse 7:31 **God articulates His desire to see us looking beautiful when we turn to Him in worship or supplication** (and to see us enjoying life with neither excessive indulgence nor waste). But who amongst us has ever been told to dress our best for prayers, whether to be performed at the mosque or at home?

And **why is all the emphasis in our societies placed on pious clothing but absolutely none on *beautiful* clothing**, despite what is said in verses 7:26 and 7:31?

Some years ago, I had the opportunity to visit one of the most famous and beautiful mosques[3] in the Middle East. I arrived appropriately dressed—or so I thought—in a floor-length skirt, loose long-sleeved top,

[1] Nasr, Seyyed Hossein (editor-in-chief) et al. 2015. The Study Quran: A New Translation and Commentary. New York: HarperCollins Publishers, 415.

[2] Most English translations of 7:31 use the phrase "...to every *place* of worship" which implies when visiting a mosque, but the meaning in Arabic can be broader and so is best translated as "...to every *act* of worship", which means wherever one may be performing the ritual prayer, even if in private at home.

[3] I do not wish to name any of the mosques in which I had uncomfortable experiences because I do not wish to shame any particular country or culture. Expectations regarding women's clothing differ not just from country to country but also from mosque to mosque and it has been very difficult for me to get it "right", as every mosque I have ever visited, whether in the East or West, has been dominated by one set of cultural expectations or another that has left me feeling either excluded, unwelcome or simply discouraged.

and carrying a shawl to place on my head before entering. I was excited to be there and was full of anticipation! The guard at the entrance assumed I was a tourist and politely told me it was prayer time and that visiting hours would resume later, and I explained in Arabic that I was in fact there for the ritual prayer. He was pleasantly surprised but then asked me if I had brought "prayer clothes" with me, and I told him I was already wearing what I would be praying in as I swung the shawl over my head. He immediately told me not to worry and to wait a couple of minutes, and sent a young boy off to fetch something. While we waited I asked him what was wrong with what I was wearing and he embarrassingly said that my skirt showed some ankle as the side buttons on the bottom of the skirt on one side stopped just that much short of covering my ankle completely. Side buttons on one side at the bottom? When had he checked out my skirt so thoroughly? I was stunned and felt humiliated, and when the guard saw the expression on my face he rushed to reassure me, ever so kindly, that he was doing this for me, *so that God would be pleased with me*. After about five-minutes of an exchange about whose responsibility I was before God, his or my own, I could feel my face burning up and was struggling to find something else to say when the boy returned and handed the guard a plastic bag, which the guard promptly handed to me with an apologetic smile, saying all was well, I could just throw what was in the bag on top of my clothes right there and the problem would be solved. I had come this far, so I told myself to stay focused on my goal of getting in and praying in that holy place, so I did as I was told. The skirt had an elastic band and just reached my knees, and when I held up the top I could see there was no point proceeding as the piece of triangular material with a hole cut out to allow for the face was so small that my face would not have gone through, and the cape-like top would not have even reached my waist. As I started to tell the guard that this outfit was clearly meant for a small girl, he promptly assured me it was alright and I could go in wearing it nonetheless. I could? What about the offending ankle that had started

all this, which the little skirt would obviously still not cover? Oh it was fine, he said, I could just keep the little skirt on top of my own skirt and throw on the tiny triangular cape over my head *somehow* and I could then march straight in. At that point I remember having an image of myself and how ridiculous I must have looked, not just felt, with part of a brown-and-beige outfit that was too small on top of a grey-and-black outfit that fit fine to three men or so, a Western woman who had accompanied me and a couple of children observing all this, and I swore to myself that *they* could keep their mosques from now on as I would never again attempt to pray in one and would only ever enter one as a tourist. Would *they* care if they knew this was how they had made me feel? What if I was so put off that I turned away from the religion altogether—is that what they want? Would they be filled with remorse and would it suddenly click for them, how ridiculous it is that it is harder for a Muslim woman to go in and pray in a mosque than for any non-Muslim to walk in and enjoy its architecture? I did not say any of this out loud but handed the guard the child's outfit as he asked me not to leave, saying that he was obliged to do this otherwise *those inside who are in charge* would cause trouble for him. I wish I could have reminded *those inside* that the Prophet had warned: **"Do not bar the female servants of God from the mosques of God"**[4] but I turned away and left, feeling all of angry, humiliated, indignant, wronged, and depressed at how low we have allowed ourselves to sink.

I honestly never thought I would have another opportunity, let alone find the inclination, to pray in this mosque ever again, but some years later that is exactly what happened. A woman who was a local told me she would take me if I still wanted to go and I jumped at the opportunity. She knew of my earlier experience and wanted to make it happen for me this time. She said she would bring the required clothing and would take care of everything, which she certainly did. While we were still in the car and approaching the mosque she handed me a thick, heavy, long black cloak with snap-buttons in the front to wear over my clothes. Then she gave me two small pieces of fabric: the white one was elastic and looked like an ankle brace, while the black one reminded me of a balaclava. I stared at them in bewilderment and then heard my friend chuckle before she proceeded to grab the white "ankle brace" and force it over my head so that all of my forehead, every last hair on my head, and my neck up to my very chin were hidden and only my eyebrows, eyes, nose and mouth showed through. I immediately felt claustrophobic—it was so tight! I could feel my eyebrows pushed together, my chin squashed up and pushing my lower teeth firmly against my upper ones, my hair plastered to my head, and the material was thick and synthetic and I soon started to sweat profusely. I began to breathe deeply, telling myself to stay calm and reminding myself that if other women can do it, so can I, and that I was there for God and so had to stay focused on Him! My friend then grabbed the

[4] Brown, Jonathan. 2014. Hadith: Muhammad's Legacy in the Medieval and Modern World. London: Oneworld Publications, 1.

"balaclava" and pulled it down over my head so it covered the top of my head and neck and draped over my shoulders, leaving my face exposed. She then did the same herself and when she was done, she was utterly unrecognisable to me. The situation felt surreal. Less than an hour or so after we came out and I was able to remove these constricting and all-round uncomfortable garments, my relief was indescribable.

Lest the direct instruction of 7:31 to dress beautifully be missed or obstructed, **the Qur'an then *immediately* continues with a warning**:

> ...continued in 7:32
> Say: who has forbidden the adornment [i.e. beautiful attire] that God brought forth for His worshippers/servants, and the good things that He provides? Say: these are for those who believe during life in this world, and for them alone on the Day of Resurrection. This is how We make clear the signs for people who would know.

And to make sure there is no misunderstanding of either 7:31 or 7:32, the Qur'an again *immediately* follows both with the following verse, which also represents a succinct summary of the only types of acts that God *does* forbid:

> ...continued in 7:33
> Say: my Lord has only forbidden indecencies, be they evident or secret, and sin, and wrongful oppression. And that you associate with God that which He has not authorised, and that you attribute to God that of which you have no knowledge.

Thus the seventh chapter of the Qur'an provides, in a small cluster of verses as just shown, the Qur'anic philosophy with regard to clothing:

- **Clothing is intended to cover one's private parts (7:26)**, which 24:30–31 below show to mean the groin area.
- **Clothing/attire is meant to be beautiful (7:26, 7:31)**
- **But no amount or type of covering can rival the clothing of reverence (7:26)**
- **Beautiful clothing/attire is a gift from God that no one can forbid (7:32, 7:33)**

With this crystal-clear Qur'anic foundation in mind, let us proceed to look at other verses in the Qur'an that mention clothing, in the order *and context* in which they appear.

Group 2: Light, 24:30–31, 24:58–60

Tell believing men to lower their gaze and guard their private parts/chastity. That is purer for them, for God is aware of what they do (24:30).

And tell believing women to lower their gaze and guard their private parts/chastity, and not to display of their (natural) adornment except that which (ordinarily/customarily) appears, and to draw their shawls over their breasts and not display their (natural) adornment except to their husbands, or fathers, or fathers-in-law, or sons, or stepsons, or brothers, or nephews, or their womenfolk, or the slaves they rightfully possess, or their male attendants who have no sexual desires, or children who have no awareness yet of women's intimate parts. And let them not strut so as to draw attention to the (natural) adornment they hide. Repent unto God, all of you [i.e. men and women], oh believers, so that you may succeed (24:31).

So the first two verses above address men and women, *in parallel*, about guarding their private parts i.e. the groin area or their chastity (repeated in 70:29–30), while restricting women to exposing their natural adornment, i.e. their breasts, only to relatives, household members and children.

For shocking as it seems to us today, it was customary for women in Medina at that time to wear tunics or vests with wide openings in the front that left the breasts exposed.[5] Verse 24:31 above put an end to this fashion among the followers of the Prophet at least in front of "strangers", as the verse clearly appears to accept the custom's continuation in front of all sorts of relatives and household occupants of both sexes. **The verse instructs believing women to draw their *khimar*, a pre-Qur'anic ornamental shawl that women used to drape loosely over their heads and neck/shoulders ,[6] over their *exposed* breasts to cover them, in effect making it clear that a woman's breasts are no longer to "ordinarily appear" before anyone outside of a still surprisingly long list of**

[5] Asad, Muhammad. 2003. The Message of the Qur'an. Bristol, England: The Book Foundation, 601; Abou El Fadl, Khaled M. 2003. Speaking in God's Name: Islamic Law, Authority and Women. Oxford: Oneworld Publications, 241; and Nasr et al. *Op. Cit.*, 875.

[6] Asad, Muhammad. Ibid.; Abou El Fadl, Khaled. Ibid., 108; and Nasr et al. *Op. Cit.*, 875.

related and unrelated men *and women* the verse makes an exception for.

This is an extraordinary accommodation by the Qur'an, despite its declared disapproval of breast-baring, to prevailing customs and what was then considered by society as acceptable flesh to show in broad public.

> Oh you who believe [men and women]: let those whom you rightfully possess [domestic staff and slaves] and pre-pubescent children ask permission (before entering) at three times: before the dawn prayer, when you undress for the mid-day heat, and after the night prayer. These are your three times of nakedness [literally "intimate parts", *'awrat*]. There is no blame on you or on them at other times if you go about attending on one another [i.e. without seeking permission first]...(24:58)

> And when your children reach puberty let them ask permission (to enter) as those before them had done [i.e. at all times]...(24:59)

Then the two verses above proceed to address men and women *together*, with regard to not exposing their *full* nakedness at home to the rest of the household.

> As for elderly women who do not seek marriage, they bear no blame if they discard their clothes without flaunting any (natural) adornment [i.e. breasts], though to refrain [i.e. from exposing their breasts at all] is better for them. For God is all-Hearing, all-Aware (24:60).

Finally, verse 24:60 picks up where 24:32 left off by taking an even more lenient position on baring the breasts by elderly women who are past their sexual phase, although the Qur'an adds that it is nonetheless better for them to keep their breasts covered even then.

But **most interpretations render "adornment" (*zeena*) in these verses of Chapter 24 to mean much more than a woman's breasts or even groin area despite no less than three instances in 24:31 that *literally* identify the topic as "breasts", "private parts" and "intimate parts"**. Overall, such interpretations extend "adornment" to a woman's very shape and/or almost all of her skin and hair and/or even any ornamental jewellery[7] she may be wearing, rather than simply the natural adornment of a woman's breasts, despite:

[7] Nasr et al. *Op. Cit.*, 876 and Asad, Muhammad. *Op. Cit.*, 596.

- The explicit reference here to drawing the shawl *over their breasts* and only showing otherwise what skin would ordinarily appear in the course of daily life;
- The explicit reference to both men and women guarding their *private parts*;
- The explicit reference to children who have no consciousness yet of *women's intimate parts*;
- The reports about *the chest-bearing women's fashion* of the time that continued late into the Prophet's mission;
- And the very *definition of clothing/attire* (which includes jewellery per 35:12) in the Qur'an as something intended by God to be beautiful, to be encouraged and never forbidden, and therefore necessarily visible (Group 1 verses of the Qur'an's Chap. 7 above).

Last but not least, it is conspicuous that few discussions of women's clothing and the Qur'an ever seem to mention the fact that men's clothing is also mentioned.[8] When the above five verses of Chapter 24 are looked at together, both the meaning of "private or intimate parts" and the Qur'an's equal expectation of what men and women's clothing must cover becomes crystal clear: **both men and women are expected to cover their private/intimate parts, i.e. groin areas, and women would ideally also cover their breasts in broad public**.

The last verse where clothing is mentioned appears in the following cluster:

> Group 3: The Confederates, 33:57–60
> Those who harm God and His Messenger (Muhammad), God has cursed them in this world and the next, and prepared for them a humiliating punishment.
>
> And those who harm believing men and believing women undeservedly, they have burdened themselves with the guilt of slander and evident sin.
>
> Oh Prophet: tell your wives and daughters and the womenfolk of the believers to cast their cloaks upon themselves. That makes it more likely that they will be recognised and not harmed. And God is ever-Forgiving, ever-Merciful (33:59).

[8] Barlas, Asma. 2015. Believing Women in Islam: Unreading Patriarchal Interpretations of the Qur'an. Texas: University of Texas Press, 158–159.

> If the hypocrites and those whose hearts are diseased and those who sow fear in the city do not cease, We will surely spur you against them, and then they will be your neighbours in it for only a short while.

The above four consecutive verses show a clear concern by God for the safety of Muhammad and his followers, and the women in particular, from the actions of the "hypocrites" and those with "sickness in their hearts" and who "sow fear/cause alarm". Verse 33:59 flows very naturally here, and in all the years I had been reading it had never given me pause of any kind, so I was surprised to learn that it is held up alongside the equally sensible 24:31 above as "proof" that the Qur'an imposed a uniform upon women. And in due course I came across, in my readings, the events of the time that add colour to this verse as formulated: apparently when women went out into the wilderness to relieve themselves they would often be harassed by men of other communities who would later deny knowledge of their identities, hence the instruction to adopt the cloak when venturing out to discourage assailants by making it harder for them to claim they had mistaken Muhammad's followers for the womenfolk of their enemies.[9]

In summary:

- **The only three verses in the Qur'an that say something specific about *women* and clothing (24:31, 24:60, 33:59)** simply tell us that women's groin area and ideally breasts also must be covered, and indicate a way for Muslim women at the time to identify themselves upfront when alone in the wild to ward off hypocritical sexual assailants.
- **One verse says something specific about *men* and clothing (24:30)**, telling us that they must cover their groin area.
- **Two other verses in the same cluster (24:58–59) address *men and women* with regard to clothing**, telling both not to be naked within their own homes around household staff and family members.

What of *Hijab*?

So what of *hijab*, the head-dress many women today wear and which comes in different styles and colours that cover varying degrees of the hair and neck?

The Qur'an mentions the word *hijab* eight times (once in derivative form)—**without it ever having anything to do with the head or hair.** In Arabic, the word *hijab* means barrier, obstacle, screen or partition, i.e.

[9] Abou El Fadl, Khaled. *Op. Cit.* (2003), 143 and 240; and Nasr et al. *Op. Cit.*, 875.

something that comes between two things to separate them from one another. Here are those verses, within their contexts.

> The Heights, 7:44–46
> And the inhabitants of the Garden will call out to the inhabitants of the Fire: We have found what our Lord promised us to be true, have you also found what your Lord promised you to be true? They will say "yes", whereupon a voice among them will proclaim that God's curse is on the evildoers,
>
> Who bar others from the path of God and would make it crooked, and who do not believe in the Hereafter.
>
> And between the two there shall be a barrier (*hijab*)...(7:46)

Thus the above indicates there will be a *hijab* between those in Paradise and those in Hell.

> The Night Journey, 17:45
> And when you read the Qur'an, we place between you and those who do not believe in the Hereafter a hidden partition (*hijab*).

In other words, there is a *hijab* between believers in the Qur'an and non-believers in the Hereafter. This is an interesting statement, as it does not distinguish between believers in the Qur'an and non-believers in the Qur'an as such, but rather forges a wider alliance among *all* those *who believe in the Hereafter*.

> Mary, 19:16–17
> And mention Mary in the Book, when she withdrew from her family to an eastern place
>
> And sought seclusion (*hijab*) from them. Then We sent her Our Spirit, who appeared to her as a perfectly fashioned human being.

So Mary placed a *hijab* between herself and her family when she left them for a place of retreat.

> The Confederates, 33:53
> Oh you who believe: do not enter the Prophet's dwellings for a meal unless you have been given leave, nor arrive at an improper time [i.e. too early]. But if you are invited then enter, and after you have eaten disperse rather than linger for conversation, for that harms/inconveniences the Prophet, but he is too shy to tell you. But God is not shy of the truth. And if you ask

any of them (the Prophet's wives) for something, ask it from behind a curtain (*hijab*), for that is purer for your hearts and for their hearts. And it is not for any of you to harm/inconvenience the Messenger of God, nor to marry his wives after him: surely that would be an enormity in God's eyes.

The context of 33:53[10] above is the following: guests at the wedding celebration of Muhammad and Zaynab (the ex-wife of Zayd) had overstayed their welcome in Zaynab's house, causing some annoyance as the Prophet even went out and came back more than once to find them still there. The main transmitter of this event was Muhammad's servant Anas bin Malik, who also said that when the guests finally left and he went to fetch the Prophet, upon returning the Prophet loosened a curtain while standing on the threshold of Zaynab's chamber for privacy and then recited this just-received verse to him. The verse is soon followed in 33:55 with an identification of those persons that the Prophet's wives need not bother with a curtain for, namely male blood relatives and their womenfolk, ***and their own domestic servants and slaves, presumably because the men among the latter would never aspire to engage their mistresses inappropriately***. It is also known that the apartments of the Prophet's wives were practically extensions of the mosque in Medina, with an endless stream of visitors pouring into whichever apartment Muhammad was spending time in on a given day, leaving no room for domestic privacy or comfort.[11]

Sād (unknown meaning but aka David[12]), 38:30–33
And upon David we bestowed Solomon: how excellent a servant [i.e. of God's]! He was ever-turning [to God] in repentance.

When the noble, swift-footed horses were presented to him in the evening

He would say: Truly I have come to love the love of good things because of[13] the remembrance of my Lord—until they became hidden from view [literally behind a *hijab*].

Bring them back to me! And he would set about stroking their legs and necks.

[10] Nasr et al. *Op. Cit.*, 1035 and Stowasser, Barbara Freyer. 1994. Women in the Qur'an, Traditions, and Interpretation. New York: Oxford University Press Inc., 90.

[11] Stowasser, Barbara Freyer. Ibid., 91.

[12] Nasr et al. *Op. Cit.*, 1101.

[13] Most translations of 38:32 imply that Solomon loved the good things *more* than the remembrance of God, but I have translated it here as *because of* the remembrance of God because it is clear in these verses that the Qur'an is giving an example of "how excellent a servant" of God's Solomon was, and not the other way round. See also Asad, Muhammad. *Op. Cit.*, 788 and Nasr et al. *Op. Cit.*, 1109 on this interpretation.

Solomon's horses became invisible when they were concealed by a *hijab* of either darkness, distance or partition, in this case.

> Clearly Spelled Out, 41:5
> And they said, Our hearts are shrouded from what you (Muhammad) call us to and there is deafness in our ears, and there is a barrier (*hijab*) between us and you. So do (as you will), as shall we.

Again, there is a *hijab* between those who were open to the Prophet's message and those who were not.

> Consultation, 42:51
> And no human being shall be spoken to by God save by divine inspiration or from behind a partition (*hijab*), or He sends a messenger to reveal what He will by His leave. Truly He is the Exalted, the Wise.

The above is about God never speaking directly to any human being but always either through a *hijab* of some sort, or through a messenger or prophet.

> Those who Defraud, 83:15
> No: on that day, they are debarred (subjected to a *hijab*) from their Lord.

In other words, the evildoers are separated from God by the *hijab* they have themselves set up through their bad deeds.

As the above verses demonstrate, ***hijab* in the Qur'an never refers to a head-dress, but is always either a physical or metaphorical barrier between two things.**

The Pushback of Jurists: Stretching the Meaning of (Natural) "Adornment" and a Couple of Specific Instructions, and Back to the Ever-Flawed Woman of Alleged *Hadith*

Simply put, **jurists from the ninth century onwards:**

- **gradually expanded the meaning of a woman's (natural) adornment over and beyond the breasts (24:31);**

- **converted the "cloak" verse from a security-via-identification measure into a divine command for all Muslim women at all times (33:59);**
- **and to varying degrees extended an ordained "elite" practice of separating the Prophet's wives from most men to all Muslim women (33:53).**

This three-fold approach[14] is, in essence, how a "dress code" for women was arrived at by jurists seeking to derive regulation from the Qur'an, which was always their primary objective as we saw in Part I.

- On the expansion of the meaning of (natural) adornment (24:31):

Surprisingly, the vast majority of early jurists *do* appear to have paid attention to the sentence *"...not to display of their (natural) adornment except that which (ordinarily) appears.."* in verse 24:31, although they applied their leniency to Muslim bondwomen/slaves and servants who had to work for a living but not to freewomen, on the basis of the former's need for practical mobility *and even custom*.[15] And there was an interesting variation among them as to what they thought appropriate for an active woman to wear: some jurists argued that a Muslim slave need only cover the area between her navel and knee so that the breasts and all else could remain exposed, others argued for covering chest-to-knee and down to the elbows, while the majority agreed that a female slave or servant need not cover her hair even during prayers.[16] I find this extraordinary, a little-told nugget that indicates that **even the zealous jurists thought that the lifestyle of the time and place is what determines what is appropriate for a woman to leave uncovered**.

By contrast, most jurists were far stricter when it came to free and higher-society women: most were in favour of a free Muslim woman covering everything but her face and hands, some made additional allowance for the feet and forearms, some pointed out that the Qur'an's intent was only to have women cover their breasts (which they had not always done as explained), while some even wanted to cover up one eye![17]

[14] Stowasser, Barbara Freyer. *Op. Cit.*, 90–93.

[15] Abou El Fadl, Khaled M. 2001. And God Knows the Soldiers: The Authoritative and Authoritarian in Islamic Discourses. Maryland; Oxford: University Press of America, Inc., 126 and 132.

[16] Ibid., 126.

[17] Ibid., 131 and 133.

Either way, what is striking about the above is that **there was a clear over-thinking of what (natural) adornment (*zeena*) means in 24:31 and 24:60. This is surprising: after all, there are two mentions of "private" and "intimate" parts (*furooj, 'awrāt*) and one mention of "breasts" (*juyoob*) in 24:31 itself.** But in the jurists' general bid to regulate every aspect of life, they would overlook this Qur'anic definition and eventually fold in everything from a woman's skin to her hair—**although none of them ever claimed that the Qur'an speaks of the hair, as indeed they could not have done**.

Equally striking is the implication that **women's attire had *not* been regulated during the first few centuries after Muhammad's death**, with this juristic debate flourishing in earnest from the ninth century onwards. In fact,

> ...*hijab* in its multiple meanings was made obligatory for Muslim women at large...during the first centuries after the expansion of Islam beyond the borders of Arabia, and then mainly in the Islamicized societies still ruled by preexisting (Sasanian and Byzantine) social traditions. With the rise of the Iraq-based Abbasid state in the mid-eighth century of the Western calendar, the lawyer-theologians of Islam grew into a religious establishment...and it was they who interpreted the Qur'anic rules on women's dress and space in increasingly absolute and categorical fashion...
>
> For the later scholars of Islam, the female face veil would be a hotly debated item; not, however, in the context of individual choice,...but within the parameters of the *hijab* as legally-prescribed 'concealment'...This restrictive position [i.e. concealment of all including face and hands] was later heightened and emphasized by, for example, Khafafi (d. 1659)....[18]

An inevitable conclusion from these historical facts is that **for the first few centuries of Islam there was no dress code or *hijab* requirement of any kind for women even while praying in mosques,**[19] so that women during that time would have prayed there in whatever they typically wore *or did not necessarily wear*, such as the yet-to-be-made obligatory hair-covering.

[18] Stowasser, Barbara Freyer. *Op. Cit.*, 93–94.
[19] Barlas, Asma. *Op. Cit.*, 55.

- On converting a security-via-identification measure on "cloaks" into a universal divine rule (33:59):

As strange as the expansion of what (natural) adornment means is the over-thinking of what the Qur'an meant by "...to cast their cloaks upon themselves", especially since the verse continues with "*That makes it more likely that they will be recognised and not harmed*" (33:59), not to mention the surrounding verses.

But it is precisely by ignoring the continuation of the verse that jurists were able to take an incident-specific Qur'anic recommendation intended to protect women from hypocritical assailants at the time and turn it into a universal law.

The over-thinking of (natural) "adornment" despite the definition given by the Qur'an right there within 24:31, and the over-thinking of "cast their cloaks upon themselves" despite the explanation given by the Qur'an right there within 33:59, in fact reinforce one another, with the ever-expanding interpretation of the former justifying the increasing coverage of the latter.

- On extending, to varying degrees, an ordained "elite" practice of separating the Prophet's wives from most other men to all Muslim women (33:53):

Once verse 33:53 had instructed that non-household men or relatives only address the Prophet's wives from behind a curtain (*hijab*), perhaps it was inevitable that Muhammad's wives would soon take this "curtain" with them outside the home. Thus we know that when travelling on camels the howdahs or litters strapped to the backs of the animals on which they sat now had curtains, and they now added a face-veil to their usual attire when out and about.[20] This occurred in the last two to three years of Muhammad's life.[21]

It is important to know that most of the traditional Qur'anic commentaries state that the *hijab* separation was applied only to the Prophet's wives.[22] Because **as the Qur'an itself tells us** in a cluster of verses in Chapter 33, **the Prophet's wives are not like other women:**

[20] Stowasser, Barbara Freyer. *Op. Cit.*, 94 and 170 and Lings, Martin. 1988. Muhammad: His Life based on the Earliest Sources. London: Unwin Hyman Limited, 241.

[21] Lings, Martin. Ibid., 214.

[22] Abou El Fadl, Khaled. *Op. Cit.* (2003), 239.

> The Confederates, 33:6
> The Prophet is closer to the believers than they are to themselves, and his wives are their mothers…

after which they became known as the Mothers of the Believers.

> …continued in 33:30–31
> Oh wives of the Prophet: if one of you commits a proven indecency, her punishment would be doubled, and that is easy for God (to do).
>
> And whoever among you submits to God and His Messenger and does good, We will bring her double her reward: and We have prepared for her a generous bounty.

The above two verses clearly express the *greater* burden of responsibility that the Prophet's wives bear in God's eyes relative to other women.

> …continued in 33:32
> Oh wives of the Prophet: you are not like other women. If you are reverent then do not be acquiescent in speech, lest he whose heart is diseased seek more. And speak honourably.

This verse is explicit that the wives of the Prophet in fact bear a *unique* responsibility. It reportedly addresses the behaviour of lukewarm converts to the new religion who would frequently approach the Prophet's wives with increasing demands that they were reluctant to take to Muhammad himself, in an attempt to take advantage of the women's kindness.[23] The Qur'an proceeds to articulate what this unique responsibility includes in the next two verses.

> …continued in 33:33–34
> And be solemn in your homes and do not flaunt [your natural adornment] in the manner of the previous Age of Ignorance. And perform the prayer and give the alms and obey God and His Messenger. For God wishes to remove all defilement from you, oh People of the (Prophet's) Household, and to purify you thoroughly.
>
> And remember/relay what is recited in your homes of God's verses and wisdom. God is truly Subtle, all-Aware.

[23] Ibid., 187.

In the above, the same expression (*tabarruj*) used earlier in 24:61 in relation to older women preferably not flaunting their breasts before the broader public is again deployed here and re-linked to the pre-Qur'anic fashion of women wearing open-breasted vests addressed in 24:31. Verse 33:33 here makes clear that while the Qur'an was tolerant of this pre-existing fashion among older women in public and among all women before male relatives and household members only, this "ignorant" fashion, as God de facto labels it, was not becoming of the wives of the Prophet, period.

And we have already seen another verse elevating the Prophet's wives above other Muslim women, which comes a little later in the same chapter:

> The Confederates, 33:53
> ... And if you ask any of them (the Prophet's wives) for something, ask it from behind a curtain (*hijab*), for that is purer for your hearts and for their hearts. And it is not for any of you to harm/inconvenience the Messenger of God, nor to marry his wives after him: surely that would be an enormity in God's eyes.

The above ban on marrying the Prophet's widows was unusual for the time and served to reinforce, along with their new title of Mothers of the Believers, the unique status that the Prophet's wives held in God's eyes. The Prophet was in fact explicitly forbidden by the previous verse (33:52) from further marriages or from divorcing one wife to take another, further underscoring the elite treatment the Qur'an was now detailing regarding Muhammad's wives.

In sum, no one can legitimately claim that the Qur'an imposes a dress code on Muslim women aimed at hiding their shape, any non-groin part of the body, hair or face. **Apart from covering our private parts (ideally including a woman's breasts) and urging us to wear beautiful outfits in general, the Qur'an is neutral on clothing for women and men alike**. If we truly care about what it tells us, we would leave women to dress as they choose without constantly judging them, one way or the other. In this regard, one of the most reassuring sights for me is that of a woman in a headscarf and another without (often in the same family)—and dressed completely differently—hanging out together socially, a sight I have seen and experienced thousands of times throughout my life in many countries in restaurants, parks, on the street and in homes.

The Pushback of Alleged *Hadith* on Women's Clothing: The Modesty-Redefined and Faux-*Fitna* Combo

As ever one is confronted with one or more allegedly supporting *"hadith"* for every controversial rule that the jurists put forward, no matter how out-of-sync with the inexorable beauty of the Prophet's soul and character it may be. So although the so-called *hadiths* that are negative about women are relatively few as previously mentioned, at least one of them manages to take on the subject of women's private parts.

Thus the Prophet allegedly said "A woman has ten private parts: when she marries, her husband covers one of her private parts and when she dies, the grave covers the rest."[24] Next to such a claim, demanding that women cover up entirely seems downright merciful! As one scholar put it: "The logical conclusion to be drawn from this tradition is that for a woman to be thoroughly modest, she ought to be dead and buried."[25]

This bizarre claim actually reminds me of a news report I read a year ago about a popular Middle Eastern singer who had turned religious and given up her music in the process, while also donning conservative clothing and a headscarf. After some time she came out of retirement, repurposing her gift towards her faith by releasing a devotional song dedicated to the Prophet on the occasion of his birthday commemoration. She publicly expressed her joy to be back, saying that God had finally answered her prayers and reconciled the conflicted feelings she had been living with, and posted pictures of her new look, including one in a beautiful pink-and-white turban covering her hair and another in an elegantly wrapped cream-and-navy headscarf. While her fans had been shocked at her announced retirement, most online commentators now applauded her move and/or expressed support, but a few were critical—and not because they were aggrieved fans. One man called a woman's voice a *'awra* (intimate part), and claimed that even if the singer had used her voice to chant the call to prayer itself, God would still curse her! A woman expressed astonishment that the singer was being applauded even though she was obviously continuing to be sinful and suggested she needed guidance, not praise. For these critics, the singer connecting with her faith and changing her entire lifestyle as part of her commitment was not enough because in

[24] Ibid., *236*.

[25] Ibid.

modern times, it seems that some of us have fallen under the influence of a truly strange, anomalous claim that a woman is only thoroughly modest when she can neither be seen *nor heard*—quite literally.

In any case while the early jurists had discussed women's clothing in the context of modesty and covering the "private parts"—however they may have defined the latter—much modern talk, by contrast, is of women being a source of *fitna*,[26] i.e. discord, divisiveness, schism etc., as discussed earlier in Part II. In other words, **women's clothing is today discussed by many jurists as if it were a public safety measure!**

Thus we hear of supposed *hadiths* attributed to the Prophet such as: "(The whole of) a woman is a private part (*'awra*) and so if she goes out, the devil makes her the source of seduction"; "I have not left in my people a *fitna* more harmful to men than women"; "Women are the snares of the devil"; and so on.[27]

Surely no one who has read the Qur'an can possibly believe that the messenger whom God chose to bring it to us could possibly have said such things.

Colour Is Good

An Asian man once asked me why black seems to be the dominant colour for Muslim women's conservative clothing in many parts. I suspect he was asking because though he came from a country that is virtually completely Muslim, women's attire there had always been colourful and local in style until recently, when gradual changes had begun to seep in—noticeable ones, as the black outfits in question are highly incongruent with the history, culture and landscape of the place and so easily stood out.

I do not know why black is the typical colour for women's cloaks and shrouds in the Middle East any more than I know why Afghan women's all-covering outfit called the burqa always seems to be blue. But I have learned that black was not worn traditionally by the young Muslim community and that Muhammad and his followers tried to wear colourful and beautiful clothes despite their poverty.[28] This applied to men and women, and it was interesting to stumble upon references to the Prophet being

[26] Abou El Fadl, Khaled *Op. Cit.* (2001), 123.

[27] Abou El Fadl, Khaled *Op. Cit.* (2003), 236.

[28] Oliveti, Vincenzo. 2002. Terror's Source: The Ideology of Wahhabi-Salafism and its Consequences. Birmingham, England: Amadeus Books, 41.

dressed in the colour saffron,[29] to the turbans of three of his Companions having been yellow, red and green,[30] and so on.

But my favourite anecdote on colour relates not to clothes, but to Aisha's hair:

"Take half of your religion from this red-haired one," Muhammad told his followers as he pointed to Aisha.[31]

Even if this incident occurred before verse 33:53 came along to instruct men to speak to the Prophet's wives only from behind a curtain (I do not know if it did or not), it is obvious that Muslim women at the time did not purposefully cover their hair as some might imagine. Since neither the "curtain" verse nor any other mentions women's hair at all anyway, it is no surprise that women were not obliged to cover their hair when praying in a mosque for at least three centuries after the Prophet's death, as already mentioned.

[29] Kahf, Mohja. 2000. Braiding the Stories: Women's Eloquence in the Early Islamic Era. In Windows of Faith: Muslim Women Scholar-Activists in North America, ed. Gisela Webb, 164. New York: Syracuse University Press.

[30] Lings, Martin. *Op. Cit.*, 182.

[31] le Gai Eaton, Charles. 2008. The Book of Hadith: Sayings of the Prophet Muhammad, from the Mishkat al-Masabih. Watsonville, California; Bristol, England: The Book Foundation, xxviii.

CHAPTER 17

Segregation: There Is No Restriction on Men and Women Mingling

Extending the "Elite" Rules Applicable Only to the Prophet's Wives to all Women, While Re-interpreting Them

There is a strong correlation between a restrictive view on women's clothing as detailed above and a restrictive view on women's participation in public life.

The over-thinking of (natural) "adornment" in 24:31 and of "cast their cloaks upon themselves" in 33:59 was bound to restrict women's public participation in society to some degree or other, depending on the time and place, or on the chosen profession or hobby.

But **it is the extension of the elite rules that had applied only to the Prophet's wives to all Muslim women, while interpreting them more strictly, that encouraged many societies to either bar women from full participation**—*although the Prophet's wives remained highly active, as the records show*[1]—**or segregate them by gender** when they did participate. We have already talked about the "curtain" verse 33:53 that was specific to the Prophet's wives yet was extended by some to all Muslim women,

[1] See Lang, Jeffrey. 1995. Struggling to Surrender: Some Impressions from an American Convert to Islam. Maryland: Amana Publications, 180 and Stowasser, Barbara Freyer. 1994. Women in the Qur'an, Traditions, and Interpretation. New York: Oxford University Press Inc., 185 on Aisha's participation in public affairs after the Prophet's death, especially in leading an army at the Battle of the Camel.

L. El-Ali, *No Truth Without Beauty*, Sustainable Development Goals Series, https://doi.org/10.1007/978-3-030-83582-8_17

but there is one other verse that played a restrictive role not just in being extended to all women but also in its *core interpretation*, over time, even as applied to the Prophet's wives themselves—retroactively. Recall the following verse:

> ✓ The Confederates, 33:33
> And be solemn (*qarna*) in your homes and do not flaunt [your natural adornment] in the manner of the previous Age of Ignorance. And perform the prayer and give the alms and obey God and His Messenger. For God wishes to remove all defilement from you, oh People of the (Prophet's) Household, and to purify you thoroughly.

But the above verse's first sentence is almost never translated as I understand and translate it above, but usually conveys one of the following meanings:

> × The Confederates, 33:33
> And remain/stay quietly/abide in your houses and do not display your finery/flaunt your charms in the manner of the previous Age of Ignorance...

This interpretation and translation are unconvincing, to my mind, for several reasons:

- If the verb at the beginning of verse 33:33 really means "to remain/stay quietly/abide", how is it that the Prophet's wives continued to go out on campaigns with him as evidenced by reports of the curtains now mounted on their camels, the face veils they now sported when they went out, and so on as we have already seen? A mere glance at an Arabic dictionary would show that the verb in question in fact means "to behave in a grave, sedate, sober or solemn manner", which makes complete sense in the context: the previous verse 33:32 tells the Prophet's wives not to be acquiescent or complaisant in speech but honourably firm with demanding visitors, and the subsequent verse 33:34 continues its articulation of how the Prophet's wives are different by bidding them to carefully memorise all that they hear recited in their homes of God's verses—a grave and solemn undertaking, indeed.
- We have already seen in Chap. 16, entitled Clothing, how the same "flaunting" expression (*tabarruj*) is used earlier in 24:61 and is tied to the pre-Qur'anic fashion of women wearing the open-breasted vests addressed in 24:31, so this cannot be a broad prohibition on

the Prophet's wives displaying their *outfits* or *personality*—as such translations imply—but is quite specifically denouncing an "ignorant" fashion the Qur'an clearly sought to limit.

To interpret and translate verse 33:33 to mean that the Prophet's wives must not leave their homes or be seen in fine attire, while also extending its application to all Muslim women, is nothing short of a double-whammy imposition on women at large that cannot be reconciled with what God tells us in the Qur'an:

- Recall that the Qur'anic instructions to dress beautifully (and therefore visibly) are applicable to all the descendants of Adam and Eve, and that God warns against anyone attempting to prevent this from being so (7:26, 7:31–33).
- Even if one still believes that 33:33 says "stay in your homes" rather than "be solemn in your homes", as I maintain, notice that this verse comes in the middle of the cluster 33:30–34 that specifically and *exclusively* addresses the Prophet's wives, not *all* "believing women" as the Qur'an often does, and so even then it would only apply to the Prophet's wives: yet we know that historically it did not cause them to remain house-bound.

The irony of all this is that it tells us, without a shadow of a doubt, that **women—including the Prophet's wives—had greater freedom to participate and mingle in society in the seventh to tenth centuries, and arguably well beyond to the sixteenth century, than they do in many parts of the Muslim world in the twenty-first century.**

Historical Evidence of Men and Women Mingling Naturally

Thus men and women were not segregated in public spaces as the popular imagination today believes. We have already seen some of the historical evidence of women's full participation in Part II. Lest there be any doubt, such mingling was not restricted to members of one's family or household: the Prophet and his Companions were known to pay social visits to women they were unrelated to, to converse freely with women whether the latter were married or single, and to receive grooming services from women outside the family.[2]

Nor did subsequent leaders in the first few generations after Muhammad's death forbid conversing or mingling with women, and it is indeed unlikely that there would have been such a large number of women religious teachers up until the sixteenth century had women been secluded or segregated.[3]

What is notable however is how resistant the Meccans in particular were, as opposed to the more open Medinans, to the increasing recognition of women's rights (e.g. in inheritance and divorce laws), and even to their attending prayers at the mosque. There are many reports of the Prophet having had to issue an explicit order that women not be barred from prayers at the mosque, and that even after this men only permitted women to attend the morning prayers, so that the Prophet had to issue a second command spelling out that he meant *all* prayers.[4]

There are also reports that tell us how Meccan men had felt from the outset upon encountering Medinan women's more emancipatory ways:

- We of Qureish (elite Meccan tribe) used to rule over our women rather than the other way round, contrary to the Helpers (Medinans who gave Muhammad and his followers refuge);
- In Mecca none of us used to speak to his wife except to ask something of her;
- We did not used to consult our women, nor involve them in our affairs;
- Their women (the Helpers'/Medinans') were learned;
- When we came to Medina and married the women of the Helpers, we found that they would talk back at us and question us.[5]

This initial resistance to women's integration overall is captured quite vividly in this remarkable admission by one of Muhammad's Companions:

[2] Lang, Jeffrey. Ibid., 179.

[3] Abou El Fadl, Khaled M. 2001. And God Knows the Soldiers: The Authoritative and Authoritarian in Islamic Discourses. Maryland; Oxford: University Press of America, Inc., 136 and 138.

[4] Abou El Fadl, Khaled M. 2003. Speaking in God's Name: Islamic Law, Authority and Women. Oxford: Oneworld Publications, 223.

[5] Al-'Asqalani, Ahmad. 2001. Fathul Bari bi-Sharh Sahih al-Bukhari (in Arabic). Riyadh: Prince Sultan bin Abdul Aziz, 191.

When the Prophet was alive we were cautious when speaking and dealing with our women in fear that a revelation would come [from God] concerning our behavior. But when the Prophet died we were able to speak and deal with them [more freely].[6]

This report by the son of Omar, no less, confirms what has already been much discussed, namely the advocacy of the Qur'an on behalf of women when various injustices would arise, accompanied by a push towards inclusiveness via affirmative action.

The challenge of women's full public participation and non-segregation today can manifest itself in different ways and often overlaps with the challenge of women dressing "appropriately", as defined by different cultural expectations. And what makes it even harder is that these cultural expectations are not only different from place to place but are often expected of women as though they were Qur'anic dictates.

I think I was around 30 when I finally plucked up enough courage to try to pray in a mosque. I was on holiday in a North African country[7] with a group of friends and was excited to visit a particularly gorgeous and old mosque that I had seen many pictures of. Since the 1980s in particular many mosques have been structurally altered or built from scratch so as to have a completely separate section for women that is totally cut off from the main hall of worship, but mercifully the older and more architecturally stunning mosques have mostly been left untouched, with one uninterrupted space for worshippers that enables women to properly see and enjoy their glorious interiors. However once I was in, I was afraid to venture into the courtyard of the mosque to look up and around at it from the centre because I (correctly) assumed that women would be expected to remain literally on the side-lines under the arches surrounding the courtyard, which would be considered the "women's section" in today's world. I looked and looked as best I could from my spot and gingerly walked around the sides to see the gorgeous artwork from different angles, conscious that two of the men in our group had gone straight to the middle of the courtyard and never stopped looking up as they turned round and round in admiration and complete abandon. I remember thinking at one point that a book I had back home provided a better view and that perhaps I should pray in a corner somewhere on my own to try to capture the

[6] Abou El Fadl, Khaled. *Op. Cit.* (2003), 223.
[7] See Chap. 16, footnote 3.

feeling of being in such a special place. But half-way through a set of prayers I heard a group of women approaching and could see them out of the corner of my eye, and they sounded agitated. I tried to stay focused on what I was reciting and kept looking down, but it soon became clear that I was the object of their agitation. As I held my ground and kept going with my prayers, a woman reached out and tugged at my long cardigan as if to say that it was all wrong. Another managed to find a short lock of hair that had escaped the scarf I had covered my hair with, picking it up and offering it up in her palm as if it were evidence. That is when I parried her arm away with my own while holding my palm up in a "stop" gesture aimed at her and the group even as I continued to look down and recite my prayers, which is when they began to move away from me, bad-mouthing me along the way. Needless to say the whole experience was anything but spiritual or inspiring. When my friends and I came out the experience of joy and peace that the men talked about stood in stark contrast to my own. I think what bothered me the most was that I must have surely looked like a Westerner to the women yet rather than be happy that I had embraced their faith, as it were, they seemed to care more about why I had not embraced their *clothes*. But the truth is that I knew it was not their fault, because if they have spent their whole lives being told that a Muslim woman dressing in a specific way is the most important thing about her, never mind what might be in her heart or how she led her life, what other reaction could I possibly expect? I decided to shrug it all off as an unfortunate cultural clash, determined to never let anyone put me off my love for God no matter what. And no one ever has, by His grace.

CHAPTER 18

Witnesses: A Woman's Testimony Is Worth the Same as a Man's, Except in Two Cases Where It May Count for *More* or *Less*

Qur'anic Verses on Giving Testimony

One of the most humiliating things to hear as a Muslim woman is the claim that the Qur'an considers the testimony of a woman to be worth half that of a man.

Setting aside common sense, how anyone can believe this despite God's relentless insistence throughout the Qur'an on the essential and primordial equality between the male and female is beyond me. Most of us have simply shrugged off this claim throughout our lives in our firm belief in a logical and just God, relegating this egregious claim to an ever-towering pile of either misunderstandings or downright manipulations of God's words.

So where does this idea come from?

The Qur'an speaks of giving testimony in the context of five specific situations[1] it clearly considered either important or was moved to address because of an incident that had arisen among Muhammad's followers at the time. These contexts relate to financial transactions, the property of orphans, sexual misconduct by women and men, accusations of infidelity against a married woman, and divorce.

[1] Barlas, Asma. 2015. Believing Women in Islam: Unreading Patriarchal Interpretations of the Qur'an. Texas: University of Texas Press, 190 and Lang, Jeffrey. 1995. Struggling to Surrender: Some Impressions from an American Convert to Islam. Maryland: Amana Publications, 165.

L. El-Ali, *No Truth Without Beauty*, Sustainable Development Goals Series, https://doi.org/10.1007/978-3-030-83582-8_18

In only one of these five cases does the Qur'an make a distinction between witnesses on the basis of gender, namely in the case that relates to financial transactions, where two women may be required to testify in lieu of one man.

Meanwhile **another one of these five cases outlines when a woman's testimony is worth *more* than a man's, namely when a husband accuses his wife of infidelity**—although we never hear anyone mentioning this extraordinary verse or highlighting the principle behind it.

Finally, **in the remaining three of these five cases—which relate to orphans' property, sexual misconduct by both women and men, and divorce, no distinction on the basis of gender is made between witnesses**.

Here are the five cases in question:

> The Cow, 2:282
>
> Oh you who believe: when you contract a debt or loan for a fixed term, write it down. Let a scribe write it down between you justly, and let no scribe refuse to write as God has taught him. So let him write, and let the debt or dictate and reverence God, his Lord, and not diminish any of it. And if the debtor is feeble-minded or weak or cannot dictate himself, then let his guardian/protector (*wali*) dictate justly. And call two witnesses from among your men, or if not two men then a man and two women that you approve as witnesses, so that if one of the two forgets/errs the other can remind her. And let the witnesses not refuse if they are summoned…

Several scholars[2] have pointed out that since **the only time the Qur'an makes a distinction between men and women as witnesses is in relation to financial transactions, it should not be taken as a general rule**.

They point out that the phrase "so that if one of them forgets/errs the other can remind her" is a reference not to the inferiority of women but rather to the fact that **women at the time did not engage in borrowing or lending themselves and were moreover mostly illiterate, making them less effective witnesses than men to a debt contract should a dispute arise**.

[2] Abou El Fadl, Khaled M. 2003. Speaking in God's Name: Islamic Law, Authority and Women. Oxford: Oneworld Publications, 157-8; Barlas, Asma. *Ibid*; Asad, Muhammad. 2003. The Message of the Qur'an. Bristol, England: The Book Foundation, 76; and Lang, Jeffrey. *Ibid*., 145, on similar views by scholars Fazlur Rahman and Badawi.

Given this, is it really surprising that the Qur'an would be so wise as to make allowance for this circumstantial shortcoming? If anything, **this verse is a measure of the Qur'an's unrelenting bid to *incorporate* women into every aspect of the community's life and affairs *despite* their circumstances. The Qur'an could have easily just said "call two men as witnesses" and left it at that—only it did not**, reaching out to bring women into the process in a manner that would not, at the same time, risk the fairness of the transaction.

For those who may still think that this verse laid down a universal rule despite the argument made thus far, I would point out two more things:

- Even the somewhat women-unfriendly (as explained in Part I) ***hadith* compilations classify many of the Prophet's sayings that had only a single woman as their source/witness as authentic.**[3]

- Those who maintain that the statement "so that if one of them forgets/errs the other can remind her" is proof of women's inferiority and why their testimony should always count as half of a man's must then also answer the following question: **how much intelligence or expertise does anyone really need to testify on the handing over of orphans' property or on sexual relations or infidelity or divorce proceedings**, the other four cases where the need for witnesses is mentioned without gender stipulation?

Finally, a comment is in order on a short and overlooked phrase that appears in the above verse that I have translated as:

✓ "...or if not two men then a man and two women..."

Most translations (but certainly not all) render the Arabic original (*fa-in lam yakūnā rajulayn*) as some variation of

× "...and if two men are <u>not available</u> then a man and two women..."

which unquestionably skews the meaning because it suggests that we should seek women witnesses *only* when two men cannot be found, rather than recognise that the verse actually offers the option. This unfortunate translation undermines women, though I actually believe it is not

[3] Lang, Jeffrey. *Op. Cit.*, 166.

necessarily intentional by most translators but rather a reflection, once again, of the psycho-social baggage we have collectively inherited that starts from the premise that women were considered below par even by the Qur'an (which was obviously not the case).

> Women, 4:6
> And test the orphans [in your charge] until they reach marrying age, then if you find them to be mature, deliver to them their property. And do not consume it wastefully and in haste before they grow up, and let whoever is rich abstain entirely [from touching their wards' property] and let whoever is poor consume honourably [with *maaroof*]. And when you deliver to them their property, bring witnesses. And God suffices as a Reckoner.

The above appears in the middle of the impassioned defence of orphans that opens the chapter entitled "Women" (verses 4:2–12) already referenced in Part III. **There is no specification of the number or gender of witnesses at the handing over of orphans' property**, and it is somewhat ironic that this verse appears early on in the long chapter where most women's issues are covered.

> Women, 4:15–16
> As for those of your (pl.) women who commit an indecency (*fahisha*), call four witnesses against them from among you. Then if they (so) testify, confine them in their houses until death overcomes them or God provides them a way.
>
> And as for the two among you who commit it, punish them both. But if they repent and make amends, then leave them be. For God is ever-Relenting, ever-Merciful.

In these two verses, the indecency in question appears to be of a sexual nature as evidenced by the reference in the second verse to two people being involved. Here, **no less than four corroborating witnesses of unspecified gender are required, the Qur'an effectively raising the bar of proof so high as to make it virtually impossible for sexual accusations to actually trigger societal punishment**.

Importantly, both parties would be considered equally guilty in this case, while both parties should be left alone if they show remorse and are promised God's forgiveness (4:16), which is also repeated later (3:135–136). However while 4:15 stipulates what a woman's punishment would be if found guilty *and is unrepentant* (confinement at home), there is no stipulation for what a man's punishment would be save that it should be commensurate: "...punish them both".

Personally, I think this must be because unlike women in those days, men would still have had to go out and make a living to support their dependents, so the Qur'an left it to society to decide what such a guilty man's punishment would be if four witnesses of his pre-marital sexual acts were indeed produced. However when enforced in some parts today, it is women who usually pay the price (and not simply by being confined to their homes), while men mostly get off scot-free. Even more unfortunate is the fact that no one today ever speaks of repentance being sufficient for both protagonists being left alone, as the Qur'an says they must. (A consolidated look at the specific question of sexual misconduct will be covered in Part V.)

> <u>Light, 24:4–9</u>
> As for those who accuse chaste women[4] (*muhssanat*) but do not produce four witnesses, then flog them eighty times and do not accept a testimony from them ever [again]. Those—they are the immoral ones. (24:4)
> ...
> And those who accuse their spouses but have no witnesses except for themselves, then the testimony of such a one is to swear (testify) four times by God that he is truthful,
>
> and a fifth time that <u>may God's curse be upon him</u> if he is lying.
>
> <u>And her punishment is averted if she swears (testifies) four times</u> by God that he is lying,
>
> and a fifth time that <u>may God's wrath be upon her</u> if he is telling the truth. (24:6–9)

In yet another example of Qur'anic advocacy on behalf of women, most of the first 26 verses of chapter 24 are an angry defence of married women

[4] Some translators take *muhssanat* in verse 24:4 to refer to chaste *married* women only, i.e. to women who are faithful to their husbands. I am among those who understand this word to refer here to all chaste women generally, i.e. including single women who do not have sex outside marriage, even though the previous two verses 24:2–3 refer specifically to unfaithful *married* persons as they stipulate a different punishment ("flogging") from the one prescribed elsewhere (in 4:15–16) for persons of unspecified marital status who engage in sexual misconduct (confinement for women, unspecified punishment for men, i.e. no "flogging" for either). This is because the subject of these verses is falsely accusing innocent women of sexual misconduct and the penalty incurred by the false accusers, *regardless* of the marital status of the woman. A consolidated look at the question of sexual misconduct is dealt with in Part V.

who are falsely accused of infidelity. Most of these verses (24:11–26) were in response to the slandering of the Prophet's wife, Aisha, over supposed infidelity committed with another man.[5] The later verses in this group go on to condemn those who were quick to accept and spread such slander.

What is usually overlooked in these verses is that in this instance a woman's testimony would actually outweigh that of a man: specifically, a wife's testimony on her own behalf would be worth more than her husband's against her.

Also overlooked in these verses is the Qur'an's a-symmetrical approach in such a case towards the husband and wife: whereas an unfaithful and unrepentant married woman would incur God's wrath, an untruthful accusing husband would incur no less than God's *curse*.

> Divorce, 65:2
> So when they (the women) have reached their terms, either you (pl.) retain them honourably or separate from them honourably. And call to witness two just people from among you, and bear witness before God [regarding what you have decided]. Whoever believes in God and the Last Day is thus counselled, and whoever reverences God, He will find them a way out (of distress).

Finally, the above verse which was already cited in Chap. 15, entitled Divorce, makes clear that **in calling witnesses to divorce proceedings, two fair-minded witnesses of whatever gender** is the simple Qur'anic instruction.

[5] Nasr, Seyyed Hossein (editor-in-chief) et al. 2015. The Study Quran: A New Translation and Commentary. New York: HarperCollins Publishers, 870.

AT A GLANCE: Some Inconvenient Truths

Clothes Should be Beautiful, Practical and Cover People's Private Parts

(a) The Qur'an articulates its foundational outlook on clothing for both men and women as follows:

- Clothing/attire is meant to be beautiful, and we are to wear our finest for worship (7:26, 7:31)
- Beautiful clothing/attire is a gift from God *that no one can forbid* (7:32, 7:33)
- Clothing is intended to cover one's private parts, i.e. groin area (7:26, 24:30–31)
- "...Yet **the clothing of reverence—that is best of all.**" (7:26)

(b) The Qur'an defines women's *zeena*, or (natural) adornment, as their breasts:

- Women's private parts and breasts are together labelled the "intimate parts" (*'awrāt*) that should be covered (24:31).
- No other part of a woman's body, such as her neck for example (or non-physical aspect such as her voice, for that matter), is regarded as an intimate part to be covered or hidden. The Qur'an even spells this out in the same verse, lest there be any confusion: **"...tell believing women...not to display of their (natural) adornment *except that which (ordinarily/customarily) appears...*"** (also 24:31).

- The Qur'an then gives an extraordinary example of what might "customarily" appear, right then and there: it makes allowance for *not* covering the breasts, of all things—*since it was customary practice among many at the time*—while limiting its acceptability henceforth in front of only family members, domestic servants and slaves, even if they are male (also 24:31). Indeed, the vast majority of early jurists were tolerant of all sorts of exposure by women that was deemed customary or practical, though this leniency was extended only to Muslim women who were servants or slaves and so worked for a living, but not to freewomen (ironically).
- The Qur'an also speaks of older women, making allowance for not covering their breasts even among the broader public in their case, *but adds that for them to refrain from doing so would be better* (24:60).

(c) On one occasion, the Qur'an recommends that the women among the Prophet's followers use cloaks as an identification measure, reportedly against the hypocritical tribes who would deny recognising them and so harass or assault them while alone. Therefore wearing cloaks is not a universal or foundational decree:

- "...those who harm believing men and believing women undeservedly, they have burdened themselves with the guilt of slander and evident sin...**tell your wives and daughters and the womenfolk of the believers to cast their cloaks upon themselves.** ***That makes it more likely that they will be recognised and not harmed...*** **If the hypocrites and those whose hearts are diseased and those who sow fear in the city do not cease, we will surely spur you against them**..." (33:58–60)

(d) The Qur'an never mentions hair, much less women's hair or any head-dress.

- The Arabic word *hijab*, which occurs eight times in the Qur'an (once in derivative form), means barrier, obstacle, screen or partition, i.e. something that comes between two things to separate them from one another (7:44–46, 17:45, 19:16–17, 33:53, 38:30–33, 41:5, 42:51, 83:15).
- One of the eight verses mentioning a curtain or *hijab* refers specifically to the Prophet's wives—not all believing women—instructing male visitors to their homes as follows: **"...if you ask any of them (the Prophet's wives) for something, ask it from behind a**

curtain (*hijab*), for that is purer for your hearts and for their hearts. And it is not for any of you to harm/inconvenience the Messenger of God, nor to marry his wives after him: surely that would be an enormity in God's eyes." (33:53) Male family members, household servants and slaves were exempted from this rule of speaking to the Prophet's wives in their homes only from behind a curtain (33:55).

So the Prophet's wives are not like other women, as the Qur'an tells us in 33:53 itself when instructing that they are not to marry anyone after the Prophet either. Indeed this point is mentioned again in the same chapter in relation to both their unique status and a number of other instructions that apply *only to them* and not to all believing women (33:6, 33:30–34).

So how did we go from the Qur'anic vision of beautiful clothing covering intimate parts (while nonetheless allowing for what may be customarily acceptable in a given society) to no less than a dress code for women, often a rather strict one covering not only the hair but all flesh and sometimes even hiding the figure itself?

Simply put, jurists from the ninth century onwards:

- gradually expanded the meaning of a woman's (natural) adornment over and beyond the breasts (24:31);
- converted the "cloak" verse from a security-via-identification measure into a divine command for all Muslim women at all times (33:59);
- and to varying degrees extended an ordained "elite" practice of separating the Prophet's wives from most men to all Muslim women (33:53).

It is important to remember that appropriate dress is viewed differently by different people and at different times and in different places. My own view is that a woman's choice of clothing, however covered up or not it might be, should be respected, and that it must indeed be her choice. The point is that the Qur'an did *not* impose a dress code as such on women, so no one can impose one on them in its name.

There Is No Mention of Women Needing to "Stay at Home" or Apart

Three trends underpinned the move to segregate women from men in many societies, limiting their overall participation.

- The interpretation and translation of the Qur'anic instruction to the Prophet's wives to "…be solemn in your homes…" (33:33) as "…*remain/stay quietly/abide* in your homes…".

Such interpreters then maintained that what's applicable to the Prophet's wives must be applicable to all believing women (as the former are surely the role models), despite the Qur'an making it crystal clear when it is specifically addressing the Prophet's wives and emphasising that they are *not* like other women.

But the latter interpretation is not only linguistically questionable but also *contextually impossible*. This is because the verse in question is sandwiched between one that tells the Prophet's wives not to be acquiescent with the constant stream of demanding visitors they had to deal with (33:32), and another that continues to lay out how the Prophet's wives are different from other women, namely by bidding them to focus on memorising all that they heard recited in their homes of God's verses, clearly as de facto trustees of the Qur'anic verses after the Prophet's death. So even if one preferred to believe that the Qur'an meant "remain in your homes" (which it did not) rather than "be solemn in your homes", one cannot possibly justify extending this alleged rule to *all* women.

- The conversion of a circumstantial verse that advises women to "cast their cloaks upon themselves" (33:59) as an identification measure against the enemy into a universal dress code in some parts of the world. This inevitably leads to a practical restriction on women's public participation to some degree depending on the situation, which serves as a step towards some form of gender segregation.

- The expansion of the meaning of (natural) "adornment" in 24:31 from the breasts to more and ever-more of a woman's body and even her attire in some cases led to jurists adopting varying degrees and types of covering-up as a dress code for women. Again this makes full public participation harder in many situations from a practical perspective, and serves as another step towards gender segregation.

The problem with all of the above, moreover, is that none of it can be reconciled with the Qur'anic directive to dress beautifully and to not dare forbid anyone from doing so (7:26, 7:31–33). For one thing, **to dress beautifully necessarily means to be *visible*.** For another, jewellery is mentioned in the Qur'an as a gift for us to wear which is to be found in rivers and seas (35:12).

A Woman's Testimony *Is* Equal to a Man's

The Qur'an speaks of giving testimony in situations involving financial transactions, the property of orphans, sexual misconduct by women and men, accusations of infidelity against a married woman, and divorce.

In only one of these five cases does the Qur'an make a distinction between witnesses on the basis of gender, namely in the case that relates to financial transactions (2:282), where two women may be required to testify in lieu of one man.

As several scholars have pointed out, this cannot therefore be regarded as a general rule. They point out that the phrase "so that if one of them forgets/errs the other can remind her" in verse 2:282 is a reference not to the intellectual inferiority of women but rather to the fact that women at the time did not engage in borrowing or lending themselves and were moreover mostly illiterate, making them less effective witnesses than men to a debt contract should a dispute arise.

Moreover another one of these five cases outlines when a woman's testimony is worth *more* than a man's, namely when a husband accuses his wife of infidelity (24:4–9)—but no one ever mentions this extraordinary verse nor highlights the principle it conveys.

And finally, in the remaining three of these five cases—which relate to orphans' property (4:6), sexual misconduct by both women and men (4:15–16) and divorce (65:2), no distinction on the basis of gender is made between the required witnesses.

PART V

Carnal Matters

Introduction

Some of the most egregious claims pertaining to women nowadays relate to sexual matters and to spousal relations, in itself something to stop and think about.

In what follows I hope to shed light on the three topics that have stood out in this regard: sex outside marriage, domestic violence, and the preoccupation of some with virgins.

CHAPTER 19

Sexual Misconduct: What the Qur'an Tells Us about Pre-marital vs Extra-Marital Sex

Qur'anic Verses on Sex Outside Marriage

This topic is obviously not a women-centric one but applies to men and women equally. I am including it in this book on women's rights in the Qur'an because of egregious practices that primarily target women in today's world and that are falsely said to be religious in nature.

As with other books of ancient scripture, the Qur'an takes a negative and strict view of sex outside marriage. We have touched upon this topic already in Chap. 14, entitled Marriage, such as in verses that insist on not treating household staff and slaves as consorts or concubines but marrying them honourably *if* they are agreeable (4:25, 24:32–3).

We have also seen in Chap. 18, entitled Witnesses, how verse 4:16 says that **those who commit a sexual indecency but are remorseful must be left alone and not harassed**, and that God moreover promises to forgive them:

> Women, 4:15–16
> As for those of your (pl.) women who commit an indecency (*fahisha*), call four witnesses against them from among you. Then if they (so) testify, confine them in their houses until death overcomes them or God provides them a way.
>
> And as for the two among you who commit it, penalise them both. But if they repent and make amends, then leave them be. For God is ever-Relenting, ever-Merciful.

L. El-Ali, *No Truth Without Beauty*, Sustainable Development Goals Series, https://doi.org/10.1007/978-3-030-83582-8_19

and

The House of *'Imran* (Joaquim, father of Mary), 3:135–136
And when those who commit an indecency (*fahisha*) or (otherwise) wrong themselves remember God and pray that their sins be forgiven—for who can forgive sins but God?—and do not wilfully persist in what they have done,

The reward of those is forgiveness from their Lord and gardens underneath which rivers flow, where they shall dwell forever. How excellent a wage for those who labour!

Meanwhile elsewhere the Qur'an mentions the obvious: that adultery, i.e. extra-marital sex (*zina*), is also an indecency (*fahisha*) (17:32), and that **adultery is also forgiven if the perpetrators repent** (25:68–71):

The Night Journey, 17:32
And do not go near adultery (*zina*), for it is an indecency (*fahisha*) and an evil way.

The Criterion, 25:68–71
And those who do not call upon another god alongside God, nor kill the soul that God has made inviolable except rightfully, nor commit adultery (*zina*)—for whoever does this shall meet recompense

and their punishment on the Day of Resurrection shall be multiplied and they shall dwell therein forever, humiliated,

except whoever repents and does good deeds: for those, God shall replace their evil deeds with good ones, for God is ever-Forgiving, ever-Merciful.

And whoever repents and does good does indeed repent unto God in true repentance.

What the above verses show is that **society is to forgive both pre-marital and extra-marital sex *even if four witnesses testify to having witnessed the act*, if the guilty parties express remorse and do good, as God Himself will forgive them**. Interestingly, all juristic views have always maintained that **the four witnesses must have observed the act of intercourse itself and not simply behaviour or a situation that *implies* it.**[1]

But **the Qur'an takes a harder line on *extra-marital sex* (*zina*) than it does on pre-marital sex (sexual *fahisha*) where *unrepentant* violators are concerned**. It suggests that **the unrepentant guilty parties be "flogged"** (to be defined below) **and not simply confined at home** until death or "until God provides a way", i.e. marriage[2] for the woman, **or a commensurate though unspecified penalty**, which logic indicates could also involve confinement till death or marriage but which may have historically involved banishment,[3] for the man:

> Light, 24:2–4
> The adulteress and the adulterer [i.e. who commit *zina*], flog each of them a hundred times, and do not let pity for them overcome you in accordance with God's religion if you believe in God and the Last Day. And let their punishment be witnessed by a group of the believers.
>
> The adulterer shall not marry save an adulteress or polytheistic/idolatrous woman,[4] and the adulteress—none shall marry her save an adulterer or polytheistic/idolatrous man. For that is forbidden to the believers.

[1] Asad, Muhammad. 2003. The Message of the Qur'an. Bristol, England: The Book Foundation, 595 and Nasr, Seyyed Hossein (editor-in-chief) et al. 2015. The Study Quran: A New Translation and Commentary. New York: HarperCollins Publishers, 868. Curiously, pre-Islamic Arabia is described elsewhere—see Smith, Huston. 2001. Islam: A Concise Introduction. New York: HarperOne, 7–8—as a chaotic place where "Drunken orgies were commonplace", although I have not come across commentary that links this fact to the Qur'anic verses on sexual misconduct.

[2] The majority view is that "until God provides them a way" in 4:15 refers to lawful marriage in the future but stunningly, some commentators actually claim that it refers to the punishment of "flogging" that would later be revealed by the Qur'an to supposedly apply to both witnessed pre-marital and extra-marital sexual misconduct, which I have hopefully shown could not have been the case. See Nasr et al. Ibid., 195.

[3] All commentaries I have seen on sexual misconduct mention banishment as one of several penalties imposed historically for this offence.

[4] While *mushrik* refers to ascribing partners to God and so can mean polytheism, in the context of the time it also meant idolaters, even if only a single false god or idol was being worshipped.

> As for those who accuse chaste women[5] (*muhssanat*) but do not produce four witnesses, then flog them eighty times and do not accept a testimony from them ever (again). Those—they are the immoral ones.

Now with regard to how the Prophet understood and instructed that the Qur'anic penalty of "flogging" be administered for proven adultery or false accusations of such, it is interesting to learn from classical jurists that **the purpose of the "flogging" appears to have been to somewhat shame rather than to cause physical damage or pain**: besides the Qur'anic instruction that the "flogging" occur before a *limited* public, commentator descriptions spoke of the requirement that a respected member of the community (and not just anybody) administer the lashes while not raising the arm above shoulder level nor using anything too hard so as not to break the skin, with the person being lashed remaining *in a standing position* and unbound.[6] Moreover, reports indicate that among the instruments used for "flogging" at the time were items of clothing and footwear,[7] "a light sandal or even the hem of a garment",[8] which supports this understanding of the goal having been limited public shaming rather than corporal punishment.

I thought I was done with defining what "flogging" actually meant (as explained above) when some days later, while in meditation, a new insight suddenly popped into my head. Throughout the process of writing this book, sitting in silent meditation to invoke God before every writing session has been a must, one without which the task ahead always seemed too daunting to pursue. These sessions would literally give me the strength to carry on, to tackle however complex a topic lay ahead. And so it was in one such session, when I was no longer thinking of the "flogging" verse at all, that the following came to mind: **of course they "flogged" with**

[5] See Chap. 18, footnote 4. As mentioned there, I am among those who understand the word *muhssanat* to refer to all chaste women and not only faithful married women, because the subject of 24:4 and subsequent verses is falsely accusing innocent women of sexual misconduct and the penalty incurred by the false accusers regardless of the marital status of the woman.

[6] Nasr et al. *Op. Cit.*, 868.

[7] Kamali, Mohammad Hashim. 2019. Crime and Punishment in Islamic Law: A Fresh Interpretation. New York: Oxford University Press, 167–168. Also, some reports state that the person administering the "flogging" must not raise his arm above his elbow, i.e. even lower than the shoulder.

[8] Smith, Huston. *Op. Cit.*, 67. I have borrowed the quotation marks around the term—as in "flogging"—from this same reference, which seems appropriate given that the act was not intended to deliver pain or physical harm as the term otherwise implies.

harmless instruments such as clothing and in order to shame, because how could God have otherwise prescribed the same number of lashes for women as for men, given our physical differences?

Needless to say, from a twenty-first-century perspective even this "gentle" form of "flogging" that is merely designed to shame the guilty to a limited extent rather than physically hurt them seems excessively humiliating and intrusive, given that personal relations today are viewed as a private rather than a public affair. But in the seventh century and within the context of the time, this would no doubt have been seen differently, falling broadly in line with societal expectations. Indeed in several *hadith* reports we are told that people came up to the Prophet to confess their sexual exploits voluntarily,[9] which reinforces, to my mind, that they did not expect to be physically tortured by being flogged mercilessly. As a surprising numerous of religious leaders and scholars have pointed out, Qur'anic penalties for sexual misbehaviour were made for a society where marriage was made easy, sexual provocations were virtually absent and piety was the norm, a far cry from the world we live in today.[10]

Now that we have looked at the verses addressing what the Qur'an considers illicit sex, you are likely to be asking yourself three questions.

First, why do we never hear of the **relatively "light" punishment** of confining guilty women at home (which, incidentally, implies that it was *not* customary for women to remain house-bound) *until something gives*, nor of a commensurate or similar "light" penalty for men (4:15–16)?

Second, whatever happened to the often-heard claim that the Qur'an instructs that the guilty parties be **stoned to death?**

Third, why are **women mentioned first**, before men, in verses 4:15 and 24:2, when the linguistic custom is the other way round as evidenced throughout the Qur'an itself?

The answers to these questions shed light, respectively, on juristic tendencies, the conflation of culture and religion, and the relentless advocacy of the Qur'an on behalf of women, as will be shown below.

[9] Nasr et al. *Op. Cit.*, 865–7.

[10] See Kamali, Mohammad Hashim. 1995. Punishment in Islamic Law: An Enquiry into the Hudud Bill of Kelantan. Kuala Lumpur: Institut Kajian Dasar, 111–115.

The Pushback of Jurists on "Light" Penalties for Sexual Misconduct: But Some Verses in the Qur'an Cancel Out Others!

It is a shocking thing to me that so **much of our juristic commentary claims that some verses in the Qur'an were abrogated—i.e. cancelled out or replaced—by other verses** within the Qur'an itself.

Every believing Muslim maintains that every word in the Qur'an is sacred, yet our own jurists often maintain that some verses should be totally ignored, as if they were not there. If so, why were these verses kept as a part of the Qur'an in the first place? Or **are they implying that God made several mistakes on several topics, later correcting Himself**, but it was all left in because both mistakes and corrections belong to Him?

Or is it that the archangel Gabriel's memory faltered and caused him to initially deliver the wrong message to the Prophet on a number of topics, triggering the need for a "replacement" verse?

Outrageous as this sounds, this is precisely what we are effectively asked to accept with regard to many a topic in the Qur'an. Many **jurists claim that the "lighter" punishments of confinement for the woman and a commensurate but unspecified penalty for the man (perhaps banishment[11]) in verses 4:15–16 were *cancelled out* by the stronger punishment of "flogging" for both parties in verse 24:2, in the process collapsing the distinction between pre-marital and extra-marital sex in these verses, respectively**. The rare expert voice that has rejected abrogation on principle has at times also conflated the two concepts,[12] treating all fornication the same. Here is why, to my mind, neither logic holds:

- Those who subscribe to abrogation (*naskh*), i.e. the idea of one verse replacing another seem to overlook verses 25:68–71 shown above: there, adultery (*zina*) is listed as one of the great sins alongside no less than a) polytheism and b) unjustifiably taking a life, so how could the penalty for it have *ever* been as light as 4:15's prescription of, effectively, mere "house-arrest" or something commensurate?
- Some scholars who reject all notions of verses abrogating one another but still miss the distinction between pre-marital and extra-marital sex in the Qur'an do so because they do not take *fahisha* in 4:15 to refer to *sexual* indecency to begin with:[13] in principle *fahisha* on its

[11] See footnote 3.

[12] Asad, Muhammad. *Op. Cit.*, 121.

[13] Ibid.

own is a general and undefined indecency, but how can 4:15 be decoupled from the very next verse 4:16, where reference is made to "two" guilty people?

In any case, the consequence of embracing the abrogation of one verse by another is that jurists now had to also maintain that there is no practical distinction between a sexual *fahisha* or indecency and *zina*, adultery, since the issue is not taken up elsewhere in the Qur'an—contrary to the popular misperception that the Qur'an positively dwells on sexual matters. I find this extraordinary, not least because I am certain that no one asked directly could possibly maintain that there is moral equivalence between the two acts, whether from a religious or social point of view.

So **where does this bizarre notion that some verses in the Qur'an were abrogated or cancelled out by others come from?**[14] Not surprisingly, it comes from assigning a specific meaning to a particular word in a couple of particular verses (2:106 and 16:101), a word that is not even a verb but a noun, and which can mean several related things depending on how it is used: *aya*.

At its most specific, *aya* is a verse in the Qur'an. At its broadest, it is a divine sign or message.

> <u>The Cow, 2:105–6</u>
> Neither the disbelievers among the People of the Book nor the polytheists/idolaters wish that any good be sent down to you (pl.) from your Lord. But God singles out for His mercy whom He will, for God is of great bounty.
>
> ✓ <u>No sign (*aya*) do We efface or cause to be forgotten</u> but We bring forth something better or similar. Did you not know that God is powerful over all things?

which is reminiscent of verses 43:46–48 about Moses showing Pharaoh greater and greater signs (*ayas*) yet which is usually translated (and interpreted even in Arabic) as follows, which clearly impacts the meaning in a very direct and serious way:

> × No <u>verse</u> do we abrogate or cause to be forgotten...

[14] "...there does not exist a single reliable Tradition [*hadith*] to the effect that the Prophet ever declared a verse of the Qur'an to have been 'abrogated' ". See Asad, Muhammad. *Op. Cit.*, 31.

and which is occasionally also translated as follows, which unfortunately encourages the viewing of earlier *religions* as no longer valid:

> × No revelation do we abrogate or cause to be forgotten…

The context of the first verse 2:105 shown above makes clear that **the word *aya* in the subsequent verse 2:106 cannot possibly be referring to a specific verse in the Qur'an but rather to a different kind of communication from God**. It must be pointed out that God here only criticises those among the People of the Book who did not like that a new prophet had come to another people, and does *not* condemn all those to whom He had previously sent His scripture, given His frequent affirmation throughout the Qur'an of the legitimacy of each one of these, His prior religions, along with their books and prophets.

Similarly:

> The Bees, 16:101–2
> And when We exchange one sign (*aya*) for another—and God knows best what He sends down—they say: you (Muhammad) are inventing! But most of them do not know.
>
> Say: the Holy Spirit has brought it down from your Lord with the truth, to strengthen those who believe and as a guidance and good tidings to those who surrender (to God).

In the above, again the context makes clear that God is not speaking here of *aya* as a specific verse of the Qur'an cancelling out another, but of a different type of divine communication that *can stand in the same place as another, because they both come from the same divine source, the Holy Spirit.*

The Pushback of Culture on the Qur'an Itself: Stone to Death, Kill for Honour or Flog with Abandon

If the Qur'an speaks of confinement and something commensurate as penalties for unrepentant women and men for pre-marital sex that is witnessed directly by four people, and of "flogging" for extra-marital sex that is also so witnessed, why do we hear so much about stoning?

There is not a single mention in the Qur'an of stoning as a penalty for anything.

On the other hand, the *hadith* compilations contain numerous—albeit wildly conflicting, confusing and even bizarre reports[15]—claiming that Muhammad as Prophet and head of state had overseen stoning for fornication (these reports do not make a clear distinction between the pre-marital and extra-marital nature of the sexual misconduct in question).

I ask the reader this: **Is it remotely conceivable that the Prophet would have defied God's command and ordered stoning to death, rather than "flogging" (to shame)**, in a worst-case scenario of unrepentant sinners who had been witnessed in the coital act by four people?

This is the same logic as what we discussed earlier in Chap. 14's section "Muhammad's Marriages": Is it remotely conceivable that the Prophet would have defied God's command and taken Mariya as a concubine, or remained unmarried to her, once verses prohibiting unmarried sex with one's servants and slaves (4:25, 24:32–33) had been revealed?

Moreover, do we care at all that the Prophet's understanding of the spirit of the Qur'an induced him, according to one report, to offer an adulterous confessor *three* opportunities to withdraw his confession?[16]

Stoning may have been the customary *pre*-Qur'anic penalty for sexual impropriety, just as taking concubines from among one's domestic staff and slaves was. Indeed there is evidence that these were indeed the norms of the time and place, at least among some communities. But to suggest that the Prophet would have implemented pre-Qur'anic rules on a given issue *after* the Qur'an had specified its own rules on the same issue is simply not credible, and indeed outrageous from any believer's perspective.

In addition, some scholars have pointed out that since the Qur'an also mentions that the penalty for an enslaved woman should be halved (4:25) while the same for a wife of the Prophet should be doubled (33:30), then stoning can never have been a Qur'anic prescription:[17] how can stoning to death be halved or doubled? A hundred "lashes", on the other hand, can be.

In any case and as already discussed above, the penalty of "flogging" *unrepentant* women or men for *witnessed* (by four people) adultery appears to have been a symbolic one designed to shame, and most contemporary religious leaders agree with scholars that it has not been an appropriate penalty for a long time given changing social environments.[18]

[15] See Nasr et al. *Op. Cit.*, 865–868.

[16] Ibid., 865 and Lang, Jeffrey. 1995. Struggling to Surrender: Some Impressions from an American Convert to Islam. Maryland: Amana Publications, 116–117.

[17] Nasr et al. *Op. Cit.*, 867.

[18] Kamali, Mohammad Hashim. *Op. Cit.* (1995), 111–115.

How some communities here and there diverge from all the above to advocating no less than murdering a daughter, sister, wife or other, usually female, relative for even the suspicion of having had unmarried sex defies all Qur'anic reason and moral proportionality. To call such murders "honour killing"—supposedly to salvage the honour of the family whose member committed such an act—is to make a mockery of justice as it places the full burden of a family's "honour" on its most *dis*empowered members, its girls and women.

Qur'anic Advocacy for Women in Response to Malicious Accusations

Lastly, why are women mentioned first, before men, in verses 4:15 and 24:2, when the linguistic custom is the other way round as evidenced throughout the Qur'an itself?

As I pondered this question in meditation, asking God to please help me understand "why" because it was so very unusual and I had not seen any commentary on this, the answer suddenly came to me: because the Qur'an was responding to an actual situation and wanted to first confirm such a sinning woman's guilt before a) pointing out that the man would be equally guilty, b) opening the door to forgiveness of both by opening the door to repentance, and c) threatening those who go around accusing women of adultery with their own punishment if they turn out to have slandered the innocent. In other words, **the entire flow of the argument is in preparation for advocacy on behalf of accused women**.

Here is how the meaning of verses 4:15 and 24:2 flows when accompanied by the verses immediately after each of them:

- Single women who commit a sexual indecency and are witnessed in the act by four people are to be confined to their homes until something gives, death or marriage (4:15)
- *But single men who commit a sexual indecency are also guilty and must also be punished* (4:16)

and

- An unfaithful married woman and an unfaithful married man are to be "flogged" equally, and before a small public, i.e. to achieve the shaming result (24:2)

- An unfaithful married man can only marry an unfaithful married woman and vice versa in future, reinforcing the shame on both (24:3)
- *While those who accuse chaste women are themselves to be "flogged", for they are the immoral ones!* (24:4)
- Recall, moreover, that the soon-to-follow verses 24:11–26 were in response to the slandering of the Prophet's wife, Aisha, over alleged infidelity committed with another man[19]

Surely the above shows that the intention of the Qur'an in these verses, which are often quoted in isolation of one another, is nothing short of advocacy on behalf of women in cases of sexual accusations. That God considers such accusations distasteful, to say the least, is self-evident.

Extraordinary *Hadith* on Illicit Sex That We Do Not Hear About

I came across a couple of thought-provoking and very telling *hadiths* in a good book on the subject that I would like to share. The writer's commentary surrounding them is also informative so I include some of it below:

> ...Aisha is reported to have said in response to a man who asked her about the character of God's Messenger: 'The Prophet's character was that of the Qur'an.'
>
> ...
>
> I was [also] guided by these opening words of a talk entitled *The Mercifulness of the Messenger of God* by the late Martin Lings, 'The mercifulness of Sayyiduna [our lord] Muhammad is affirmed by the Qur'anic verse *We sent thee not save as a mercy to the worlds.*'
>
> ...
>
> Abu Hurayrah[20] reported that the Messenger of God said, 'Forgiveness was granted to a prostitute who came upon a dog panting and almost dead from thirst at the mouth of a well. She took off her shoe, tied it with her head-covering, and drew some water for it. On that account she was for-

[19] Ibid., 870.

[20] That such a report is attributed to Abu Hurayra is in itself telling, as while he was the most prolific *hadith* transmitter, he was known to *not* be the most women-friendly, to put it mildly, with some of the most egregious *hadiths* on women attributed to him (whether correctly or not), and reports that both Aisha and Omar had clashed with him over some of his demeaning reports. See Chap. 3, footnote 24.

given.' He was asked if people received a reward for what they did for animals, and he replied, 'A reward is given in connection with every living creature.' (Bukhari)

But the one which led to the most exhaustive reflection and ultimately helped me to move closer to an understanding of the depth of the Prophet's humanity was this one:

Ibn Abbas reported that a man came to the Prophet complaining, 'My wife rejects no one who lays a hand on her!' The Prophet told him, 'Divorce her.' But the man told him, 'I really love her.' So the Prophet said to him, 'Then, hold on to her.' (Abu Dawud [aka al-Sijistani])[21]

I am certain that most readers will be as surprised by the above as I was initially. But on further reflection I realised that the Prophet here was in fact not only giving life to the spirit of the Qur'an, but literally carrying out its instruction. Besides the clear evidence of the Prophet's compassion for the wronged husband, **the above is also instructive in that his reaction was not to move to judge and punish the wayward wife: rather, the Prophet chooses to advise either (honourable) separation per the Qur'an or marital reconciliation (despite the wife's repeated infidelity), in accordance with the spirit and indeed letter of a verse specifically addressing infidelity (4:35)**, which we will take a close look at in the next chapter.

[21] From the introduction by Jeremy Henzell-Thomas to le Gai Eaton, Charles. 2008. The Book of Hadith: Sayings of the Prophet Muhammad, from the Mishkat al-Masabih. Watsonville, California; Bristol, England: The Book Foundation, xxv–xxvi. As he also points out in the introduction in xxviii–xxix, the *hadith* on forgiveness of the prostitute is reminiscent of the famous incident in the Gospel of St John 8:7 in which the Pharisees bring a woman charged with adultery to Jesus and he replies: 'He that is without sin among you, let him cast the first stone at her', and then says to the woman: 'Neither do I condemn thee: go and sin no more.'

CHAPTER 20

Domestic Violence: The Qur'an Does Not Instruct Husbands to Hit Their Wives for "Disobedience" or Anything Else

Qur'anic Verses That Prove That Wife-Hitting Is *Not* Prescribed

Arguably the most contentious verse in the Qur'an relating to women is verse 4:34, which some incorrectly claim instructed husbands to hit their wives if they disobey them. Before delving into this one, let us ask ourselves one question: Does this make sense in light of all the verses we have looked at so far that relate to women? Does it make sense that God would sabotage His own efforts at establishing equal social dignity and responsibility for women and men alike by suddenly telling husbands they can hit their wives?

Throughout this book, I have tried to emphasise how important it is to not single out a verse in isolation, to not look at a single tree, lest the message or forest as a whole be missed. At the risk of repeating myself, this means two things:

- A verse must be considered not just in its entirety but alongside the verses preceding and following it before we decide what it means, otherwise we might inadvertently go down the wrong track or simply miss the point. Certainly, some verses and phrases are standalones, but many are not.
- A verse on a specific topic must also be considered alongside all other verses in the Qur'an *that deal with that same topic*.

L. El-Ali, *No Truth Without Beauty*, Sustainable Development Goals Series, https://doi.org/10.1007/978-3-030-83582-8_20

Verse 4:34 might be a familiar verse number to the reader by now because we have actually discussed it already, in Part III under Chap. 11's sections "Guardianship" and "Participation", and in Chap. 12, entitled Inheritance and Chap. 15, entitled Divorce. This is because it is a relatively long verse that touches on several topics all at once, both directly and indirectly.

Let us now look at 4:34 alongside its neighbouring as well as other verses in the Qur'an that deal with one particular topic that it also addresses: *nushooz*.

> Women, 4:34–35
> Men are upholders/maintainers (*qawwamūn*) of women with whatever God has favoured some [men] with over others [other men], and with whatever they spend of their wealth [on the women]. Therefore righteous women are devoutly pious (*qanitāt*), keeping private what God has ordained be so-kept. As for those (women) whom you fear (have committed) a promiscuous act (*nushooz*), admonish (pl.) them, abstain from them in bed, strike them. But if they heed you (pl.) [i.e. your admonishment], then do not (pl.) look for a way against them. For God is Exalted, Great.
>
> And if you fear a breach may occur between the two of them [i.e. the husband and wife in question], then send an arbiter from his family and an arbiter from her family. If the two of them wish to fix things, God will bring about agreement between them. For God is all-Knowing, all-Aware.

When 4:34 is read all the way to the end and the ensuing verse 4:35 which continues the narrative is read together with it, the effective phrase "strike them but *not* if they heed your counsel" is obviously revisiting the question of adultery discussed in the previous chapter, where a *repentant* unfaithful wife (or husband) is to be forgiven by society (25:68–71) and not flogged/struck to cause shame even if there are witnesses to the fact. In other words, **the whole of verse 4:34 is addressing *society as a whole*, the last part dealing specifically with adultery[1] and not just any husband-wife situation,** while verse 4:35 goes on to deliver on God's

[1] See Abou El Fadl, Khaled M. 2006. The Search for Beauty in Islam: A Conference of the Books. Maryland: Rowman & Littlefield Publishers, Inc., 109–112. Also see Brown, Jonathan. 2015. Misquoting Muhammad: The Challenge and Choices of Interpreting the Prophet's Legacy. London: Oneworld Publications, 280 regarding Ibn 'Ashur on how a legal approach to "strike them" in 4:34 necessarily requires that a person involved in a case not also be its judge and enforcer.

promise to forgive an adulteress (or adulterer) by intervening Himself to reconcile the couple in question—a divine act of compassion towards us reminiscent of that of a loving and concerned grandparent.

So verses 4:34–35 are in fact a *case study* offered by the Qur'an on *how* to implement the penalty for adultery thoughtfully. That the subject of these verses, *nushooz*, refers to "a promiscuous act" (for lack of a better expression) is confirmed in two ways:

- Within verse 4:34 itself, by the instruction to men/husbands to "abstain from them (women) in bed"; and
- By another verse later in the same chapter where the word *nushooz* appears again, this time in relation to men. As we have seen throughout this book, **the Qur'an does not let a single opportunity go by without establishing *moral symmetry* in God's approach to women and men**. The verse where *nushooz* is applied to men is 4:128 and its neighbouring verses (which reinforce the meaning of 4:34 as maintained above) will be familiar as we visited them also in Part III where we discussed how monogamy is the norm in the Qur'an and how polygyny was related to "orphaned", i.e. widowed or bereaved women:

<u>Women, 4:127–130</u>
They consult you about women. Say: God instructs you about them, and what is recited to you in the Book regarding the orphaned women—whom you do not give what has been decreed as their rightful due yet whom you desire to marry—and the helpless among the children: that you should uphold justice for the orphans...

And if a woman fears that her husband (has committed) a <u>promiscuous act (*nushooz*)</u> or neglected her, there is no blame on either of them if they fix things in reconciliation, for reconciliation is best. <u>Souls are prone to greed</u>, but if you (pl.) do good and are reverent, God is surely aware of all you do. (4:128)

<u>You (pl.) will not be able to deal justly between women, however much you wish to. But do not turn away from one altogether</u> so as to leave her suspended [i.e. in limbo, neither happily married nor free to move on]; and if you come to an agreement and are reverent, God is Forgiving, Merciful.

<u>But if the two separate, God will compensate each of them</u> from His abundance. For God is all-Embracing, Wise.

In other words, verses 4:127–130 above tell us that people are greedy by nature and so men are likely to take more than one wife, which the Qur'an was allowing only in the case of widowed or bereaved women left without support (discussed at length in Part III under Marriage/monogamy). **At the same time, God makes clear His lack of enthusiasm for men taking another wife by literally calling it an act of *greed*, and goes so far as to state unequivocally that He does not think men can ever be fair that way**. But if the first wife and the husband can still make their relationship work, God will understand and if they cannot and decide to separate, God promises to also understand and, moreover, compensate both: the initial wife for ending up divorced for not wanting to share her husband, and the husband for agreeing to separate rather than be de facto unfair to his wife.

This is how the "strike them" part of verse 4:34 should be looked at, namely in its own context as well as together with other verses dealing with the same act, namely *nushooz* or promiscuous act. **The two *nushooz* verses 4:34 and 4:128 apply to women and men, respectively and are two sides of the same coin: the Qur'an could have referred to the illicit sexual act by a married woman in 4:34 as *zina* (adultery), but it does not do so *precisely* to establish symmetry in its approach to men and women, as it could not logically have also called a man taking a second wife *zina* (adultery) since the Qur'an itself was allowing polygyny under certain conditions**.

In fact if we line up the verses mentioning *nushooz* next to one another, their symmetry not just in content but also in language is striking and again reinforces the meaning above, namely that **"strike them" refers to the societal penalty of "flogging" to shame in cases of witnessed and unrepentant adultery, and is not authorisation of domestic violence by a husband against his wife**. Here they are in slightly shortened form to drive the point home:

> …As for those (women) whom you fear (have committed) a promiscuous act (*nushooz*), admonish (pl.) them, abstain from them in bed, strike them. But if they heed you (pl.) [i.e. your admonishment], then do not (pl.) look for a way against them. For God is Exalted, Great. (4:34)
> And if you fear a breach may occur between the two of them [i.e. the husband and wife], then send an arbiter from his family and an arbiter from her family. If the two of them wish to reconcile, God will bring about agreement between them. For God is all-Knowing, all-Aware. (4:35)

and

> And if a woman fears that her husband (has committed) a promiscuous act (*nushooz*) or neglected her, there is no blame on either of them if they reconcile, for reconciliation is best. Souls are prone to greed, but if you (pl.) do good and are reverent, God is surely aware of all you do. (4:128)
> You (pl.) will not be able to deal justly between women, however much you wish to. But do not turn away from one altogether so as to leave her suspended... (4:129)
> But if the two separate, God will compensate each of them from His abundance...(4:130)

Notice how in 4:35, God explicitly supports reconciliation between the couple if they so wish despite the wife's infidelity—precisely what the Prophet is reported to have done in the *hadith* quoted at the end of the previous chapter when the wronged husband declares that he still loves his unfaithful *and* promiscuous wife regardless.

So why has "strike them" in verse 4:34 not been interpreted or explained to us this way? Even **past[2] and present religious authorities, who thankfully roundly reject the idea that husbands are allowed to hit their wives, mostly argue their case *indirectly***:

- By pointing to the Prophet as an emancipating, kind and respectful husband who moreover instructed his followers to not hit women and to always treat them with respect.
- And/or pointing to the "gradual" instructions of the verse where the striking only takes effect *if* counsel is not heeded *and* marital abstention ("abstain from them in bed") does not do the trick.
- And/or, especially in contemporary scholarship, by arguing that the word "strike" is used in different ways in the Qur'an and may in this instance mean "strike or turn away" or "withdraw completely".

But the *direct* answer lies in the fact that jurists and commentators have not usually interpreted *nushooz* to refer to anything sexual, opting for far broader concepts:

[2] Pre-modern jurists were in fact surprisingly unanimous in rejecting the chauvinist interpretation of "strike them" in verse 4:34, while the majority of pre-modern courts also "were surprisingly receptive to women seeking redress or protection from spousal abuse." See Brown, Jonathan. Ibid., 274–287.

- When *nushooz* is applied to women (4:34), it has mostly been translated as rebelliousness or arrogance, but also more mildly as ill conduct, discord, or animosity, all of which take the "strike them" out of the societal realm and into the private domain of the husband vis-à-vis his wife, hence the problem.

  (When *nushooz* is applied to men (4:128), it has usually been translated as ill treatment, cruelty or animosity.)

But **the subject in both 4:34 and 4:128 is in fact one and the same: a second partner in addition to the current spouse**. As already mentioned, the promiscuous act of a married woman would constitute an unmarried and therefore *illicit* act from the Qur'anic point of view, hence the mention of a penalty in the case of the woman in 4:34. But the promiscuous act of a married man is not necessarily an unmarried/illicit act and in 4:128 it in fact refers to the specific case where men were permitted, though discouraged, by the Qur'an to take another wife.

It is this resistance to interpreting and translating *nushooz* as a promiscuous or extra-spousal act in both the case of men and women that has led us down this path where some think that domestic violence is approved by the Qur'an. In my view, much of this resistance is likely due, once again, to the inertia created by the repetition of the same thing over and over again down the generations.

The Pushback of Myth on the Qur'an Itself: But God Told Job to Hit His Wife—It Says So in the Qur'an!

During a workshop I was running overseas a few years ago on human rights and the Qur'an, I had been speaking about verse 4:34 partly along the lines detailed above when a woman participant raised her hand and said: But God told the prophet Job in the Qur'an to hit his wife!

I am not often left speechless, but I recall being so taken aback that I hesitated for a few seconds before saying anything. Then I asked: In the Qur'an? Yes, she said emphatically, and suddenly I became aware of many participants in the room gently shaking their heads in agreement. I looked around at the room full of women and I will never forget the big, concerned eyes and gravity of expression everyone seemed to have. None of the participants spoke or read Arabic or English and in fact I was holding the workshop through a translator, so I understood that whatever Qur'an they had read must have been in their own language. But I did not want to jump to conclusions, so I told the group that I had read the Qur'an dozens of times during the course of my life and that I could assure them that nowhere in it does God tell Job to hit his wife, that I did not recall Job's wife ever being mentioned even, but that I would look into it and get back to them after I returned home and had had a chance to investigate.

And indeed, while Job is mentioned four times[3] in the Qur'an as one of God's prophets, I could not find a mention of his wife. One of these mentions is this sequence:

> <u>Săd (unknown meaning but aka David), 38:41–44</u>
> And remember our servant Job, when he called out to his Lord: Satan has afflicted me with weariness and suffering!
>
> Stamp your foot [came the reply]: Here is cool water to wash with and to drink.
>
> And We bestowed upon him his family, and with them others like them, as a mercy from Us and as a reminder for those of understanding.
>
> And take a bunch of grass in your hand and strike with it, and do not break your oath. Truly We found him steadfast—an excellent servant, ever turning (to God).

The verses above clearly speak of the long-suffering Job's resilient faith and steadfastness in the face of relentless onslaught by Satan. Mention of Job's family is made and it is highly positive, with no mention of his wife or any other woman or individual for that matter.

But to my dismay, as I looked up more and more English translations, I found that some of them had inserted either the words "your wife", (your wife), or (her) into verse 38:44 after the word "strike", to the following effect:

> × And take a bunch of grass in your hand and strike <u>your wife/(your wife)/(her)</u> with it, and do not break your oath. Truly We found him steadfast—an excellent servant, ever turning (to God).

[3] Job is mentioned in the Qur'an as one of God's prophets in verses 4:163, 6:84, 21:83–84 and 38:41–44.

which is in stark contrast to the original, which thankfully many popular translations did effectively maintain as:

> ✓ And take a bunch of grass in your hand and strike with it, and do not break your oath. Truly We found him steadfast—an excellent servant, ever turning (to God). (38:44)

Why would anyone do this, and how can such audacious tampering ever be justified?

Apparently several classical commentators, mostly from the twelfth to the fourteenth centuries,[4] had argued that Job's wife at one point got fed up with all the trials her husband was going through and reproached him for continuing to believe in God, an account they had most probably encountered in the Bible, in Job 2:9.[5] *But* these commentators then added their own imaginings to the biblical account: that Job had replied in anger that if he ever got his health back he would strike her a hundred times for such blasphemy, but that when he did get better he regretted this "oath", and that God had therefore instructed him to take a handful of grass and hit his wife with it instead, so that he would neither be "breaking his oath" nor really harming her at the same time.[6]

At worst, I suppose we should be pleased that even this interpretation shows God trying to protect the wife!

But the truth of the matter is, besides the fact that there can never be any justification for importing foreign words into a Qur'anic verse, this bizarre interpretation is utterly unconvincing:

- These commentators or "interpreters" did not substantiate their expanded understanding of this verse *in any way*.[7]
- The verses before 38:44 which speak of Job do not refer to his wife—the only other reference is to Satan. And Job's wife is not mentioned at all anywhere in the Qur'an.

[4] Nasr, Seyyed Hossein (editor-in-chief) et al. 2015. The Study Quran: A New Translation and Commentary. New York: HarperCollins Publishers, 1111 and lvii–lix.

[5] Asad, Muhammad. 2003. The Message of the Qur'an. Bristol, England: The Book Foundation, 789.

[6] Nasr et al. *Op. Cit.*, 1111.

[7] See Nasr et al. *Op. Cit.*, 1111 and Asad, Muhammad. *Op. Cit.*, 789.

- In fact, there is no mention of Job's wife anywhere in *hadith* either,[8] so this interpretation cannot even be blamed on inauthentic *hadith*, the usual cause behind women-unfriendly interpretations.
- And lastly, not keeping an oath is not always condemned in the Qur'an so this argument rings hollow: for example, "God will not take you to task for the frivolous in your oaths..." (5:89), and "Do not make God an obstacle, through your oaths, to doing good and being reverent and reconciling between people...God will not take you to task for the frivolous in your oaths..." (2:224–225)

There can be no doubt, therefore, that 38:44 simply means what one initially understands it to mean: that God is telling Job to take a handful of grass and strike with it symbolically *at Satan* to brush away his tormentor and not lose faith.[9] In fact the Arabic words used (*la tahhnuth*) mean both "do not break your oath" and "do not lean towards the wrong", which is what giving in to Satan's whisperings would constitute.

This incident with Job is reminiscent of another involving Abraham, who threw pebbles at Satan when the latter tried to tempt him into disobeying God's command to sacrifice his son, a symbolic act re-enacted by millions annually as one of the rites at the annual pilgrimage (*hajj*) in Mecca.

[8] Nasr et al. *Op. Cit.*, 1111.

[9] An alternative interpretation of verse 38:44 is that "take a bunch of grass" relates to some herbal cure being recommended to the ailing Job. See Nasr et al. *Op. Cit.*, 1111.

CHAPTER 21

Virgins: There Are No 72 Virgins Waiting for Anyone in Paradise

Qur'anic Verses on Women and Men in Paradise

This is yet another of the cringe-inducing topics outrageously laid at the door of the Qur'an, but what can one do. Like a couple of others before it, this myth must unfortunately also be addressed because of how prevalent it has become since 9/11.[1]

Common sense and the Qur'an itself tell us that the promise of Paradise is made to both women and men who earn it through the choices they make during their lives on earth, and that the rewards are the same for both. We have seen this self-evident truth explicitly articulated in various verses of the Qur'an cited in this book already, and there are many more.

So why is it that when we come to *descriptions* of this Paradise, we suddenly perceive the three dozen or so instances of these in the Qur'an as if they were addressing only men? Societal programming, that is why. **Layers of patriarchal fog have accumulated over our minds over the centuries that have left us effectively *programmed* to hear any description of Paradise in the Qur'an as though it were addressing only men**—which is logically impossible. The Qur'an does occasionally address men specifically—such as when it describes *female* spouses—but where it uses

[1] According to Brown, Jonathan. 2015. Misquoting Muhammad: The Challenge and Choices of Interpreting the Prophet's Legacy. London: Oneworld Publications, 238, the leader of Al Qaeda, Osama Bin Laden, had promised 72 virgins to Muslim "martyrs" in Heaven.

L. El-Ali, *No Truth Without Beauty*, Sustainable Development Goals Series, https://doi.org/10.1007/978-3-030-83582-8_21

the generic plural it is undoubtedly addressing both women and men in its promises of the rewards of Paradise.

Descriptions of heaven in the Qur'an occur in a single verse or in a group of verses at a time. There is a lot of repetition, while some elements are mentioned only once or twice. Here are the key elements of these physical descriptions:

- Gardens underneath which rivers flow, plenty of shade, two upper and two lower gardens, and two groups of the righteous (the foremost or those "brought near", i.e. to God, and those "of/on the right").
- Abundant and varied fruit, cups ever-filled from a spring providing a refreshing drink, four types of potable rivers: of never-stale water, ever-fresh milk, delicious wine, and clear honey (47:15).
- Silk and embroidered clothing, jewellery, precious stones, reclining on couches in contentment.
- Boys and immortal youths, described as hidden pearls and as scattered pearls floating around, attentive to the inhabitants of Paradise as though they were their own children, filling their cups and generally waiting on them (52:24, 56:17).

And then there are the descriptions that reference either earthly women or other female beings in heaven, or both:

- **Purified mates/spouses** for every person in Paradise are mentioned in verses where the same phrase re-appears such as:

  The Cow, 2:25; The House of *'Imran* (Joaquim, father of Mary), 3:15; Women, 4:57
  ...And there [in the gardens underneath which rivers flow] they shall have purified spouses (*azwāj*)...

And as described in Part II, the word *zawj* and its plural *azwāj* used in the verses above and elsewhere means a "pair" or "one of a pair", i.e. mate, so it is one spouse each, for those who may wonder.

Culturally, **verses referring to having a "purified spouse" in heaven are usually assumed to be addressing men only because of a fundamentally incorrect association of purity with virginity**, thereby attaching it to women. The ubiquitous concept of **"purity" (*tahara, zakat*) in the Qur'an is never used to refer to virginity**. It is used in relation to:

- The souls of God's prophets, for example:

  The House of *'Imran* (Joaquim, father of Mary), 3:42
  And when the angels said: Oh Mary,[2] God has chosen you and purified you [i.e. your soul] and chosen you above the women of the worlds.

  The House of *'Imran* (Joaquim, father of Mary), 3:55
  When God said: Oh Jesus, I am making you die (*mutawaffeeka*)[3] and raising you to Me and purifying you from those who disbelieve, and placing those who follow you above those who disbelieve until the Day of Resurrection [i.e. Judgment Day]...

- People on a righteous path and the inhabitants of Paradise, as in:

  The Congregational Prayer, 62:2
  It is He who sent forth among the illiterate a messenger [Muhammad] from among themselves, to relay to them His messages (*ayas*) and purify them and teach them the Book and wisdom, though they were before then lost in evident error.

  Ta Ha (unknown meaning), 20:76
  The Gardens of Eden under which rivers flow, where they shall dwell forever: that is the reward of those who purify themselves.

  The Cow, 2:25 (and similarly 3:15 and 4:57)
  And give good tidings to those who believe and do good deeds that theirs are gardens underneath which rivers flow...where they shall have purified spouses and dwell forever.

[2] See verse 21:91 mentioned in Chap. 10, on Mary being included in the Qur'an as one of God's prophets.

[3] As every Arabic speaker knows from everyday speech, a person who has *tawaffa* has "died". But most English translations of the Qur'an opt for indirect meanings in 3:55 such as "to be taken away" instead of the actual "be made to die". See the note in Nasr, Seyyed Hossein (editor-in-chief) et al. 2015. The Study Quran: A New Translation and Commentary. New York: HarperCollins Publishers, 146 and also Asad, Muhammad. 2003. The Message of the Qur'an. Bristol, England: The Book Foundation, 89.

– Things, e.g. rainwater or a house of worship:

The Pilgrimage, 22:26
And when We assigned for Abraham the site of the House [the *Kaaba* in Mecca], saying: Do not associate anything with Me and purify My house for those who would make the rounds, and those who would stand, and those who would bow, prostrating themselves.

– And actions, e.g. almsgiving or ablutions:

The Banquet (i.e. The Last Supper), 5:6
Oh you who believe: When you get up to pray wash your faces and hands up to the elbows, and wipe your heads and your feet up to the ankles. And if you are physically unclean[4] then purify yourselves…

- **Reunification with one's earthly spouse** in Paradise is mentioned in verses such as:

Thunder, 13:23
Gardens of Eden that they [the righteous] shall enter, along with those who were righteous of their parents[5] and spouses and offspring. And the angels shall enter upon them from every gate—

Ya Sīn (uncertain meaning), 36:55–56
Those who have earned Paradise on this day are busy rejoicing,
They and their spouses reclining on couches in the shade.

[4] To be "physically unclean" and so require purification before prayer (beyond the just-described simple ablution that involves simply wiping the face, head, forearms and feet with water) refers to the need for actual washing after answering a call of nature or after sexual intercourse, as defined in the rest of verse 5:6 and also in 4:43. The Qur'an does not include menstruation in its definition of being "physically unclean" and therefore requiring purification/actual washing before prayer, though custom has always included it to the point that women are prohibited or excused, depending on one's perspective, from even performing the daily prayers while menstruating.

[5] Most popular translations render *ābā'* in 13:23 as "fathers" rather than "parents". But every Arabic speaker will readily recognise the word here to essentially mean "forefathers" and so includes mothers, and moreover the verse is clearly speaking of a person's more proximate ancestors and descendants (as evidenced by the mention of one's spouse, a contemporary) irrespective of their gender, so the forefathers in question are also proximate, i.e. parents. Besides, we would have expected to see the word "sons" used instead of the gender-neutral "offspring" for consistency had God meant to include righteous male relatives but exclude righteous female relatives from Heaven, surely the implication of such translations. See also the note in Asad, Muhammad. Ibid., 406.

Forgiver, 40:8
Our Lord: admit them [the righteous] to the Gardens of Eden that You promised them, along with those who were righteous of their parents and spouses and offspring…

Ornaments of Gold, 43:69–70
Those who believed in Our messages (*ayas*) and who surrendered [to God]: Enter the Garden, you and your spouses, to be made joyous.

Disappointingly, most (but not all) translations use the word "wives" in the above and previous verses rather than "spouses", as though God was only addressing men. This is not justifiable because the Qur'an here does not use the feminine plural version (*zawjāt* or even the ubiquitous *nisa'*, i.e. women, or wives) but the generic masculine plural (*azwāj*) of the word *zawj* or mate, which linguistically (and logically) means both husbands and wives.

That said, the Qur'an sometimes does speak specifically of **earthly *women* in Paradise**:

- "Those (women) of limited/short glances" (37:48, 38:52 and 55:56), i.e. righteous women, which is reminiscent of verses 24:30–31 covered earlier in Part IV where *both* believing men and believing women are advised to "lower their gaze" in modesty.

- The Event, 56:35–37
  We shall have created them (women) anew,
  Thus made them virgins.
  Loving, (and) of equal age/quality (*atrāb*).

In the above verse the Qur'an is promising that earthly women in Paradise will be newly created, perfect and young again, *as will men be born anew and made young again* since **the women will be of matching age and substance *to the men***. To reduce virginity here—this bigger concept of being born anew—to a mere sexual state while applying it exclusively to women is to miss the point, which is **re-gifted youth and freshness on an eternal basis for women and men alike**.

- "Glorious and of equal age/quality" (78:33)—while there is nothing in this sentence that implies that its subject is feminine, it has almost always been taken to refer to women while "glorious" is usually translated as "voluptuous" or even "buxom",[6] a rendering that is unfortunately in keeping with the narrowing and therefore sexualisation of the broad and profound descriptions of Paradise.

- **Union with a *hoor* spouse in Paradise**, by default (given all the above and the emphasis on "pairs") for those without an earthly spouse as mate, is mentioned in such verses as:

Smoke, 44:54
So (it shall be); and We shall have married them [literally "paired" them with, i.e. *zawwajnahum*] to beautiful-eyed *hoor*.

Smoke, 52:20
Reclining on couches in rows; and We shall have married them [literally "paired" them with, i.e. *zawwajnahum*] to beautiful-eyed *hoor*.

Hoor, or *hooris* in its anglicised form, are heaven-made beings also likened to hidden pearls, having a beautiful whiteness of the eye that contrasts with an intense blackness of the iris (e.g. 56:22).[7] But some translations render the description as "wide-eyed" rather than "beautiful-eyed", which has a very different connotation that I find culturally telling. Meanwhile the word *hoor* is strikingly similar (in its Arabic word construction) to the term used in the Qur'an to refer to the disciples of Jesus, the *hawariyyun* (61:14).[8] This confirms that the term *hoor* essentially and unsurprisingly refers to pure beings, and in fact Muhammad himself was described as *hoori*-eyed by a female contemporary,[9] which would have been unlikely if only females were thought to constitute this category of pure beings in Paradise. **That there should be male and not only female**

[6] See the note in Asad, Muhammad. *Op. Cit.*, 1055–6 on verse 78:33, as well as any Arabic dictionary where *ka'b* as a noun can mean either heel or lower part (clearly not the meaning here) or glory, dignity, honour, i.e. nothing to do with the female figure.

[7] Asad, Muhammad. *Op. Cit.*, 944 and Nasr et al., *Op. Cit.*, 1213.

[8] At the risk of oversimplifying just a touch, the root of every word in Arabic consists of three letters, so different words containing the same three letters in the same order are usually related and express the same concept, but from different angles or points of emphasis. On *hawariyyun* in reference to the disciples of Jesus and its essential meaning, see also the note in Asad, Muhammad. *Op. Cit.*, 89.

[9] Kahf, Mohja. 2000. Braiding the Stories: Women's Eloquence in the Early Islamic Era. In Windows of Faith: Muslim Women Scholar-Activists in North America, ed. Gisela Webb, 162. New York: Syracuse University Press.

heavenly beings or *hoor* makes perfect sense: if God promises to pair the single people in Paradise with *hoor*, then surely there will be single women and not only single men in Paradise in need of being paired up in this way, right?

That said, and just as it sometimes speaks specifically of earthly women in Paradise, the Qur'an does speak specifically at times of ***hoor women* in Paradise**:

- "*Hoor* (female) in palatial pavilions" (55:72), although this is usually translated as "*hoor* confined/restrained in pavilions", which is surely counter-intuitive in the delightful and carefree Paradise the Qur'an describes. Linguistically, the root word at play here is *qasr* which can mean either "palace" or "limitation, restriction": given the repeated descriptions of Paradise as a luxurious, beautiful, happy place free of all concerns for all of its inhabitants, does it make sense to then basically "restrict" the movement of these female heavenly beings to a particular structure there? Does it not make more sense that the verse is saying that they are enjoying these pavilions that are more like palaces? The usual interpretation and translation surely undermine the essence of the Qur'an's extensive description of Paradise as an idyllic place for *all.*
- "(Female *hoor*) untouched by human or *jinn*" (55:56 and 55:74), the *jinn* being a species invisible to human beings that the Qur'an often mentions. Like human beings, the *jinn* have free will and are therefore capable of both right and wrong, beauty and ugliness, greatness or lowliness. Mention of the *jinn* here makes it clear, to me at least, that "untouched" means never having been vulnerable to the *imperfections or failings* of either humans or *jinn*, a far more profound and comprehensive characteristic than to simply be virgin in a sexual sense—surely a more aptly loft concept when speaking of Paradise and of the two species, humankind and *jinn*, that the Qur'an addresses.

In summary, women and men are promised the same things in Paradise. "Purified spouses/mates" for everyone (2:25, 3:15, 4:57), whether one's righteous spouse from one's time on earth (13:23, 36:56, 40:8, 43:70) or a spouse from among beings referred to as *hoor* or *hooris* (44:54, 52:20). And as already mentioned, the word *zawj* in its plural *azwaj* used in these verses and elsewhere means a "pair" or "one of a pair" of either sex, i.e. mate, so it is one spouse each.

Virginity as relating to people being born again and made equally and eternally young in Paradise applies to both women and men by definition. For those who would insist on a narrower and more sexual meaning, or on "purified spouses" referring to sexual virginity and of women specifically, it is worth remembering that at least 10 and possibly 11 of the 12 women the Prophet married during his lifetime were not virgins, and that chastity was prescribed for men and women alike[10] as we have seen in Chap. 14, entitled Marriage and Chap. 19, entitled Sexual Misconduct.

It is legitimate to ask why the Qur'an sometimes focuses its description on the women of Paradise specifically, be they earthly or *hoor* women. I have not come across any commentary on why this is the case, which is unsurprising given that most commentaries assume that the Qur'an is addressing men anyway, as if women were appendages. My own thought on this issue is that perhaps men were a harder sell at the time and needed to be wooed more proactively than women, being the tribal and clan leaders of their communities and the defenders of the prevailing idolatry: in fact as mentioned in Chap. 14, Marriage, the earliest converts to the new religion were in fact the underdogs, namely young men and women of no influence, and slaves.

My other thought on the question of women in Paradise, whether earthly or *hoori*, is to recall the Prophet's own description of them (among other beings and things) after the miracle of his heavenly visit in the company of the archangel Gabriel, which could not be further from the popular preoccupations I have reluctantly addressed in this chapter:

> ...if a woman of the people of Paradise appeared unto the people of earth, she would fill the space between Heaven and here below with light and fragrance.[11]

[10] See also Barlas, Asma. 2015. Believing Women in Islam: Unreading Patriarchal Interpretations of the Qur'an. Texas: University of Texas Press, 155.

[11] Lings, Martin. 1988. Muhammad: His Life based on the Earliest Sources. London: Unwin Hyman Limited,102.

The Pushback of Alleged *Hadith*: 72 Virgins Are Promised...Or Perhaps 70

Just to get it out of the way, the number 72 does not occur anywhere in the Qur'an. There are three mentions of the number 70 in varied contexts—all unrelated to women or even *hoor*—which sometimes appears as a stand-in for the word "many"[12] in the way we might today say "dozens", for example.

There is an alleged *hadith* attributed to the Prophet that promises a martyr several things, including 72 *hooris* as wives.[13] While we are at it, there is another alleged *hadith* that promises the lowliest believer, who does not even have to be a martyr, the same thing—along with 80,000 servants![14] Yet another allegedly states that a martyr gets 70 *hooris* as wives and is allowed to intercede on behalf of 70 members of his family.[15] And so it goes.

Firstly, and as discussed above at length, a female *hoori* according to the Qur'an is first and foremost a heaven-made, purified being untouched in every way—physical, mental or spiritual—by humans or *jinn*. To reduce a female *hoori* to a mere "virgin" and use the two terms interchangeably is a cultural bias that speaks for itself.

Secondly and unsurprisingly, none of these *hadiths* have ever stood on solid ground anyway, even going back to their original inclusion in the *hadith* corpus, which as we discussed in Part I at length had scooped up every last claim anyone ever made if they assigned it to the Prophet. Questions of problematic transmitters, whether intentional or not, with regard to this group of alleged *hadiths* on *hooris* were well-documented from the outset by scholars who researched the infractions and even expressed regret for their previous confidence in some transmitters.[16] In any case, collective common sense had always pretty much dismissed such reports, until modern communications gave a fringe and agenda-driven claim a global voice.

[12] The number 70 appears as either a specific number or as a substitute for "many" in verses 7:155, 9:80 and 69:32.

[13] Brown, Jonathan. *Op. Cit.* (2015), 302.

[14] Ibid., 242.

[15] Ibid., 304.

[16] Ibid., Appendix IV, 302–305.

AT A GLANCE: Carnal Matters

Putting Illicit Sex Back in Its Place

- Like other books of scripture, the Qur'an is against all sex outside of marriage, whether pre-marital or extra-marital/adultery (3:135–136, 4:15–16, 17:32, 25:68–71).
- But no "accusations" of sex outside marriage should be entertained unless four eye-witnesses come forward to support such a claim (4:15, 24:4). Logically, **this de facto relegates sexual relations to the private rather than the public domain save for extreme cases, such as public lewdness**. Indeed jurists have always maintained that the four witnesses must have observed the act of *intercourse* itself in the first place, and not simply a situation or behaviour that *implies* it. Yet even if sexual accusations are sustained by four credible eye-witnesses, people should be forgiving towards both pre-marital and extra-marital sex offenders if the guilty parties express remorse and do good, as God Himself will forgive them (3:135–136, 4:16, 25:68–71). Logically, then, should anyone be found guilty of illicit sex, **it is sufficient for the guilty party or parties to express regret for society to be *obliged* to leave them be**.
- In the case of *unrepentant pre-marital* sex violators who have been observed in the very act of intercourse by four eye-witnesses, the Qur'an then has this to say:

  – For the woman, confinement at home until death or until God provides a way out (4:15), usually interpreted as a marriage proposal from someone that the woman accepts.

- For the man, punishment is to be commensurate per the Qur'anic directive "punish then both" (4:16), but there is evidence that historically men were treated more leniently by their societies and that this might have simply involved banishment from the village or town in their case.

- In the case of ***unrepentant extra-marital*** sex violators who have been observed in the very act of intercourse by four eye-witnesses, the Qur'an then has this to say:

  - Both women and men are to be "flogged" one hundred times before a limited group of the public (24:2), which was carried out using such symbolic instruments as clothes or footwear. The apparent choice of instrument in the Prophet's time sheds light on why the Qur'an did not lessen the number of "floggings" for women relative to men given the physical differences between the two sexes, as we would have expected it to do. It also highlights the fact that the intention was to shame rather than to cause corporal harm or pain, which is further confirmed by mention of the need for there to be a few people present.
  - Adulterers, whether men or women, are to only marry fellow adulterers after that, or pagans/idolaters, i.e. they are further punished by not being entitled to marry other fellow believers (24:3).
  - Accusing married women of adultery without producing four eye-witnesses is so abhorrent in God's eyes that such an accuser should also be "flogged" but by a slightly reduced number of eighty times, and no testimony should ever be accepted from them ever again (24:4).

No Husbands Hitting Wives—Ever

As has been stated more than once, this book is premised on two fundamental ideas:

First, that a verse in the Qur'an must be considered ***not just in its entirety but alongside the verses preceding and following it*** before we decide what it means.

Second, that a verse must also be considered *alongside all other verses that deal with the same topic* to complete our understanding of the Qur'anic perspective on that topic.

If we are diligent enough to do the above with verse 4:34, it soon becomes crystal clear that the claim that this verse instructs or allows husbands to strike their wives in certain situations is simply false.

When the rather-long verse 4:34 is read all the way to the end and the ensuing verse 4:35 which continues the narrative is read together with it, the effective phrase "strike them but *not* if they heed your counsel" is obviously revisiting the question of adultery summarised under illicit sex above, where a *repentant* unfaithful wife (or husband) is to be forgiven by society (25:68–71) and not flogged/struck to cause shame even if there are witnesses to the fact.

In other words, verse 4:34 is addressing *society as a whole*, the last part dealing specifically with adultery and not just any husband-wife situation, while verse 4:35 goes on to deliver on God's promise to forgive an adulteress (or adulterer) by intervening Himself to reconcile the couple in question—a divine act of compassion towards us reminiscent of that of a loving and concerned grandparent.

So verses 4:34–35 are in fact a *case study* offered by the Qur'an on *how* to implement the penalty for adultery thoughtfully. That their subject is indeed a promiscuous act (*nushooz*) by a married woman is confirmed by other verses in the Qur'an addressing the same act (i.e. *nushooz*) by a married man (4:127–130).

And in fact if we line up the two sets of verses on promiscuous acts by men and women next to each other, there is a remarkable symmetry not only in content but also in language and turns of phrase.

Lastly, nowhere in the Qur'an does God tell the prophet Job to strike his wife, a previously minor myth that has been perpetuated by some translations. In fact, Job's wife is not mentioned anywhere in this holy book.

Paradise Regained

The Qur'an tell us, over and over again, that the promise of Paradise is one that God has made to both women and men who earn it through the choices they make during their lives on earth, and that the rewards are the same for both.

Every woman or every man is essentially promised a "purified spouse" in Paradise (2:25, 3:15, 4:57), where "purity" has nothing to do with female virginity and *everything* to do with proximity to God, i.e. Godliness and nobility of soul (3:42, 3:55, 62:2, 20:76, among others).

This "purified spouse" in heaven may be one's *earthly spouse*, if that man or woman had been righteous (13:23, 36:55–56, 40:8, 43:69–70), or a *hoor or paradisal spouse* (44:54, 52:20), a made-in-heaven being.

Now the Qur'an does sometimes address men specifically—such as when it describes earthly and paradisal (*hoor*) spouses that are *female*. Here is some of what it then tells us:

- Earthly women in Paradise have "short glances" (37:48, 38:52 and 55:56)—just as believing women *and men* on earth have, since they also "lower their gaze" (24:30–31).
- Earthly women in Paradise will have been born anew, made perfect and young again—and yes, virgin—*just as earthly men in Paradise will be also*: for the two will be "of equal age/quality" to one another (56:35–37), meaning of matching youth and substance. **Thus this is not about "female virginity" but about the promise of re-gifted youth and freshness in Paradise on an eternal basis *for women and men alike*.**
- Paradisal women (*hoor* who are female) will have been **"untouched by human or *jinn*"** (55:56 and 55:74), the *jinn* being a species invisible to human beings that the Qur'an often mentions. Like human beings, the *jinn* have free will and are therefore capable of both right and wrong, beauty and ugliness, greatness or lowliness. Mention of the *jinn* here makes it clear that "untouched" **means never having been vulnerable to the *imperfections or failings* of either humans or *jinn*, a far more profound and comprehensive characteristic than to simply be virgin in a sexual sense**—surely a more aptly loft concept when speaking of Paradise and of the two species, humankind and *jinn*, that the Qur'an addresses.

And as a reminder, the word *zawj* in its plural *azwaj* used in all these verses and elsewhere means a "pair" or "one of a pair" of either sex, i.e. mate, so it is indeed one spouse each in Paradise.

Lastly, the myth of "72 virgins in Paradise" for a (presumably male) martyr is just that, appearing nowhere in the Qur'an.

Epilogue

phoenix
noun

1. a mythical bird of great beauty fabled to live 500 or 600 years in the Arabian wilderness, to burn itself on a funeral pyre, and to rise from its ashes in the freshness of youth and live through another cycle of years: often an emblem of immortality or of reborn idealism or hope.
2. a person or thing that has become renewed or restored after suffering calamity or apparent annihilation.

In this book, I have tried to pull out all the verses in the Qur'an that are relevant for a comprehensive understanding of women's nature and rights in the Qur'anic worldview, and that might additionally shed light on some myths and misconceptions. It is my profound hope that the reader will have found both comfort and inspiration from visiting or revisiting God's words with the earnestness they surely require.

As I write this epilogue in 2019, I am conscious that it has been 527 years since the fall of Granada, the last remaining Muslim territory in Andalusia, Spain, to the Catholic monarchs Isabel I of Castile and Ferdinand II of Aragon in 1492, which ended 700 years of North African Muslim rule in the Iberian peninsula.

L. El-Ali, *No Truth Without Beauty*, Sustainable Development Goals Series, https://doi.org/10.1007/978-3-030-83582-8

It is also 566 years since the fall of Constantinople to the Ottomans, which ended 1100 years of Christian rule of then-Byzantium, or modern-day Istanbul.

The decline in the Islamic civilisation of the Middle East intellectually, spiritually, artistically and scientifically appears to have begun soon after these twin defeat and victory. Perhaps the defeated North Africans of Andalusia became preoccupied with regaining their former power, and the victorious Ottomans became expansionist in response to a combination of what they had observed happen in Andalusia and their own new-found power, having basically put an end to the long-reigning and seemingly invincible Byzantine Empire. Whatever the motivations or prime preoccupations at the time, one thing is clear: as a community across the entire Middle East, we became more preoccupied with outer glories at the expense of our inner, qualitative growth, contrary to what had been recognisably the preoccupation during the time of the Prophet and the subsequent Muslim reign in Andalusia which began less than a century after his passing. Today most of our communities and countries have fallen behind in many of the areas that really matter—such as education, social justice, and indeed legal justice or the law—without which we cannot hope to fulfil our potential intellectuality or spirituality at a time when we are facing great challenges in economic, governance and extremism-related matters.

I am reminded again of the verse: "…God does not change the condition of a people until they change what is in their souls [or hearts]…" (13:11).

Surely it is time for greater individual and collective instrospection.

Appendix: On Contraception and Abortion

Obviously, neither contraception nor abortion is mentioned in the Qur'an, the holy book having been revealed in the seventh century long before such topics became mainstream possibilities. But given the extensive debate surrounding these issues among some non-Muslim religious communities in the West, as well as resistance to family planning in much of the developing world, it is perhaps appropriate to comment on them since these are very relevant issues today for women everywhere.

As for contraception, it has always been regarded as acceptable by Islamic authorities, who base their decision on *hadith*.[1]

There are two "sound" *hadiths* attributed to the Prophet where he appears to give either verbal or tacit approval of the practice of *coitus interruptus* and, by extension, contraception.[2]

The most often-cited *hadith* when supporting the use of contraception is the one where the Prophet appears to have given tacit support for it, which was relayed by one of his Companions:

[1] Brown, Jonathan. 2014. Hadith: Muhammad's Legacy in the Medieval and Modern World. London: Oneworld Publications, 10–11 and al-Hibri, Azizah. 2000. An Introduction to Muslim Women's Rights. In Windows of Faith: Muslim Women Scholar-Activists in North America, ed. Gisela Webb, 62. New York: Syracuse University.

[2] Hassan, Riffat, 2000. Is Family Planning Permitted by Islam? In Windows of Faith: Muslim Women Scholar-Activists in North America, ed. Gisela Webb, 232. New York: Syracuse University Press.

L. El-Ali, *No Truth Without Beauty*, Sustainable Development Goals Series, https://doi.org/10.1007/978-3-030-83582-8

> "We used to practice *coitus interruptus* during the time of the Prophet when the Qur'an was being revealed."[3]

The lesser-known *hadith* on this topic is one where the Prophet articulates his support for it:

> "...It is not a lesser infanticide. You may practice it, but if God has predetermined for a child to be born, it will be born."

There is one weak *hadith* denouncing *coitus interruptus* and, by extension, contraception, which alleges that the Prophet stated that it *is* a "lesser infanticide", but this has always been dismissed as a weak or unreliable report.[4]

Perhaps most interestingly, there is a *hadith* that appears in several compilations that says that the Prophet forbade the practice of *coitus interruptus* without the wife's consent.[5] I find this report very consistent with Qur'anic advocacy on behalf of women in marriage, whether from a conjugal relations or a right-to-motherhood point of view. That said, neither getting married not having children have ever been considered mandatory in Islam,[6] and as previously mentioned some classical scholars and jurists are known to have never married, while others have married but chosen not to have children.

As for abortion, some of us grow up hearing that most scholars are in agreement that abortion is acceptable during the first three months of pregnancy, although more recently medical data has led some jurists to begin to question whether abortion should be allowed even during this time *unless* the mother's rights are at stake.[7]

The reason for Islamic jurists' traditionally accepting attitude of abortion is the belief that a foetus does not immediately receive a soul upon conception, that it only becomes *en*souled[8] sometime later. I have not heard or read of any *hadith* being cited in support of the three-month view, but in reviewing Qur'anic verses, that may be the source of this belief, three stand out.

[3] Brown, Jonathan. *Op. Cit.* (2014), 10 and Hassan, Riffat. *Ibid*. See also al-Hibri, Azizah. *Op. Cit.*, 62.

[4] Hassan, Riffat. *Op. Cit.*, 232–3.

[5] Ibid., 233.

[6] Ibid.

[7] al-Hibri, Azizah. *Op. Cit.*, 62–3.

[8] Hassan, Riffat. *Op. Cit.*, 234.

- Verse 2:233 says that an infant's nursing period is two years for mothers who wish to nurse their infants for the full term.
- Verse 31:14 charges children to be good to their parents, and speaks of how mothers suffer first when carrying their child and then because the period before "weaning" or of "utter dependence" of a child is two years.
- And then verse 46:15 mentions that the "gestation and weaning" of an infant is a total period of 30 months.

Combining the last verse with the previous two implies that the infant comes into existence, so to speak, three months after conception (followed by up to six months of gestation in a full-term pregnancy plus 24 months maximum of weaning), which is the point at which it receives a soul. It is interesting that the Qur'an does not define the gestation period even as it does define the weaning period, but lumps the two together into 30 months, as if to allow for the fact that some babies are born prematurely. While I have not seen any commentary myself that links these verses to jurists' acceptance of abortion in the first three months, this reasoning appears plausible to me as the source of that view.

That said, I have also read that the allowable period for abortion by most schools of jurisprudence is in fact not three months but 120 days, or four months.[9] This view, which is also widespread, is based on a couple of *hadiths*[10] that were classified as "authentic" (in terms of their chain of transmission), and which essentially say the following:

- The constituents of every human being come together in the womb for 40 days.
- Then it is a clot for another 40 days.
- Then it is a lump of flesh for another 40 days.
- Then the angel is sent to breathe Spirit into it.

And God knows best.

[9] Ibid., 234. Reportedly the Islamic schools of jurisprudence that allow abortion up to 120 days are the Sunni Hanafi, Shafi'i and Hanbali, and the Shia Zaidi school, though there are differences between them as to whether this can be at will or if a good reason is needed, e.g. the mother's health or a potentially deformed child. The schools that oppose all abortion are the *majority* of the Sunni Maliki school, and the Shia Ja'fari school. See also www.dar-alifta.org/ar/ViewFatwa.aspx?ID=14601&LangID=1 (in Arabic).

[10] Bukhari compilation. No. 3208, www.sunnah.com/bukhari/59; and Muslim compilation. No. 2643, www.sunnah.com/muslim/46.

References

Abdul Rahman, Aisha (aka Bint al-Shate'). 1979. The Wives of the Prophet (in Arabic). Beirut: Dar al-Kitab al-Arabi.

Abou El Fadl, Khaled M. 2001. And God Knows the Soldiers: The Authoritative and Authoritarian in Islamic Discourses. Maryland; Oxford: University Press of America, Inc.

Abou El Fadl, Khaled M. 2003. Speaking in God's Name: Islamic Law, Authority and Women. Oxford: Oneworld Publications.

Abou El Fadl, Khaled M. 2006. The Search for Beauty in Islam: A Conference of the Books. Maryland: Rowman & Littlefield Publishers, Inc.

Abou El Fadl, Khaled M. 2007. The Great Theft: Wrestling Islam from the Extremists. New York: HarperOne.

Al-Albani, Muhammad. 1400H. Al-Ajwiba al-Nafi'a 'an As'ilat Lajnat Masjid al-Jami'a (in Arabic). Beirut: Al-Maktab al-Islami. Referenced on www.dorar.net.

Al-'Asqalani, Ahmad. 2001. Fathul Bari bi-Sharh Sahih al-Bukhari (in Arabic). Riyadh: Prince Sultan bin Abdul Aziz.

Al-Baleek, Imad. 2017. Meet the First Female Minister of Commerce in Islam (in Arabic). Al Arabiya news website www.alarabiya.net, October 19.

Al-Batyawi, Aziz. 1981. Sunan al-Umran al-Bashari fi al-Sira al-Nabawiyya (in Arabic). Amman: Al-Ma'had al-'Alami lil-fikr al-Islami.

Al-Matroudi, Ibrahim bin Salman. 2013. Al-Riyadh newspaper No. 16326. www.alriyadh.com/815375 (in Arabic). March 6.

Al-Mubarakfuri. 1421H. Tuhfat al-Ahwadhi bi-Sharh Sunan al-Tirmidhi (in Arabic). Egypt: Dar al-Hadith.

L. El-Ali, *No Truth Without Beauty*, Sustainable Development Goals Series, https://doi.org/10.1007/978-3-030-83582-8

Al-Qari, Ali, and Al-Tabrizi, Muhammad. 2001. Mirqāt al-Mafateeh: Sharh Mishkāt al-Massabeeh (in Arabic). Dar al-Kutub al-Ilmiyya.

Arberry, Arthur J. 1982. The Koran. Oxford: Oxford University Press.

Asad, Muhammad. 2003. The Message of the Qur'an. Bristol, England: The Book Foundation.

Barlas, Asma. 2015. Believing Women in Islam: Unreading Patriarchal Interpretations of the Qur'an. Texas: University of Texas Press.

BBC. 2009. Slavery in Islam. www.bbc.co.uk/religion/religions/islam/history/slavery_1.shtml. September 7.

Bin Muhammad, HRH Prince Ghazi. 2013. Conjugal and Sexual Love. In Love in the Holy Qur'an. Cambridge, England: The Islamic Texts Society.

Brown, Jonathan. 2014. Hadith: Muhammad's Legacy in the Medieval and Modern World. London: Oneworld Publications.

Brown, Jonathan. 2015. Misquoting Muhammad: The Challenge and Choices of Interpreting the Prophet's Legacy. London: Oneworld Publications.

Brown, Jonathan, and Ali, Abdullah Hamid. 2017. Slavery and Islam: What is Slavery? www.yaqeeninstitute.org/jonathan-brown/slavery-and-islam-what-is-slavery/#ftnt1. February 7.

Dar al-Iftaa Al-Missriyyah. 2016. Official multilingual website of the Egyptian authority on *fatwas*, or religious opinions. www.dar-alifta.org (in Arabic). Accessed October and November 2019: www.dar-alifta.org.eg/AR/ViewFatwa.aspx?ID=14761&LangID=1&MuftiType=0, www.dar-alifta.org/ar/Viewstatement.aspx?sec=new&ID=5144, www.dar-alifta.org/ar/Viewstatement.aspx?sec=new&ID=5142, www.dar-alifta.org/AR/Viewstatement.aspx?sec=&ID=5656, www.dar-alifta.org/ar/ViewFatwa.aspx?ID=14601&LangID=1

Dukes, Kais. 2009–2017. Language Research Group, University of Leeds and https://quran.com, https://corpus.quran.com. Accessed 2017, 2018, January–March 2019.

Ibn Abdel Barr, Al-Hafedh. n.d. Sahih Jami' Bayan al-Ilm wa Fadlihi as compiled by Al-Zuhairy (in Arabic). Cairo: Maktabat Ibn Taymiyya.

www.islamqa.info. 1997. Multilingual website. Accessed October and November 2019: www.islamqa.info/ar/answers/311718

www.islamweb.net. 2002. Multilingual, multi-discipline website. Accessed October and November 2019: www.islamweb.net/ar/fatwa/115147, www.islamweb.net/ar/library/index.php?page=bookcontents&ID=3717&bk_no=2&flag=1, www.islamweb.net/ar/library/index.php?page=bookcontents&ID=5596&bk_no=56&flag=1, www.islamweb.net/ar/library/index.php?page=bookcontents&flag=1&bk_no=79&ID=318

Kamali, Mohammad Hashim. 1995. Punishment in Islamic Law: An Enquiry into the Hudud Bill of Kelantan. Kuala Lumpur: Institut Kajian Dasar.

Kamali, Mohammad Hashim. 2019. Crime and Punishment in Islamic Law: A Fresh Interpretation. New York: Oxford University Press.

Khutab, Mahmoud. 1965. Leaders of the Conquest of Persia (in Arabic). Beirut: Dar al-Fath.

Lang, Jeffrey. 1995. Struggling to Surrender: Some Impressions from an American Convert to Islam. Maryland: Amana Publications.

le Gai Eaton, Charles. 2008. The Book of Hadith: Sayings of the Prophet Muhammad, from the Mishkat al-Masabih. Watsonville, California; Bristol, England: The Book Foundation.

Lings, Martin. 1988. Muhammad: His Life based on the Earliest Sources. London: Unwin Hyman Limited.

Lings, Martin. 2005. A Return to the Spirit: Questions and Answers. Kentucky: Fons Vitae.

Lings, Martin. 2007. The Holy Qur'an: Translations of Selected Verses. Cambridge, England: The Royal Aal Al-Bayt Institute for Islamic Thought and The Islamic Texts Society.

Mawsou'at al-Nabulsi lil-'Ulum al-Islamiyya. 2018. Official website of Mohammed Rateb Nabulsi of Syria. www.nabulsi.com (in Arabic). Accessed October and November 2019: www.nabulsi.com/web/article/3791. October 28, 1984. www.nabulsi.com/web/article/10260. June 11, 1989.

Moussa, Ali Helmy. 1982. Computer Application to Arabic Words in the Qur'an. Journal of 'Ālam al-Fikr (in Arabic), Volume 12, No. 2. Kuwait: Ministry of Information.

Mu'assasat al-Dorar al-Sunniya. 1442H. A committee of religious scholars in Saudi Arabia. www.dorar.net/hadith (in Arabic). Accessed October and November 2019: webpage addresses cited contain Arabic alphabet.

Nasr, Seyyed Hossein (editor-in-chief) et al. 2015. The Study Quran: A New Translation and Commentary. New York: HarperCollins Publishers.

Oliveti, Vincenzo. 2002. Terror's Source: The Ideology of Wahhabi-Salafism and its Consequences. Birmingham, England: Amadeus Books.

Oxford Islamic Studies Online. n.d. Women and Islam. Oxford University Press. www.oxfordislamicstudies.com/article/opr/t125/e2510#. Accessed November 2019.

Pickthall, Marmaduke. 1992. The Koran. London: David Campbell Publishers.

Reda, Nevin. 2005. Women Leading Congregational Prayers. Canadian Council of Muslim Women paper.

Rida, Muhammad Rashid. 1404H. Huquq al-Nisa' fil-Islam (in Arabic). Beirut: Al-Maktab al-Islami.

Sherwood, Marika. Britain, slavery and the trade in enslaved Africans. https://archives.history.ac.uk/history-in-focus/Slavery/articles/sherwood.html#5. Accessed November 2019.

Siddiqi, Muhammad Zubayr. 1993. Hadith Literature: Its Origin, Development and Special Features. Cambridge, England: The Islamic Texts Society.

Smith, Huston. 2001. Islam: A Concise Introduction. New York: HarperOne.

Stowasser, Barbara Freyer. 1994. Women in the Qur'an, Traditions, and Interpretation. New York: Oxford University Press Inc.

www.sunnah.com. 2011. *Hadith* compilations in English and Arabic. Accessed October and November 2019: www.sunnah.com/tirmidhi/12/17, www.sunnah.com/urn/637830, www.sunnah.com/urn/1262960, www.sunnah.com/bukhari/59, www.sunnah.com/muslim/46.

The Economist. 1997. An Engineering Mystery: Why pagodas don't fall down. December 18.

The Economist. 2020. Bygone Civilizations: Secret gardens. February 1.

United Nations Development Programme. 2017. Human Development Report.

Union of News Agencies (UNA), formerly The International Islamic News Agency. www.iinanews.com.

Webb, Gisela (editor). 2000. Windows of Faith: Muslim Women Scholar-Activists in North America. New York: Syracuse University Press.

Za'i, Hafiz (editor). 2007. English Translation of Jami' At-Tirmidhi, Volume 6. Riyadh: Maktaba Dar-us-Salam.

Index[1]

[1] Note: Page numbers followed by 'n' refer to notes.

L. El-Ali, *No Truth Without Beauty*, Sustainable Development Goals Series, https://doi.org/10.1007/978-3-030-83582-8

Made in the USA
Las Vegas, NV
19 January 2022

41798115R00187